D0408941

JUN   1991   2

3 9090 00587995 8

SURREY PUBLIC LIBRARY

NEWTON BRANCH

MARKETING
YOURSELF

ALSO BY DOROTHY LEEDS

Smart Questions
PowerSpeak

MARKETING YOURSELF

THE ULTIMATE
JOB SEEKER'S GUIDE

DOROTHY LEEDS

HarperCollins*Publishers*

SURREY PUBLIC LIBRARY

MARKETING YOURSELF. Copyright © 1991 by Dorothy Leeds. All rights reserved. Printed in the United States of America. No part of this book may
be used or reproduced in any manner whatsoever without written permis-
sion except in the case of brief quotations embodied in critical articles and re-
views. For information address HarperCollins Publishers, 10 East 53rd Street,
New York, NY 10022.

FIRST EDITION

Designed by Alma Orenstein

Library of Congress Cataloging-in-Publication Data

Leeds, Dorothy.
  Marketing yourself: the ultimate job seeker's guide / by Dorothy Leeds.—
1st ed.
      p.   cm.
  Includes bibliographical references and index.
    ISBN 0-06-016312-7 (cloth)
    1. Vocational guidance.   2. Job hunting.   3. Assertiveness (Psychol-
ogy)   4. Persuasion (Psychology)   I. Title.
HF5381.L3464   1991
650.14—dc20   89-46543

91 92 93 94 95 DT/HC 10 9 8 7 6 5 4 3 2 1

To Anna Pearl Robertson,
with all my love forever

Contents

Acknowledgments

With thanks and deep appreciation to:

Sharyn Kolberg, whose diligence, perception, and creativity helped make this book a reality. She is a perfect right arm.

Tom Miller, for his guidance, patience, and support. He is everything an editor should be, and more.

The Sales and Marketing Executives of Greater New York and **Ed Flanagan** for paving the way.

Jeff Slutsky, the greatest Streetfighter of all, and a pretty good marketer, too.

Ann Wolbrom, for her support, good cheer, and dynamite administrative assistance.

George Walther, a very knowledgeable and gracious man, who knows more about the telephone than anyone in this world.

All those who so graciously gave of their wisdom and time, especially: Robert Blinder, Susan Boren, James B. Clemence, Dr. Richard E. Emmert, Joe Gandolfo, Joe Girard, Roberts T. Jones, John Kelman, Aven Kerr, William Olsten, Judd Saviskas, Ellen Schneider, Arthur Denny Scott, Martin Shafiroff, Robert Shook, Steve Stein, and Walter F. Whitt.

Special appreciation to my family, Nonny, Ian, and Laura, for their continued love, support, and forbearance.

Introduction

What is the ultimate job seeker's fantasy? Everyone I asked told me, "Getting paid well for doing what I love to do."

Why aren't we all living out our job fantasies? Because, up until now, the way to get the jobs we want has been a mystery. I have written this book to turn mystery into mastery.

No matter what kind of job you're looking for, no matter what your experience (or lack of it), no matter where you are right now, this book will show you exactly how to get the job of your choice—with the salary, perks, and benefits you deserve. All you have to do is learn how to sell and market yourself, the two most essential skills you'll need for getting a job in the 1990s and beyond.

The purpose of this book is to teach you those sales and marketing skills and show you exactly how they apply to getting the job of your choice.

My own expertise in sales and marketing is the fruit of fifteen years of study, experience, and training. I have made my living passing this knowledge on to others. I have built up an extensive marketing organization of my own, and in the course of speaking and consulting all over the country, I've trained over 20,000 executives and salespeople.

Having had five successful careers (so far) in my life, I'm an expert on the subject of how to get the job of your choice. I have an insider's understanding of what it's like to go out and look for a job.

When I first started out, I studied other successful job seekers. What was their secret? Some were better educated than I was, but others weren't. Some had nicer clothes or were more charming or had more advanced technical skills. Their only common trait, the one area in which they all stood above the crowd, was their *ability to sell and market themselves*.

But the most revealing discovery was that these people had no innate sales and marketing abilities. They taught themselves: They read, practiced, and, through trial and error, mastered the techniques that got them started on their successful career paths. What I learned enabled me to get a high-level position in the competitive world of advertising—with no prior experience or training in that field!

My goal in writing this book is to eliminate the trial and error part of the process for you. Here, in one complete, easy-to-follow, step-by-step guide, you'll find all the information you need to fulfill your own dreams, goals, and ambitions.

I didn't rely on my experience alone for this information. I went to the experts—company presidents, CEOs, human resources managers, high-level corporate executives—to find out what they look for in a potential employee. I asked the top sales and marketing professionals in a variety of fields what made them so good at what they do. I studied economic trends, population growth, and what's hot and what's not in the job market for this decade and beyond.

By combining this information with the sales and marketing techniques in this book, you'll be among the top contenders for any job you go after.

Marketing Yourself is divided into five sections:

PART ONE: "HOW TO GET THE JOB OF YOUR CHOICE: SELL, DON'T SETTLE"

- Get the inside track to success by selling and marketing yourself.
- Learn how your attitudes and emotional responses to sales and marketing may be holding you back, and what to do about it.
- Build the confidence you need to go out and sell yourself.

PART TWO: "THE SUCCESS FACTORS: THE TEN MOST MARKETABLE SKILLS"

- Ten qualities and personal characteristics every employer is looking for—universal skills that will make you an ideal candidate for any job you choose, plus examples, quizzes, and assessments to help you measure and improve your own success factors.

PART THREE: "KNOW YOUR PRODUCT"

- Learn how to hook your "product" into the real reasons people get hired, and show employers you've got what they need.

- Make your personal job search easier by specifying and clarifying your own career goals.
- Sell yourself successfully using your most marketable skills and accomplishments—whether you've had a lifetime of career success or have never had a job before.

PART FOUR: "KNOW YOUR MARKET"

- Keep yourself motivated, activated, and on target by developing your own personal marketing plan.
- Recognize current economic trends, how they affect you and the way you work.
- Discover thirty of the hottest job markets in the country today, where those jobs are, and what skills you need to get them.

PART FIVE: "CLOSING THE SALE"

- Use inside secrets from top sales professionals to "clinch the deal."
- Put step-by-step marketing procedures and specific sales techniques to work for you:
  - Locate the people who most want to hire you.
  - Make employers the offers they can't refuse.
  - Sell yourself effectively in any interview situation.
  - Eliminate key areas of interviewing anxiety.
  - Negotiate for more than money.
  - Get the jobs you really want.

This book was written for each of you as an individual. Because the job search is a unique experience for each of us (we all have different goals, ambitions, and priorities), the book is filled with personal assessment quizzes and individualized worksheets to make each step particular to your specific needs. It's designed to be a guide to your future, a handbook of practical information and profitable strategies for success throughout your working lifetime.

This book is also designed to assure you that it is possible to build the career of your choice. It doesn't matter how old you are now or whether you're looking for your first job or your twenty-first. The journey is the same. If you plan well and travel with an open mind and a flexible attitude, your trip will be both pleasurable and satisfying. Unexpected detours abound, and you may have to alter your route as you go. Or you may find a more interesting, less traveled highway and decide you'd rather explore that path instead.

Whether you've never had a job before, want to move up the corporate ladder, or want to change careers midstream, *Marketing Yourself* will help you build the skills to deal with whatever career changes and choices you face now and in the years to come. It's like riding a bicycle: Skills you'll learn here will serve you for a lifetime.

An exciting future awaits us. A whole new century: The Century of Choice and Change. Think of all the changes the twentieth century has seen, as America has moved from an agricultural society to a manufacturing society. We have extended and expanded our abilities and imaginations.

Now we are moving from a manufacturing society to a service society, into the information age and the age of sales and marketing. We're still expanding our abilities and extending our imagination. If you want to take advantage of everything this changing and challenging world has to offer, you can't sit back and wait for things to happen; you have to make them happen and that takes marketing. Selling and marketing skills will help you to be prepared for unexpected change and to have more confidence in yourself and your abilities. You will learn to measure your value and use that knowledge to get what you want.

My motto is, "Success is turning knowledge into positive action." What you do with the information in this book is up to you. At the beginning of each chapter you'll find a basic principle of sales and marketing that encapsulates the significance of the information that follows. These thirty principles will provide you with the basis of a strong and practical understanding of sales and marketing.

I guarantee that if you learn *and apply* these principles to the job search, you'll gain the confidence, self-knowledge, and skills to build the career you've always wanted and to be a happier—and wealthier—participant in the workforce of today and tomorrow.

PART ONE

How to Get the Job of Your Choice

Sell, Don't Settle

1

Marketing Yourself

The Ultimate Job Seeker's Skill

Sales and Marketing Principle #1

Marketing success depends on the quality of the product plus the ability of the salesperson.

If you're looking for an ordinary "another day, another dollar" job, you don't have to read this book. It doesn't take any special skill to get that kind of job. But if you're serious about finding the right job for you, one that will make you happy and pay you what you deserve, it's time to get down to business—the business of selling yourself.

If you're looking for a magic formula for getting the job of your choice, look no farther. There is no magic formula.

There is a secret, but it's not magic. And I'm going to tell you what that secret is, right here, right up front.

It's sales and marketing.

It's learning the specific skills and techniques that successful salespeople have been using for years and applying them to the job search.

The sales and marketing techniques you'll learn in this book will help you to:

- Reach the people most interested in hiring you
- Understand the real reasons people "buy"—and why employers will want to buy what you have to sell
- Ask for more and get it
- Build the career you've always dreamed of having

3

BIRTH OF A SALESPERSON

Success in today's changing workplace depends on action, not reaction. You have to do more than send out résumés in response to ads. There are many intelligent, creative people seeking challenging, well-paying jobs. You have to become a salesperson if you don't want to be left behind.

"But wait a minute!" you say. "Who said anything about becoming a salesperson? That's not my career choice!"

Oh, but it is—even if it's not.

Why? Because the most important knowledge you need in order to succeed in your career is how to sell yourself.

According to Arthur Denny Scott, senior vice president of personnel at Goldman, Sachs and Company, "Going to the right college or even having the right skills isn't enough anymore. You have to be a salesperson—and I don't mean a huckster. I mean you're going to have to market your ability to contribute to the organization."

The secret of getting ahead, of obtaining the competitive edge, is your ability to persuade potential employers that *they need you*. That's what selling and marketing are all about.

> **Selling** is simply showing someone else how your product or service will help him or her fill a need or solve a problem.
>
> **Marketing** is the process of getting a product or service from the seller to the buyer.

Learning to market yourself is learning how to connect the product (you) with the buyers (employers). "Buyers" are looking at an overall package when they make their decisions. How you sell and market that package can make the difference between you and the competition.

It doesn't matter if you're old or young, if you're just graduating from college or if you're changing careers after twenty years on the job. I'll show you how to discover your strong points and emphasize your assets in order to build the career you always dreamed about.

What you are going to do from here until the end of this book is to:

- Identify your strengths, talents, and interests
- Increase your self-confidence as you discover your value to others
- Become a salesperson and learn how to market and promote your personal assets

Seem like a tall order? Perhaps. But not when you consider that your career, like any business, takes time, care, and effort. It is a process, not a result. It would be presumptuous to think you could discover all there is to know about yourself by reading this book, or that you could possibly be "finished" when you read the last page. This process will continue for a lifetime.

NO HARD SELL IN THE NEW AGE

Why is it that selling and salespeople have developed such a shady reputation over the years? A successful salesperson used to be a charmer, someone who could sweet talk you out of your last dollar. A credulous buying public welcomed promises of health, wealth, and happiness, even at a tremendous price.

The "hard sell" has been around for hundreds of years. It used to be that a salesperson would say anything—lie, cheat, bamboozle—anything to make a sale. What has happened to the hard sell in the new age? Selling isn't what it used to be. *Flimflam, sucker,* and *scam* aren't a part of the new sales vocabulary. The hard sell is losing its grip as new concepts in selling have emerged. The kinder, gentler type of salesperson, who asks questions and listens instead of bulldozing his or her way through a sale, is the wave of the future. Honesty is the best policy in the information age.

So why do we shudder at the thought of having to go out and sell anything at all, no less ourselves? We're shy. We're modest. We're embarrassed to talk about ourselves. But think of it this way: If you owned a business, would you simply open a store, sit there, and wait for customers to come to you? If you did, you'd go out of business in a very short time. To succeed, you'd have to tell someone about your product. You'd have to get the word out; and if the *owner* of the business is reluctant to sell, who else will do it for you?

If you picture a salesperson as the old-time huckster referred to earlier, you're not going to be comfortable learning the sales techniques you'll need to make your career dreams a reality. Selling is an art that, once learned, can benefit you in every area of your life.

A "new" salesperson has emerged in the business world because the customer has changed. People are more savvy than they used to be—not as gullible or as easily convinced. So the new salesperson sees himself or herself as someone whose purpose is to help others solve their problems.

That's exactly what you're doing when you're looking for a job. You're trying to match up your talents and abilities with an employer who has a problem you can solve or a need you can fill. The same techniques that sales and marketing experts use can be applied—with equal success—to the job search. This book will show you how to do just that.

THE CAREER ENTREPRENEUR

What is it that makes one salesperson more successful than another? There are many answers to that question, but here is one of the most important: Whether he works for himself or for someone else, the successful salesperson usually demonstrates great ingenuity and creativity in finding new markets and territories to conquer. It's this willingness to look beyond the tried and true, this entrepreneurial spirit, that gives one salesperson the competitive edge over another.

An entrepreneur is someone who sees an opportunity, weighs all the alternatives, considers the risks, and takes decisive action. The smart employee of the 1990s is a career entrepreneur, constantly looking for new markets in which to sell himself.

When Josh was a little boy, he wanted to be a farmer. As he grew older, he began to realize the difficulties facing American farmers today. But he couldn't deny his love of the land or give up his dream altogether. So he researched the "dying" agricultural market, chose his area of study, and became an agricultural engineer. Today he studies and develops new and improved hybrids that will strengthen farmers' productivity and profits. Josh took advantage of a growing field even in an industry that's supposedly in decline.

Josh made a successful career choice because he had an eye toward the future. He chose a field based on a growing technology.

This was a smart marketing move. Josh already has the makings of the new entrepreneur. If you want to be among the successful, you have to weigh your alternatives, consider the risks, and take decisive action in the business of planning and promoting your life and your life's work.

As you develop a career marketing strategy, whether you work for a large company or work for yourself, you'll need that entrepreneurial spirit, managing yourself as if you were running a small business. The information in this book provides you with the secrets you need to market yourself successfully in any field you choose. You need to have an aggressive marketing plan, just as any small business would. You need to know your "product" inside and out, and how to bring that product to the buying public. You need to know where your industry or field of interest is headed, so that your product remains a marketable commodity in a rapidly changing world. And you need to have the skills of salesmanship to convince the buyer of the value of the product.

SUCCESS IS TURNING KNOWLEDGE INTO POSITIVE ACTION

My motto is "Success is turning knowledge into positive action," and it can be applied to any situation. Other people may present you with opportunities, but you're the only one who can make something happen. Ultimately, you're your own boss, whether you work for someone else or not. In an April 1989 article in the *New York Times,* Harris L. Sussman of the Digital Equipment Corporation stated, "As a career counselor, I tell people that everybody is ultimately self-employed. And if you don't think that way, then you've given up control over the decisions in your life to somebody else. There are dozens and dozens of paths to follow."

THE SPIRIT OF THE 1990s

There is a new spirit that's revitalizing the way we work in this country. It has nothing to do with mysticism or spiritual rebirth. It has to do with what we want out of work, what we choose to do with our lives, and how, when, and where we choose to do it.

It's in this spirit that marketing prowess is becoming the hallmark of career success in the 1990s. Jim Hansberger, senior vice president of Shearson Lehman Hutton and one of Atlanta's top financial consultants, says, "People who recognize it's salesmanship that distinguishes them from the competition are the ones who are going to forge ahead. To make it successfully into the twenty-first century, we must be market-oriented and sales-minded."

Using the sales and marketing principles set forth in this book, you will prepare for the future and achieve your goals. You'll become a career entrepreneur in the business of selling the ultimate product—yourself.

2

The Sales Readiness Quiz

Sales and Marketing Principle #2

Attitude is more important than aptitude for sales and marketing success.

Do you have a "sales personality"? Are you "market-oriented" and "sales-minded"? According to the experts, those are the qualities you'll need to get the job of your choice.

What follows is not a test of your knowledge of sales techniques. It's a quiz to evaluate your sales personality and your attitude toward selling in general.

Be honest with yourself as you take this quiz. Go with your instincts, not with what you think the answer should be. You can't fail this quiz. It's meant only as a guide to help you judge your sales readiness.

Don't be concerned if you don't rate as high as you'd like. Read this book, do the worksheets, follow my suggestions, then take the quiz again. I guarantee you won't be disappointed a second time.

SALES READINESS QUIZ

1. You are planning a vacation with a friend. You want to go to Paris and your friend wants to go on a cruise. Would you:
   A. Talk dynamically about Paris and what you love about it
   B. Debate or ignore every reason he presents for going on the cruise
   C. Try to find out what it is about the cruise that appeals to your friend most
2. What is the most difficult aspect of getting a job?
   A. Finding the right job opportunities
   B. Asking for the job at the interview

    C. Calling to make the appointment
3. When you picture a salesperson in your mind's eye, do you see:
    A. A person who is trying to help you solve a problem
    B. An arm-twisting used-car salesperson
    C. A smooth persuader whose main motive is to sell you his or her product or service
4. Your main goal at a job interview is:
    A. To get the job
    B. To get as much information as possible
    C. To ask questions
5. When you solve a major problem at work, do you:
    A. Go in and ask for a raise
    B. Write it down and bring it up at performance appraisal time
    C. Give it little notice and assume your boss is keeping an apprecia-tive eye on all your accomplishments
6. You are planning to buy three pairs of expensive shoes in a small boutique. Do you:
    A. Pay for them
    B. Ask at the beginning if they'll give a discount if you buy all three
    C. After trying on shoes for three hours, say, "I might buy if you give a discount for buying three pair"
7. The last time someone said no to you, did you:
    A. Ask why he or she said no
    B. Take the no as an irrevocable decision
    C. Keep trying to persuade him or her to say yes
8. In a group of very aggressive, talkative people, do you:
    A. Hold your own comfortably
    B. Sit back timidly, content to listen
    C. Speak up occasionally because you don't want to be left out
9. If someone asked you to describe your best feature, would you:
    A. Talk nonstop for hours
    B. Blush and not know where to start
    C. Discuss briefly two or three admirable traits
10. If you hear about a job opening do you:
    A. Send a résumé
    B. Call personnel to get more information
    C. Try to contact the person you'd actually be working for
11. How would you prepare for a job interview?
    A. Role-play with friends or colleagues
    B. Develop a list of questions to ask
    C. Think about what you'll be asked and prepare some answers
12. When sending out a letter with your résumé to a prospective em-ployer do you:
    A. Send a form letter
    B. Send no letter
    C. Write a tailored letter for each job
13. If you call a prospective employer and he or she immediately says "We're not hiring today," what do you think is the reason?

A. The employer took an instant dislike to you
B. It's not the right time
C. He or she doesn't have a good reason to talk to you

14. If you were selling computers and needed customers, would you:
    A. Call up all your friends
    B. Attend a seminar on "Computer Basics for Small Business Owners"
    C. Open the phone book and start calling

15. You have applied for a job you really want and have been turned down by personnel. Would you:
    A. Call and try to get another appointment
    B. Accept the decision and try another company
    C. Try to find out who you would be reporting to and make an appointment directly with that person

16. Why do you think people "buy"?
    A. Because it makes them feel good
    B. Because their buying is based on a logical decision
    C. Because they like the salesperson

17. You are going on an important interview. Do you:
    A. Research the company
    B. Wing it
    C. Figure you'll ask questions to learn what you need to know at the interview

18. A friend gives you a referral. Do you:
    A. Take the name and number and say, "I'll call next week"
    B. Take the name and number and call immediately
    C. Ask your friend for more information about the job and the boss

19. Why is listening such an important part of the sales process?
    A. You get important information
    B. You find out the hidden concerns
    C. It shows that you care

20. What is the best way to stay in control during a sales presentation or a job interview?
    A. Always have a planned question
    B. Keep talking in a very persuasive manner
    C. Answer every objection or concern that is raised

21. At the end of a job interview, do you:
    A. Say thank you and leave
    B. Ask for the job
    C. Ask when you'll be hearing from the employer

22. You've been searching for a job for six months and have been rejected twenty times. Do you:
    A. Get angry and take it out on friends and family
    B. Begin to doubt your own abilities
    C. Reevaluate your interviewing skills

23. In an interview situation, which would you see as a strong signal of acceptance?
    A. If the interviewer asks, "When can you start?"

B. If the interviewer says, "This would be your desk"
C. If the interview goes on for a long time
24. You get a letter from a satisfied customer commending you or a colleague complimenting your performance. Do you:
 A. Show it to your family, friends, and colleagues
 B. Acknowledge it, feel good, and stash it away
 C. Make copies and send it to your boss, her boss, your department head, even the president or chief executive officer
25. Who do you think gets to the top in most organizations?
 A. People who work the hardest
 B. People who fit into the corporate culture
 C. People who sell themselves most effectively

RATE YOUR SALES READINESS

1. A = 3   B = 1   C = 5
The worst way to sell anything is to ignore or argue with the other person (B). You only hurt his feelings or make him want to cling stubbornly to his own position. Talking dynamically about Paris (A) may help, but the real secret to selling is to appeal to what the other person wants or needs. By finding out what's most appealing about the idea of a cruise (C), you'll know what the other person really wants. If he says, "There's a lot of dancing on board ship," for instance, you can counter with a list of places to go dancing in Paris.

2. A = 3   B = 5   C = 3
Even the most experienced salespeople sometimes have difficulty "asking for the order" (B). When you're in an interview (the ultimate sales situation), an essential sales skill is knowing how to be assertive without being aggressive. Finding job opportunities (A) is not difficult if you take advantage of research tools available in the papers, the library, and personal contacts. Calling to make the appointment (C), also an important skill, is not difficult if you utilize the three *P*'s: patience, practice, and perseverance.

3. A = 5   B = 0   C = 1
Your own notion of what a salesperson is will determine your ability to succeed in today's job market. If you see salespeople as arm twisters (B), you won't feel very good about having to sell yourself. If you see a person who's trying to help you solve your problems (A), that's the kind of salesperson you'll be during your job hunt. Smooth persuaders (C) will probably always do well in this world. But they will always finish second to someone genuinely concerned with solving other people's problems.

4. A = 5   B = 5   C = 5

All three of these answers are good. You want to come away with a job offer so you can decide whether or not to take the job (A). You want to get as much information as possible so you can make a smart decision about the job (B). And you want to go in prepared to ask questions (C) in order to accomplish A and B.

5. A = 5   B = 3   C = 1

If you go right in and ask for a raise, you're sales-oriented and interested in building your value (A). This is the best approach, in step with today's more assertive approach to life. Waiting for performance appraisal time is good (B), but that may be a long time off. My philosophy is that it's more important to keep yourself in the eye of the organization. You do this by letting people know when you've done something valuable. If you give it little notice (C), no one else will notice it, either. If you don't sell yourself, nobody else will.

6. A = 1   B = 3   C = 5

Negotiation is an important selling skill. The best time to ask for a discount is after a salesperson has invested time showing her wares (C). At that point, she'd rather give you a deal than lose the sale. You get three points for being able to ask for a discount when you come in (B). You're on the right track, but you don't want to tip your hand at the beginning. You get one point (A) for being successful enough in the first place to be able to afford paying full price for three.

7. A = 5   B = 1   C = 3

It's important to know why someone says no (A) if you want to get a yes the next time. It might even tell you how to proceed to change the no to a yes this time. If you keep trying to make the sale (C) you're not easily dissuaded and have enough confidence in yourself to try again. If you take every no as an irrevocable decision (B), you're not giving yourself a chance to learn what your mistake might have been.

8. A = 5   B = 2   C = 3

Congratulations on holding your own (A) and feeling comfortable about it. Competition for jobs will be great, and the better your communications skills, the easier you'll find it to sell yourself and the better your chances of getting the jobs you want. Speaking up occasionally (C) gets you three points for realizing that you need to at least make an effort to participate. You get two points for listening (B) because you may gain valuable information. But you'll need to learn to hold your own in a conversation if you're going to compete in the job market.

9. A = 1   B = 3   C = 5

Talking nonstop about your product (in this case yourself) is not a very effective sales technique (A). Your customers will see you are being pushy or unconcerned with their welfare. If you blush and don't know where to start (B), it means you're unprepared for the question. You wouldn't start selling cars without knowing anything about them. You'd prepare yourself for the questions your customers will most likely ask. If your answer was (C), it shows you think enough of yourself to be able to discuss your good qualities without being obsessive or obnoxious.

10. A = 1   B = 2   C = 5

If you emulate successful salespeople, you'll take the initiative, be more assertive, and go directly to the person who makes the final hiring decision (C). Since you've heard about the position, use your source to get your foot in the door: "Johnny Jones suggested I call. . . ." Calling personnel to get more information (B) is less helpful but shows you're willing to do some research. If you just send a résumé to personnel (A), you're not taking advantage of your inside knowledge.

11. A = 5   B = 5   C = 5

This is another question where all three answers are good. Doing well at job interviews takes skill, and the way to build a skill is to be well prepared and practice, practice, practice. So all three answers will be helpful to you.

12. A = 2   B = 0   C = 5

Sending a résumé with no cover letter at all (B) tells a potential employer that you have no special interest in him or his company. The sales-oriented approach is to let the employer know why he should read the résumé and call you in for an interview. You do this by sending a letter tailored specifically for him (C). Sending a form letter is almost as bad as no letter at all (A).

13. A = 1   B = 3   C = 5

In selling terms, you've encountered *sales resistance* in this situation, which occasionally occurs when the customer doesn't like the salesperson (A). But in this case you hadn't been speaking long enough for the employer to dislike you (unless you were rude or obnoxious). It's possible that the employer was busy and you caught her at a bad time (B). But the most common reason for resistance is that the salesperson hasn't established the value of the product or service (C)—in other words, hasn't presented a strong enough reason for the customer to buy (or for the employer to keep talking to you). If this happens often when you call, it means you need to change your approach. See Chapter 26.

14. A = 4   B = 5   C = 1

Calling all your friends (A) is an excellent way to start because networking is one of the best ways to find buyers for your product. Attending a seminar for new business owners (B) shows you have strong sales sensibilities. People who would attend such a seminar are "qualified" buyers—they're definitely in the market for your product, so your chances of making a sale here are very good. Just opening the phone book (C) and making calls may bring you a few customers, but you'll probably waste most of your time and effort. In the job search, the more qualified buyers you reach, the better your chances of getting the job you want.

15. A = 3   B = 0   C = 5

If you have been turned down by personnel and just accept their decision (B), you are too easily discouraged. Successful salespeople try to close the sale (get the person to buy) at least five times before they even consider giving up. Going directly to the decision maker (C) demonstrates sales smarts and persistence, both necessary and desirable qualities for the job search process. Trying to get another appointment through personnel (A) is not as effective but does show you're resilient and not easily put off.

16. A = 5   B = 1   C = 3

Emotions play a big part in both selling and hiring processes. People buy (or hire) for emotional reasons (A); the product fulfills a need or desire they have. That's why, in order to sell yourself to an employer, you'll have to show him how you'll solve his problems or fulfill his needs. People also buy from people they like, trust, and respect (C). You can't make someone like you, but you can show that you are a person worthy of trust and respect. Logic almost always plays a lesser role in the decision-making process (B).

17. A = 5   B = 0   C = 3

Although asking questions (C) is an essential part of the interviewing process, most people are impressed by what you *already* know about them. Before you go on any "sales call," learn as much as you can about the company and the person you're going to see (A). You'll stand out from other applicants. If you try to wing it (B), you put yourself at a definite disadvantage—you'll know nothing about the company or the job before sitting down with the interviewer.

18. A = 1   B = 3   C = 5

The best answer in this case is to ask your friend for as much information as you can get before you make the call (C). You want to find out something about the person you'll be calling (who he or she is, what his or her position is in the company, etc.), what the job is like, and why this job is open. Calling immediately (B) shows you have initiative, but you'd be better off researching the company first. If you say "I'll call next week" (A), you're probably just putting it off and may lose the opportunity.

19. A = 5   B = 5   C = 5
All three answers are true. There's an old sales saying that goes, "Customers don't care how much you know until they know how much you care." In a hiring situation, the interviewer wants to know that you care about the job and the company (C). Listening carefully also gives you important factual information (A) and may reveal the hidden concerns of the individual interviewer (B)—the real reasons you will or won't get hired.

20. A = 5   B = 1   C = 3
Here is another sales maxim: "The person who asks the question controls the conversation." Going into the interview with a series of planned questions (A) keeps you in control of the situation and makes sure you get all the information you need to make a smart decision. What you think is talking in a persuasive manner (B) may come across as conceited and pushy. Without asking questions, you could end up talking for hours and never satisfy the employer's real concerns. Clearly answering objections or concerns (C) is essential to a successful interview but doesn't give you the same control that asking questions does.

21. A = 1   B = 5   C = 3
It's important that you "ask for the sale" or, in this case, the job (B). Ask in a pleasant, civil way so that you don't turn people off. Saying thank you and leaving (A) is not going to help you get the job unless you're the most sought-after person in the world. Asking when you'll be hearing from the employer (C) shows a little more assertiveness and is better than just saying thanks and leaving. But more than likely you'll be told, "We have several candidates to choose from. We'll call you." You won't get very far with that, so it's always best to ask a closing question.

22. A = 0   B = 1   C = 5
The best answer here is to reevaluate your interviewing skills (C). Twenty interviews can give you a lot of good experience in different types of situations that may arise. Go over your experiences and ask yourself what you did right and what can be improved. If you begin to doubt your own abilities (B), you're taking rejection too personally. A negative decision may have nothing to do with your personality. Getting angry at

yourself or at anyone else (A) doesn't improve your skills or your chances at the next interview. Don't give up trying; the next interview could be the one you've been waiting for!

23. A = 3   B = 5   C = 1

Most people take a long interview as a sign of definite interest (C). In fact, this often signifies nothing more than a disorganized interviewer, someone who doesn't really know what he's looking for. Don't assume an hour-long interview means you're a shoo-in. If, however, the interviewer starts to visualize you in the job and consistently refers to "your" desk, "your" co-workers, etc. (B), it's a pretty good clue that there is a strong interest. "When can you start?" (A) is a possible sign of interest, but it may also indicate that the employer is in urgent need of someone and may not be able to wait until you're available.

24. A = 3   B = 1   C = 5

Are you secure enough to take hold of your future and make sure the right people see what others think of you? Since only the rich and famous have public relations agents, we have to assume that role for ourselves. The best answer is (C). Showing the letter to your friends and colleagues (A) will make you feel better and perhaps add to your reputation but may not do much where your boss is concerned. Feeling good is always nice (B), but why pass up opportunities to increase your visibility?

25. A = 3   B = 4   C = 5

Although we're in the middle of the information age, we're also at the beginning of the age of marketing. Even our presidents have to "sell" themselves if they want to get elected. You must be well-versed in sales and marketing skills to get ahead (C). Corporate fit is and will continue to be important (B) but work is becoming less structured in many situations. Hard workers (A) are not to be discounted—but they are not necessarily the people who get ahead. In a small or newly organized company this may be the case, but unless other people know how hard you work, or unless you "fit in" with the rest of the team, your hard work will not always be appreciated.

SCORING THE SALES READINESS QUIZ

96–120 points

Good for you! You've scored high in sales readiness—which means you're one step ahead of the competition already. You have a positive attitude toward selling and a personality that makes you a natural for marketing yourself.

71–95 points

You are well on your way toward the sales and marketing orientation required for success in today's market. You're thinking in the right direction, and with just a little improvement, there'll be no stopping you!

46–70 points

You're not quite at the level you should be, but you're getting there. It would help you to be a bit more assertive and to have more confidence in yourself. All it takes is a shift in attitude and a willingness to learn. You're on the right track.

45 points or less

You need to reevaluate your attitudes and perceptions regarding sales and marketing. Doing the exercises and following the principles put forth in this book will be a great help in improving your sales readiness and increasing your marketing power.

3

Sold on Yourself

Sales and Marketing Principle #3

If you don't believe in the value of your product, no one else will either.

SELLING YOURSELF WITHOUT SELLING OUT

Do you cringe when I talk about selling yourself? Are you still thinking in terms of the huckster we talked about in Chapter 1? Do you think that selling yourself somehow implies a loss of dignity or a weakness of character? Or perhaps you think you're so good that you don't need to sell yourself? I hope you can answer, "None of the above."

You don't become successful by sitting back and waiting for great things to happen to you. Marketing yourself is the only way to get the word out there. Do you think Michael Jackson or Madonna never did any marketing? Or Donald Trump? Or anyone else at the top of his or her profession? They all had to sell themselves to get where they are today.

And as for loss of dignity or weakness of character, this is a very distorted notion of what selling yourself is all about. Selling yourself does *not* mean selling out. Those people who sell out are those who *don't follow their dreams*—those who give up because the path they've chosen turns out to be a little rockier than they had first imagined.

When you were a child, people often asked you, "What do you want to be when you grow up?" You answered with a clear (if temporary) vision of your future self—doctor, dancer, firefighter, astronaut, movie star, president.

If someone had asked you, "What do you think you can be when you grow up?" would you have answered differently?

Probably not. Because when we are young we can envision ourselves as we want to be: on stage at Radio City Music Hall or on the pitcher's mound at the final game of the World Series. We can imagine ourselves performing delicate brain surgery or designing the world's longest suspension bridge. We can picture ourselves strong, confident, capable, and

18

unafraid. The gap between what we want and what we think we can do is very small.

For most of us, this gap begins to widen as we grow older. The first time someone tells us "You're not smart enough" or "You're not tall enough" or "Girls can't do that," we may shrug it off. The second and third times, however, we begin to doubt ourselves and start believing what we are told. We build up an inventory of "cannots," "should nots," and "it's never been done befores." The clear pictures we had as children become cloudy and fade.

Sometimes we have to back up a bit to go ahead. This book is about going back to those visions of what you really wanted to do and replacing the old inventory of negatives with an objective and positive assessment of your talents and achievements. You are America's finest resource, harboring a wealth of untapped or undervalued potential waiting only to be discovered.

DON'T SETTLE FOR LESS

Instead of going after what we want, we have been taking what we can get. A very famous book called *Think and Grow Rich,* written by Napoleon Hill, contains the statement, "Ninety-eight out of every hundred people working for wages today are in the positions they hold because they lacked the definiteness of decision to plan a definite position, and the knowledge of how to choose an employer."

You don't have to be among those ninety-eight unhappy people. By setting goals that are important to you and will make you happy, you will have the "definiteness of decision." And by following the marketing concepts in this book, you'll know how to "choose an employer."

The success of any sales and marketing effort depends in large part on the salesperson's expectations. If you go into a situation convinced that you will fail—that you won't make the sale or won't get the job— you probably won't.

Most of us have been "programmed" to equate mistakes with failure. We use the fact that we have made a mistake as proof positive that we are unworthy or unable to attain success. We tend to fall back into old attitudes when dealing with new situations, and we often rely on the conditioned response which says, "Oops! Sorry! This can't be done!" We believe this inner voice and give up before we have even tried.

Belief in failure can become a conditioned response. But so can belief in *success!* Olympic athletes train more than their bodies to earn that gold medal; they prepare their minds as well. Before they begin a race they envision their performance. They rehearse their success before it happens.

Paint a clear, detailed picture of what you want to accomplish for yourself, and then take each small step necessary to follow through. Barbara Sher and Annie Gottlieb, in their book *Wishcraft: How to Get What You Really Want,* write, "Most of us have a distorted notion of how things actually get done in this world. We think that accomplishment only comes from great deeds. Great deeds are made up of small, steady actions, and it is these that you must learn to value and sustain."

Your ability to succeed in selling yourself doesn't depend on what has happened in your past, but on how you see your future. Convince yourself that you will be successful and you'll convince others as well.

LEARNING TO ROOT FOR YOURSELF

No one can hope to be a good salesperson unless he has a strong belief in the product he's selling. Enthusiasm is catching. If you have a positive attitude about yourself and your ability to do the job, the potential employer will feel this too. As every salesperson can attest, even the most successful strike out sometimes. But as Eleanor Roosevelt once said, "No one can make you feel inferior without your consent."

You're probably not going to get every job you go after. But don't let anyone put you down or make you feel inadequate. Only you can let that happen. See rejection for what it is: a temporary refusal. A no in one place is equal to a yes waiting for you somewhere else.

A friend once went through a particularly tough interview and was then turned down for a job she really wanted. Two days later she received a phone call. The employer had had time to think back over the interview and asked if she would come in and talk to him again. He was in a much better mood this time around and she was offered the job. He had simply changed his mind. Employers are human too; they have their good days and their bad days, just like you.

Recently, I was looking to hire a salesperson for my office. There were two candidates I really liked. I had a difficult time making up my mind. As it turned out, the person I hired had to leave the job after three weeks due to some personal problems. I quickly called Linda, the second candidate, and offered her the job.

So don't take a no as a permanent, scarring rejection or an indicator of things to come. Go into each situation feeling confident about yourself and enthusiastic about the job—but not desperate for it. A buyer is always suspicious of a salesperson desperate to make a sale. Even if you're down to your last few dollars, never act needy. Every time you set out to "make a sale," remind yourself that you are a unique, special individual with a lot of talent and a genuine contribution to make.

But First, a Word about the Real Competition

In searching for a job or career opportunity, you are often advised to take note of the fierce competition and told how you must stand out from the crowd, must achieve that competitive edge.

There is no disputing the numbers. There will always be a certain number of people applying for the same job as you or wanting to do what you want to do. Sometimes these numbers will be great. At times you may get discouraged and begin to think you haven't got what it takes.

You may start to measure yourself against those around you, to see everyone else as being more, or smarter, or better than you are. You might occasionally feel inferior and therefore not worthy or deserving of success. Perhaps you've had failures in the past and you point to them and say, "Experience tells me I'm not able." It's important, however, to keep things in perspective. You may feel that you're not able, but remember this is *not a fact*. It's only the way you *feel*. Most of us have experienced these kinds of feelings at one time or another.

Keep in mind one of the most important principles of sales and marketing: *If you don't believe in the value of your product, no one else will either.*

This doesn't mean you're not concerned with the competition. You are. But the competition you need to be most concerned about comes from within. According to Joe Girard, listed in the *Guinness Book of World Records* as the "World's Number One New Car Salesman," "Before you can sell yourself successfully to others—and thus sell your ideas, your wishes, your needs, your ambitions, your skills, your experience, your products and services—you must be absolutely sold on yourself: 100%."

Don't let the negative voices within you compete with your talents and abilities. You can gain the competitive edge over these voices within that say you're unable to do this or that, that you're not creative or have no mathematical ability or can't speak in front of people.

These voices can be very convincing. You take them as fact. A voice says "You have no mathematical ability" and you give up trying to balance the checkbook. Albert Einstein failed algebra in school. Did this prove he had no mathematical abilities? If he had believed that was true, the Theory of Relativity might never have been born.

The "You Don't Have to Be Einstein" Equation

Philip, a friend, once came to me in a panic. His supervisor had resigned and Philip had a chance to go after the position. This was the opportunity he had been waiting for. There was one hitch, however. As head of the department, he would be required to present semi-annual reports to the board of directors. Philip had always admired his supervisor's presentation and believed he could "never get up in front of those people and speak the way she did." Philip didn't feel he could "sell himself" for this position.

He came to me for help in public speaking. I knew I could help him, give him voice and speech exercises, and build his confidence. But I also knew he would never be able to sell himself believing that he had to "speak the way she did." Philip was competing with an exaggerated image of someone whose abilities he admired. Until he replaced this image with a belief in his own ability, he would always fall short of his expectations.

You act on your beliefs. If you believe you can't, you can't. Subtract one little apostrophe and one small letter of the alphabet and you can change your life. Remember this equation: CAN'T − 'T = CAN. You don't have to be Einstein to appreciate its simplicity.

When I introduced Philip to the "You don't have to be Einstein" equation, his image of himself changed. He was able to "make the sale" because his beliefs had altered. And by the time his first board meeting came around, Philip was able to give a strong, confident presentation. "To think I was afraid to go after this job!" he told me later.

We all have conflicts between our aspirations and our apprehensions. Tom Hopkins, in his book *How to Master the Art of Selling,* says, "Perhaps we can't eliminate this ongoing battle. But we can decide whether we'll lose every day, lose usually, win usually, or win every time. We can't, of course, win every sale. . . . That's okay. What isn't okay is to constantly lose out to our same old unresolved fears and anxieties."

Don't let yourself be ruled by your past. Take the good with you in your search for a new job and leave the bad behind. And there's no point in worrying about whether or not you'll be perfect in the future. If you build your faith on the ability to act in the moment, the future will take care of itself.

BELIEVE IT OR NOT, THE BOSS IS ROOTING FOR YOU

You may not believe this, but most customers *want* a salesperson to be successful. As you'll see in Chapter 28, even as we're saying "But I really can't afford your product," what we often mean is, "Please show me the real value of your product so I can justify spending the money."

The same principle applies to your job search sales and marketing campaign. The prospective boss wants you to make the sale. She wants to end the search. Perhaps she has made a hiring mistake in the past; she certainly doesn't want to repeat that experience. She may have seen a lot of other people and may be beginning to despair that she'll never find the person she needs.

And You Think You're Nervous!

The interviewer is very often just as nervous as you are. Sam Feinberg, a reporter for *Women's Wear Daily,* has stated that 95 percent of interviewers don't know how to interview. It's probable that you are (or certainly can become) much better at it than they are.

The interviewer has more at stake than you do. Let's take a look at a prospective boss: Jane, a bank vice president in charge of professional development and continuing education. She has had an opening for a new training manager for almost three months, and Jane's boss is impatient for her to hire someone soon. Other people in the department are complaining about how overworked they are. Jane feels pressured because she couldn't keep the previous employee and because of the complaints from her boss and department personnel. She wants to fill the position quickly, but she still wants to make a good decision. And you think you're nervous!

Look at the job search from the boss's point of view. You'll be a much better salesperson once you've put yourself in your client's shoes.

Jane was hired by the bank because of her abilities and her experience in employee education, not because of her interviewing skills. Like many employers, Jane is not totally clear about what she wants. Most bosses have a general idea—someone who's committed, a self-starter, responsible, energetic—but they haven't really formulated much of a game plan. By remaining calm and confident and asking pertinent questions, you will help a confused employer get a clearer picture of what she needs.

The employer also wants to make a good impression on you. After all, if you're an outstanding candidate, you may have several job offers from which to choose. She wants you to choose her. Employers suffer from fear of rejection, too. So go in to the interview with empathy and understanding. Reassure the employer that you are the best person for the job. Whatever you can do to reduce the interviewer's anxiety will make it easier for her to say yes to you.

On Equal Terms

Some salespeople hesitate to contact a prospective customer because they feel they might be bothering him or her or intruding on important work. In my sales seminars, I always remind participants that they are there to offer a useful service to a customer; if they didn't have something the customer wanted or needed, they wouldn't be there. No salesperson need ever feel inferior or intrusive.

Remember that you and your prospective employer are equals. The fact that you don't have a job and he or she does means only that and nothing more. Don't ever feel less important because you're looking for a job. You have something of value to offer; that's why you're there. If the interviewer doesn't treat you as an equal, you should have serious doubts about working for him anyway.

Realize that the employer, like the customer, is a person with a problem to be solved and that you are there to solve it. You are there to sell yourself as the person who can anticipate his needs and fill them better than anyone else.

SHIFTING VALUES AND THE NEW WORK ETHIC

Why do we care about anticipating anyone else's needs? Why do we work at all? I've heard many people say the real reason they work is to make a lot of money. Yet if you describe a job that really doesn't interest them, those same people will often say, "You couldn't pay me enough to do that job!" Your job search marketing efforts should reflect your personal goals and reasons for working.

The goals we set for ourselves include more than status symbols and financial success. In the 1990s we're not only reexamining how, when, and where we work; we're also looking at why.

A few years ago I ran into my neighbor, George, loading several boxes into the elevator of our building. George had been an accountant with the same large firm for over twelve years and often complained loudly about his job. I asked George how things were going at work.

"I hate work," he said. "I guess I'm just basically lazy. I don't want to get up in the morning. I work with numbers all day. I come home and veg out in front of the TV. Work is just boring. But it pays pretty well— enough for me to have bought myself a present," he said, pointing to the boxes on the floor beside him. They contained an elaborate stereo system, he explained, and he started to tell me about all of the system's amazing features. I asked him who was going to put the system together for him.

"Oh, I am," he said, and his eyes began to sparkle. His voice became animated and his whole body came alive as he described how carefully he'd chosen each of the components and how he couldn't wait to get started putting the complicated system together. It would take him hours, he said.

"Sounds like a lot of work," I said.

"What do you mean?" he asked. "Just look what I get when I'm done: a terrific sound system like I always wanted, not to mention the pride and sense of accomplishment knowing I did it myself. Work? That's not work!''

Webster's New Collegiate Dictionary defines work as "Sustained physical or mental effort to overcome obstacles and achieve an objective or result." According to this definition, putting the stereo system together was work. It took sustained physical and mental effort to put together such an elaborate electronics setup and it achieved a definite result. But George didn't see it that way.

Does George remind you of anyone you know? Do you ever feel the way he does about getting up in the morning? Just what does work mean to you? Is it something you look forward to? Or do you start off every week with the Monday morning blues? Are you dissatisfied with your present job?

Although most people spend more than 96,000 hours of their lives working, only a minority derive satisfaction and excitement from their work. The average person is resigned to the idea of having to work and looks forward to retirement to do what he or she wants. People look for satisfaction and fulfillment *outside* the workplace; there's a sharp division between work and nonwork.

But today employers are realizing that employees who are excited about their work are more productive, more creative, and more dedicated. I asked Robert Blinder, senior vice president and director of corporate resources at Prudential-Bache, what he looks for in his employees. "I look for intelligent, hard-working, knowledgeable people," he said. "People who like what they do so much that they'll be happy spending a lot of time doing it."

We're less willing to spend 96,000 unhappy hours working in order to have "a life" at some later time—we're willing to work hard, as long as we can also have the quality of life we desire.

My neighbor George found this out. When his accounting firm was bought out by an even larger one, George was offered early retirement. He accepted a generous settlement and joined a small electronics repair service that specialized in stereo systems, TVs, and VCRs. The business is doing very well and George has a new attitude about work. Now when I run into him in the elevator, he tells me he is "exhausted, but happy." He used the *knowledge that he already had*—even though it was something he had always considered a hobby—to *take positive actions* toward making his work a more integral and satisfying part of his life. This is the new work ethic.

More of Ourselves

What do we get out of this new work ethic? Optimistic as it may sound, what we get is much more of ourselves and for ourselves.

It has been proven that job stress can lead to burnout, illness, and the destruction of personal relationships. As a society, we have measured success in terms of money, power, and title. Many "successful" people are neither happy nor satisfied, however. "Yuppies" who work seventy hours a week for the money and the status burn out very quickly because they equate self-worth with money, not the work itself.

In the industrial age, our parents and grandparents worked long, hard hours at uninteresting or unrewarding jobs. They had little independence or responsibility. They went to work, got their paychecks, and came home. There are still people like that, who like to have everything laid out and controlled for them. However, if you're interested in becoming a happier, more productive, and better paid member of the workforce, then I am speaking to you. The new work ethic provides you with the crucial ingredients to form a positive relationship *between your work and your sense of self-worth*.

We have explored several important themes in this chapter:

■ *To sell yourself you have to believe in yourself.* Have confidence in yourself, and others will have confidence in you. You can't stand out from the crowd until you can stand up for yourself. Rejection is a normal part of the job search process, not a personal indictment. Learning to learn from your mistakes and experiences is an important part of the selling process.

■ *Success is attained by setting goals and following through.* Sometimes we're afraid to set important goals because they appear distant and unreachable. Don't think of yourself as starting from Point A and magically arriving at Point B; instead, envision yourself going through each step, learning from any mistakes, and, most of all, *enjoying the process*.

■ *When your work is more valuable to you, you're more valuable to your work.* The new work ethic tells us to look for work that adds to our sense of self-worth. When work becomes more than just a fast buck, it's a true expression of how we value our time and energy.

■ *You'll never be "selling out" if you follow your instincts and have faith in your dreams.* Selling yourself to others only proves that you have confidence in yourself and are willing to stand behind your beliefs. When you don't believe in yourself, you're only selling yourself short.

PART TWO

Success Factors

The Ten Most Marketable Skills

Do you know what today's employers are really looking for? What they really want? What kind of person they see as an ideal employee?

If you want to sell yourself as a valuable commodity in the job market, you need to develop the success factors you'll find in the following ten chapters. These are the skills and personal characteristics that make you stand out from the crowd, increase your negotiating power, and get you the job you want.

You are the most important resource a company can have, the most important investment it will make. Each hiring decision costs a company time and money—and a wrong decision can lose clients, hurt morale, and damage public image. So if you want a job with challenge and opportunity, you will have to prove to the company it's making the right decision by hiring you.

Every job has particular skill requirements. Engineers, chemists, technicians, researchers, teachers, editors, salespeople, doctors, lawyers, investment bankers—whatever profession you pursue has specific educational and training prerequisites. Assuming you have the needed skills, what will make a company want to hire you rather than the person sitting next to you with the same education, training, and experience?

THE PARTNERSHIP PRINCIPLE

Being an equal partner means sharing the responsibilities as well as the rewards. It means having respect for the work you do and requiring respect for work well done. You take an interest in your work, the company takes an interest in you, and everyone takes an interest in the quality of the service. It's a win–win situation.

Employers aren't looking for people to be robots. They can get robots for that. They're looking for real people, with real skills and an interest in being part of the team. The old "us against them" attitude within the corporate structure hierarchy doesn't stand up in the face of new technologies. Computers and telecommunications give many workers equal access to the same information, and equal opportunities to be original and highly productive.

If this is true, then you can see why companies are going to be screening candidates for more than their skills and experience. They are going to be looking for the success factors, the ten skills and personal characteristics we will explore that will bring you success in *any* job or career. The stronger your success factors are, the easier it will be to market yourself to potential employers.

I've included some suggestions for ways to develop these success factors, to take this knowledge and turn it into positive action. Most of these tips involve little more than reevaluating your attitudes toward your work—and yourself.

4

Success Factor #1

Adaptability

Sales and Marketing Principle #4

An effective marketer isn't resistant to change, but views it as a challenge and an opportunity.

KEEP YOUR EYE ON THE CHAMELEON

Perhaps the most important personal quality necessary for success today is adaptability: the ability to adjust yourself easily and willingly to differing conditions. Your attitude toward change can make the difference between getting ahead and standing still.

If you see change as a challenge, a chance to prove yourself, your value to a potential employer will rise markedly. Susan Boren, vice president of human resources at Dayton Hudson Corporation, has this to say about adaptability: "Personal adaptability is vital to us. As business changes we need employees who can change also. And they must view change as an opportunity."

Change as opportunity could be the secret to success in the years ahead. Myra and Joan are both rising young executives in XYZ Corporation. They have both received memos stating that management is installing a new computer system which everyone will be expected to learn so that important data can be accessed whenever needed.

Myra is thrilled at the prospect. She has been annoyed at having to wait for someone else to bring her information she needed. Now she will be able to do it herself. She sees this not only as a way to be more productive, but also as an opportunity to learn a new skill to add to her growing list of accomplishments.

Joan, on the other hand, thinks, "I'll never have time to learn this system and I'll probably never use it anyway. If I need some data, I'll just have someone bring me the information I need.'' She spends several sleepless nights worrying and calls in sick the day of the scheduled installation. When it comes time for promotion, Joan can't understand why Myra is chosen over her, when she has put in more hours than Myra and produced all of her work on time.

I see this scenario over and over again as new systems and technologies are introduced. Joan would receive a low rating in this important success factor. She is inflexible. She has a narrow vision of the future. Are you more like Joan, or like Myra? Are you easily upset by anything that seems to threaten the status quo?

Some careers demand more flexibility than others, of course. Accountants, for example, who will be in great demand over the next few years, often see several different clients during a given week. They usually set up in a makeshift or borrowed work area. My accountant, Beth, also works for a gas station where she usually has to share a table with auto parts and cans of motor oil. The next client she visits may set her up in a vice president's office or in a corner of the mail room. She had to learn to adapt her way of working to the change of clients and physical surroundings in order to do her job.

CONQUERING THE UNKNOWN

We all have our own ways of working, ways that give us comfort and security. When presented with an unexpected problem, we tend to react according to our usual patterns. Why is it often so difficult to break out of these patterns? It usually has to do with *fear of the unknown*. The way we know works. Who knows what will happen if we try another way? We imagine all kinds of tragic and humiliating consequences. The reality is, the results may not be exactly what we had in mind, but they are rarely tragic or humiliating. Once you begin to make a fairer assessment of a particular set of circumstances, you can begin to change your habitual reactions and take the appropriate new action.

When you encounter a problem, make up a worksheet like the one that follows and answer these questions:

How is this situation unique? _____

_____

_____

What is the best way to handle this particular situation (or person)? ___

_____

_____

What is my usual mode of dealing with problems? _____

_____

_____

What works? _____

_____

_____

What doesn't? _____

_____

_____

When was the last time I handled something in a new way? _____

_____

_____

In terms of my bottom-line objective, how would I like this situation to turn out? _____

_____

_____

How can I get out of my own way and make that happen? _____

_____

_____

If you are by nature overly resistant to change, it's important to analyze your behavior when change is introduced. Learn to recognize your resistance, and ask yourself why it's so important to hold on to your usual way of doing things. There's no need to jump on every passing bandwagon, but you should be able to weigh the old against the new in a spirit of open-mindedness.

Adaptability benefits you as much as it does the company. Suppose that you unexpectedly lose your job. If you are an adaptable person, your ego may be bruised but you'll be able to learn from your experience, evaluate your skills, create a marketing plan, and go on to a better opportunity. You'll have a practical strategy and will feel good about your ability to move on. And if you feel good about yourself, you won't be devastated by unforeseen changes in your life.

TURN YOUR FEARS AROUND

Can you turn your fears around and make change work for you? Take the following quiz and see how you feel about change.

When you contemplate making changes in your work or personal life, you:

---

1. Think you have to give up everything you know and start all over again.
   True _____   False _____
2. Feel that you're being forced to do things you don't want to do.
   True _____   False _____
3. See yourself as a creature of habit and believe that you can't teach an old dog new tricks.
   True _____   False _____
4. Think if you try something new you might make a mistake.
   True _____   False _____
5. Think that change involves pain and hard work.
   True _____   False _____

If you answered "True" to any of those questions, you're probably resistant to change and could use some work on changing your attitude. Here are some helpful hints to combat the myths in the quiz you've just taken:

1. *You think you have to give up everything you know and start all over again.* Not true. When you adapt one thing to another, you take what is usable from the first and apply it to the second. No need to reinvent the wheel. Concentrate on developing transferable skills—like the ten success factors—so that you can apply skills you already possess to different areas.

2. *You feel that you are being forced to do things you don't want to do.* If you're always waiting for "the other shoe to drop," it will. Which do you think is a more painful experience: being evicted from an apartment you can't afford, or choosing to look for a smaller, less expensive space? Altering your entire lifestyle after you've had a heart attack, or starting a moderate program of good food and exercise when you're still perfectly healthy?

There was a big to-do last year when Deborah Norville was brought in to replace Jane Pauley on the *Today Show*. In an interview, Ms. Pauley said that although at first she was upset and apprehensive about the change, she soon began to view it as an opportunity for her to embark on a new era in her life. She now had a chance to explore new options she might not have seen otherwise. She was actually glad that circumstances had forced her hand.

It's always more difficult to make changes when they're imposed on us by outside sources. Think of change as a catalyst for improving your life, not as a hardship forced on you by circumstances.

3. *You see yourself as a creature of habit and believe that you can't teach an old dog new tricks.* Hugh was always extremely predictable. Others in his office said, "You can set your clock by Hugh." They often did. He arrived every morning at five to nine, had the same black coffee and cherry danish, ate in exactly five minutes, and promptly began his day. He left for lunch on the dot of twelve and returned at one on the dot. He stopped work exactly at five.

Hugh was forty-nine when the company was bought out by a larger firm. They wanted to promote Hugh, but Hugh didn't want a new position. He felt comfortable in the job he had, so why change? But the company changed around him, and eventually Hugh had to face an even bigger change—his job was phased out, and he was forced to leave the company. This made Hugh take a long, hard look at himself, his habits, and his attitudes toward change.

Rapid changes are overtaking businesses all over the country. Employers are looking for people who can handle change with ease and enthusiasm. When it comes to developing your adaptability, don't think about changing old habits—think about forming new ones. Make it a habit to try one new thing every day. Take a different route home from school or into work or back from dropping off the kids at day-care. Have lunch in a brand-new restaurant and order something you've never tasted before. Read a book about a subject you've never even heard of. Small changes sometimes bring big surprises. And before you know it, you'll be looking forward to the "change of the day."

4. *You think if you try something new you might make a mistake.* Well, you might. Everybody makes mistakes. We learn to learn from our mistakes, to analyze what went wrong and go on from there. Corny as it may sound, those who are successful in coping with change learn to pick themselves up, dust themselves off, and start all over again.

5. *You think that change involves pain and hard work.* It might. It depends on your attitude. It may be difficult for you to accept some of the ideas and suggestions I make in this book. But the big question is this: Are you unhappy? Because if you are, then how much is your happiness worth? Is it worth some temporary discomfort as you go

through a transition period? Is the result worth the effort? That's one you'll have to answer yourself.

What positive actions can I take today to improve my adaptability success factor? _____

_____

_____

5

Success Factor #2

Commitment

Sales and Marketing Principle #5

With so many similar products and services today competing for the same markets, the commitment of the salesperson is often the deciding factor.

I PLEDGE ALLEGIANCE TO MYSELF

The subject of loyalty and commitment comes up often in my management seminars. One manager expressed to me the feelings of most top executives: "I'd rather have a hard-working, committed person who stays with the company for two years than an unmotivated, complacent employee who's around for the long haul."

Our definition of commitment on the job is changing as we move into a new century and different ways of working. Arthur Denny Scott of Goldman, Sachs and Company sees the "diminishment of corporate loyalty" as the way of the future. Scott, who worked for IBM for twenty-eight years, says, "More and more, loyalties are toward personal interest, to a profession or a career. Engineers may remain engineers, for example, but move around from one place to another. Going to work for IBM used to be like a marriage, and that kind of relationship will no longer exist."

As we move from the era of "corporate marriage" into the "divorce age," companies and employees are becoming less willing or able to make such long-term commitments. Years ago, when you joined XYZ Corporation, XYZ expected a long-term (perhaps lifetime) commitment from you, and you expected long-term support (financial and otherwise) from the company. Changing technologies, as well as the trend toward buyouts, mergers, and takeovers, make long-term commitments very rare.

But the fact that long-term commitment is changing doesn't mean there is no commitment at all. It means that, although we may not be able to promise we'll stay with a particular company for the next twenty years, we must be *committed to doing the task at hand* and giving it our best. The emphasis is changing from quantity to quality.

GOOD HABITS START EARLY

Commitment is a habit that can be developed at any stage. If you are still in school, your commitment can be to your schoolwork or to the after-school job you have (even if it's for little or no wages). My neighbor's son, Howard, worked at many summer and after-school jobs throughout high school and college—and received several offers for full-time employment from these companies after graduation. Why? Because he's committed to doing well at whatever he's doing, and employers translate this as a willingness to work hard and a concern for the company's benefit as well as his own.

Companies both large and small appreciate that attitude. In my own organization, I had a part-time employee, Lisa, who had to go out of town for a few weeks. She was so concerned that she arranged for her own replacement, brought him in the week before she left, and trained him herself. Needless to say, this extra effort was greatly appreciated and told me a lot about Lisa's success factors.

Large companies also appreciate this sense of commitment. One of the changes we're seeing in today's workforce is the increased use of temporary workers; one of the reasons "temps" are becoming so popular is that many of the temporary workers are very committed to doing a good job, whether they're at a place for a day, a week, or a month. Most people who work as "temps" do so because it fits their current needs and lifestyle. They know that the agency will use them often if they're reliable and perform well on each assignment.

Take Allen, for example. Allen was a temp worker for a large publishing concern; the company had a policy manual several inches thick and conducted all of its business strictly by the book. One of these rules was that the company never hired part-time employees on a permanent basis. Allen was a very hard worker, committed to doing a good job while he was there. He even made several suggestions for improving procedures for other temporary employees. The company wanted to hire Allen full-time, but he was going to school at the time and couldn't take a full-time position. Yet, because of Allen's commitment to producing quality work, this conservative "play by the rules" corporation eventually hired him permanently, something he was repeatedly told could never happen.

Allen became a valuable asset to his department. When he finished school and looked back over his accomplishments, Allen found many other events in his life that demonstrated a high level of commitment. Discovering he had this valuable, marketable skill gave Allen extra confidence and was a strong selling point for potential employers.

Every industry has been affected by changes in definitions of loyalty and commitment. According to Dr. Richard E. Emmert, executive director of the American Institute of Chemical Engineers, "People are changing jobs several times through the course of a career; companies are less paternalistic, employees less loyal. There are more people working through service firms and as independent contractors rather than directly for the company needing the service."

In the future, many companies will consist of a large network of freelancers and consultants, individuals and small groups of people who are working independently toward a common goal. Whether you do this within a corporate structure or actually go into business for yourself, your survival will depend on your commitment to doing the work.

INVEST IN YOUR COMMITMENT

What is your commitment to work? Think about how your attitude affects your performance. What can you do to improve your current situation? Try to see how committing yourself to your work will pay dividends down the road. If you can't make a commitment to what you're presently doing, it may be time for a change.

Look at your present responsibilities at home, at school, or on the job:

Do you go about them half- or wholeheartedly? _____

_____

_____

How would your boss, your parents, or your teachers answer that question? _____

_____

_____

When was the last time you really extended yourself? _____

_____

How did it make you feel when you did? _____

_____

_____

Even if no one else recognizes the difference in your attitude, it will make a difference to you.

Do you have problems making commitments? Break down your resistance into manageable chunks. It's possible to do something for one hour or one day that may seem impossible to do forever. You can honestly make a pledge to do your best and have the discipline to do what is needed for the immediate situation, one task at a time. It's necessary to have goals and make plans for the future, but no one says you have to accomplish them all at once.

TAKE A REALITY CHECK

Another aspect of commitment in today's workplace concerns reliability and responsibility. You must keep the promises you make to yourself as well as to others. People don't expect you to be perfect, but they do expect you to be there on time and to be focused. If you're disorganized and scattered, try breaking your time down into manageable pieces so that tasks do not become overwhelming. Keep an appointment book or notebook with you always and jot down ideas the moment they occur so that you won't forget anything. Take a reality check every once in a while to make sure you haven't made promises you can't keep and haven't taken on too many projects all at once.

Steve, a college classmate of mine, was bright, industrious, and creative. He would consistently turn in interesting and original term papers—two weeks late. His enthusiasm for a new sport or hobby was extreme and catching. He would get all of his friends involved; then his interest would shift and he would leave his teammates wondering what had happened to their staunchest supporter.

Steve made the dean's list every semester. His sophomore year, he managed to get interviews with five of the country's top law firms for summer internship programs—then was late for three of the appointments; went to the wrong address for the fourth, and forgot about the fifth one altogether. This problem has continued throughout Steve's working life. He is now a moderately successful lawyer, but he will never rise to his potential because he is not reliable.

All actions and decisions have corresponding consequences. Commitment entails the acceptance of those consequences. "The lack of maturity in making decisions is a big problem in the financial services industry," says James B. Clemence, director of management development at Peat Marwick. "This major problem has come about because young, inexperienced college graduates, who don't yet understand the concept of accountability, are being given very responsible positions (at very large salaries). But they haven't learned to accept responsibility for themselves and their actions."

Being a responsible, committed worker means being answerable for your actions. We are now moving into an "adult stage" of work, where each individual will be held accountable.

GROWING UP IN AMERICA

America was born as an agricultural society; basic needs of survival had to be met when we cut the umbilical cord with the mother country. The industrial age saw us grow into the "toddler" stage of our work development. We were a curious people, experimenting and expanding our world—but at work in the mills, factories, and sweatshops we were told what to do, and how to do it, and in most cases we had no say in the matter. The Company was our parent, and managers were our babysitters.

We are now coming out of the "adolescent" stage, a painfully familiar stage to most of us. This is comparable to the time in your life when you have this recurring argument with your parents: You want to borrow the car, and they don't want to let you.

"Look, Mom, Dad," you plead, exasperated, "you always say you expect me to act like an adult, but you still don't trust me enough to give me any responsibility!" You repeat this argument often enough until at last the folks come to see that you are right and give you the keys to the car. If you're smart, you're very careful and prove that their trust is justified.

This stage in the world of work means that corporations are expecting more and more of their workers but have yet to give them (except in the most progressive companies) the authority to take independent action.

Work in this country is now heading into its most exciting and challenging stage: Corporate America is beginning to treat its employees as adults, to trust and respect their individual talents and abilities. Walter F. Whitt, senior vice president, Human Resources, at McGraw-Hill, says that "corporations are beginning to permit employees to be more auton-omous, to be more accountable and to have a broader range of responsi-bilities. There'd be less emphasis on rote-type 'good work' and a lot more on thinking and decision-making capabilities."

The new ideal for the corporate structure is to have ideas generated at all levels and rising to the top like a balloon—with management choos-ing the best of these as solutions. This will replace the "trickle down" style, where a single solution to a problem, good or bad, was made by top management and issued on down the line.

Susan Boren, vice president of human resources at Dayton Hudson Corporation, feels that her company is "placing more and more value on real communication with our employees. Hudson's was for a long time a family business, and we felt we had to 'take care' of our workers. We still care about our employees, but now they're more our partners than our children. We listen to their ideas and treat them with more respect, as adults who must take care of themselves."

Just as it is in the family situation, this trust and respect is not given unconditionally or indiscriminately. It is given only to those who earn it.

Corporations that have traditionally given responsibility only to senior executives are realizing that in order to provide service to their custom-ers, the responsibility and authority to make decisions must be decen-tralized. Susan Boren sees Dayton Hudson continuing to embrace this philosophy: "In the next twenty years, we will be continuing to empower people at lower levels, to provide them with enough information for them to make good decisions in order to provide better service."

NOT "WHY ME?" BUT "WHAT NOW?"

The "company man" of the industrial age, who conformed with every company rule and did exactly what he was told and no more, wasn't willing to take any responsibility for himself or his actions. Adaptable, creative, independent people are willing to take more risks—and live with the consequences.

Do you have a "why me?" attitude? Do you think you're unlucky and that bad things just happen to you? If so, you'll need a change of attitude to succeed in the future. Instead of focusing on "why," starting thinking about "what." Don't think "Why do I always act this way?" but rather, "What can I do differently this time?"

Janet heard a rumor in her medical lab that her particular field of research was being discontinued. She'd been working at this lab for eight years, and she had accepted orders from her supervisors and never said a word. She had been passed over for promotion, but didn't complain

good posture or do you slouch over, head down and shoulders forward?

Millions of dollars are spent every year by marketing experts on design and packaging. They know that the way a product is presented has a lot to do with how it is accepted. The same goes for you. When you go in to sell your services to a potential employer, are you aware of the impression you're making, physically and verbally?

If you walk into an interview with uncombed hair, a slouch, and a shuffle, you'll have to work very hard to get the employer to see beyond the "packaging." Ask your friends or family for feedback about how you present yourself and how they perceive your body language and posture.

2. *People respond from their point of view, based on past experience.* Languages develop differently in different parts of the world because of each culture's unique circumstances. The Eskimos, for example, have over 100 words meaning *snow*. There is one that means "snow that is for drinking water," one for "snow spread out over the land," another for "snow that has just fallen," and 97 more for other types of snow. Snow is of primary importance in Eskimos' lives, and their language reflects that.

All communication depends on your point of view.

Words mean different things to different people. Here is a list of words that may have strong emotional impact. Write down your feelings about each word:

Criminal: _____

Lawyer: _____

Boss: _____

Television: _____

Work: _____

Religion: _____

Money: _____

Now ask two other people to write down their reactions and compare. You'll find that the three sets of "answers" are very different from one another.

Effective selling requires effective communication, so be sure that you are communicating in the way you intend. If you describe yourself as a workaholic, for instance, one potential boss may see that as a positive trait, while another may see it as negative. Be sure to express yourself clearly and precisely—and ask a potential employer to clarify anything he says that seems ambiguous to you.

3. *People respond according to their needs, not yours.* This is an essential rule of successful selling. When you go to buy a car, you go because

you want or need a new car—not because the salesperson wants to sell it to you. If you don't want that car, it's going to be a very difficult sale.

If you ask your boss for a raise, you'll get it because your boss needs you—not because you need the extra money. And if you get a job, you'll be hired because the company needs you, not because you need employment.

As we discussed in Chapter 1, you get a job because you fill an employer's needs, not your own. You won't sell yourself by saying, "Hire me. I need a job." You will sell yourself by saying, "Hire me. I can help you solve your problem."

4. *The only way to find out where people are coming from and what their needs are is through a planned process of questioning and active listening.* Asking the right questions and knowing how to listen are two of the most effective communication tools. The right question will get you the information you need when you need it. Why? Because people love to answer questions. They feel compelled to answer them. People automatically pay more attention to a question than they do to a statement.

Questions are very powerful. Even the shyest person will respond to a question directed right at him; ask the right question and you'll wonder why you ever thought he was shy!

Knowing how to listen will allow you to receive information as it's intended to be communicated. Epictetus, the Greek philosopher, once said, "God has wisely given us two ears and one mouth so we may hear twice as much as we speak."

Here is a simple quiz to help you improve your listening skills:

THE LISTENING QUIZ

When talking to people, do you:	Usually	Sometimes	Seldom
1. Prepare yourself physically by facing the speaker and making sure you can hear?	____	____	____
2. Watch the speaker as well as listen to him?	____	____	____
3. Decide from the speaker's appearance and delivery whether or not what he has to say is worthwhile?	____	____	____
4. Listen primarily for ideas and underlying feelings?	____	____	____
5. Determine your own bias, if any, and try to allow for it?	____	____	____

6. Keep your mind on what the
   speaker is saying? ____ ____ ____
7. Interrupt immediately if you
   hear a statement you feel is
   wrong? ____ ____ ____
8. Make sure before answering
   that you've taken in the other
   person's point of view? ____ ____ ____
9. Try to have the last word? ____ ____ ____
10. Make a conscious effort to
    evaluate the logic and credibility
    of what you hear? ____ ____ ____

Score: Questions 1, 2, 4, 5, 6, 8, 10: 10 points for "usually," 5 for
"sometimes," 0 for "seldom." Questions 3, 7, 9: 0 points for "usually,"
5 points for "sometimes," 10 for "seldom."

If your score is below 70, you have developed some bad listening
habits; if it is 70 to 85, you listen well but could improve; if it is 90 or
above, you're an excellent listener.

"WHAT WE'VE GOT HERE IS A FAILURE TO COMMUNICATE"

In the age of the service society, working well with other people is the
best way to success. And working well with other people is 100 percent
communication. Can you even imagine a job done in total isolation?

How we communicate with the people we work with is as important
as the work itself. "You can have the personality of a tree stump and
work on an assembly line," says Arthur Denny Scott of Goldman, Sachs
and Company. "But in a service society personal relations become much
more important. If you've only valued physical skills, you'll be in deep
trouble. You must be able to project yourself into the mind-set of the
other person and see things from his perspective."

Communication covers a wide area, but the basic skill involves getting
your thoughts or ideas across to another party—on a one-to-one personal
basis, to ten or twelve people across a boardroom table, or to millions of
viewers across a TV screen. The way you communicate says a lot about
you, especially when you are in the process of marketing yourself. We
communicate in obvious ways and ways that are not so obvious; all of
these ways can be studied, practiced, and mastered.

If you send a potential employer a letter filled with grammatical errors
and misspellings, you surely won't get a positive response. If you go in
to an interview and introduce yourself with a flimsy handshake, then sit

on the edge of your chair nervously cracking your knuckles, your qualifications and past experience will be of very little value to you.

If, however, you are well spoken, project confidence, and write sharply, a certain lack of experience might be overlooked.

It often happens in a job search scenario that your initial contact with a potential employer is your direct mail marketing letter (see chapter 23). Expressing yourself clearly, concisely, and correctly will create a powerful first impression—and make you a serious contender for any job. Put yourself in an employer's position. Suppose you received a letter that began:

> Daer Sir:
> I am lloking for a job as a secrtrary. Do you need won?

I doubt you would read any further. You certainly wouldn't care about the letter writer's previous experience, and you would have to question how motivated this person would be on the job if he or she can't take the time to proofread an introductory letter.

In this case, it's not the thought that counts. People notice even small mistakes, so putting that extra effort into written communication is well worth the time.

Practice, as always, makes perfect, so keep writing and rewriting until you are satisfied that there are no errors. Use a dictionary, a thesaurus, and guides to style and grammar. An original idea is no good to anyone if you're the only one who can understand what you've written.

Oral communication is equally important. How many times have you made judgments about people based on nothing more than the way they sound over the telephone? It's not necessary to become a public speaker to succeed in business, but having a good strong voice inspires trust and implies confidence and competence.

The importance of communication skills cannot be overemphasized. Almost every one of the "hottest" jobs listed in Chapter 20 includes good communication skills as one of the requirements for success.

What positive actions can I take today to improve my communication skills? _____

_____

_____

7

Success Factor #4

Creativity

Sales and Marketing Principle #7

Selling is creative problem solving—how best to get what you want while giving the customer what he or she needs.

PLAYING AROUND, SERIOUSLY

A friend, an office manager in a small dental clinic, once said to me, "I don't see myself as a very creative person." Yet I've always admired her ingenuity and resourcefulness. Faced with seemingly insurmountable difficulties, she always manages to find an effective solution. She was surprised when I told her I thought this showed great creative talent.

How do you view creativity? Just because you're not a Picasso or a Hemingway doesn't mean you're not creative. Creativity is really about different ways of looking at things. Picasso had a particular vision of the world and expressed it through his art; Hemingway expressed his vision through the written word; Beethoven and Bruce Springsteen both use music to share their views. Albert Einstein and Madame Curie expressed their creativity in scientific terms. Luckily for the rest of us, all creativity does not require genius. It begins with taking an objective look at a problem or an obstacle, and combining imagination and reason to discover a solution.

Most people don't think they're creative at work. As a consultant, when I ask most managers what they do, they tell me they plan, control, organize, staff, and lead. When I ask them if their job is creative, they say no. But a manager's main job is to deal with problems, and creativity applies to every kind of problem that exists. Every time you find a new way to work something out, you're being creative, manager or not.

47

It doesn't take much creative thinking for a job on an assembly line. But as we develop into more and more of a service society, the need for creativity in the workplace increases. Walter F. Whitt, vice president of corporate human resources at McGraw-Hill, sees management becoming more creative, "more entrepreneurial, more willing to take calculated risks—people who are not constrained by narrow vision and who are able to think conceptually."

DEVELOP YOUR CREATIVE FLOW

There are no right or wrong answers to the quiz that follows. These twenty-five questions will give you an idea of how you view yourself and your creativity.

1. Do you enjoy "the creative process"—experimenting with new ideas or new ways to do things?
2. Do you accept things as they are because you think "it's always been done this way"?
3. Do you feel following the rules is more important than getting the job done, or are you willing to bend a little?
4. What do you do when you don't like something, or you have to wait too long, or you see time or materials being wasted? Do you complain? Or look for ways to fix it?
5. Are you naturally curious?
6. When you see something that is particularly useful or ingenious, do you think of ways you can adapt it to your own job or personal life?
7. When faced with a problem, do you stick with it until it's solved?
8. Do you consider many different options before taking action?
9. What was the last good idea you had? What made it a good idea? How did it come to you?
10. Do you ever just sit and daydream or doodle on a piece of paper? Do you enjoy it, or do you feel you're wasting time?
11. Are you judgmental about your efforts before you even finish a project?
12. Do you get frustrated with yourself if you can't solve a problem immediately? Or do you give yourself a chance to come up with a better solution?
13. Have you found any new and interesting ways to stimulate your creativity? Walking in the woods? Taking a bubble bath? Meditating?
14. Do you read in your spare time? What do you read?
15. Are you familiar with resource materials and facilities? Do you know where the library is? The local college? Do you read trade journals or business publications?

16. Do you enjoy playing games?
17. What do you think about the job you do? Do you see creative opportunities in your work?
18. Are you open to new ideas and suggestions from others—no matter who they may be?
19. Are you supportive of someone else who comes up with a good idea?
20. What's your biggest problem at work right now?
21. Have you tried breaking that problem down into smaller, more manageable challenges?
22. Do you know anyone else who's had a similar problem and may be able to help you out?
23. Do you tend to think that creativity is reserved for "artists" and doesn't apply to you?
24. What do you do when a problem has you stumped? Do you give up easily?
25. Do you ever see solving a problem as fun?

LOOKING AT PROBLEMS FROM ANOTHER ANGLE

The next time you're faced with a problem to solve, try to look at it as an exercise in creativity. Step back and analyze it objectively without being judgmental. Ask yourself, "What is *interesting* about this problem?" Look at it from that angle, and see what solutions evolve. Then try another angle. Try the angle that struck you immediately, the one you decided against because it seemed too simple. Or too difficult. Or ridiculous.

Don't worry about the details or try to figure out how much it will cost. Just consider the big picture and look for a broad conceptual approach. Don't reject any possibility just because it's flawed. Creativity involves the ability to go beyond routine solutions to come up with a new idea or a new application of an old one.

The more creative you are, the more valuable you will be to any organization. On the job, consider any problem as an invitation to flex your creative muscles. You—and your employer—just might be pleasantly surprised.

What positive actions can I take today to improve my creativity skills?

_____

_____

8

Success Factor #5

Decision Making

Sales and Marketing Principle #8

Marketing often requires quick and confident decisions. That doesn't mean you have to be right all the time—we learn from all of our choices.

THE DECIDING FORMULA:
RESEARCH, ANALYSIS ... AND TRUST

Jason was in a period he called "between lifestyles." He had been working as a photographer's assistant for several years, thinking he would someday go out on his own. Discouraged, he felt that he was not moving along fast enough, that photography was no longer his main interest. He wanted to get married and start raising a family (and his fiancée wanted to be an at-home mother). But he was not very confident he could support a family on an assistant's salary. Jason decided to switch careers.

A friend offered him a job as a jewelry salesman. Jason accepted the offer and spent the next year and a half trying to convince himself that he had made the right decision, even though his job was making him increasingly unhappy. He felt obligated to his friend and was afraid of making another wrong move. Finally he realized that he missed being around photography. This time Jason was much more careful in his decision-making process. He made a list of all the things he enjoyed most about photography, as well as the reasons he had left it a year and a half earlier. Then he listed those things he liked and disliked about selling jewelry.

He discovered he had learned a great deal about selling but not very much about jewelry (he had no real interest in it). He was, however, deeply interested in cameras. He put salesmanship and cameras together

and is now one of the most knowledgeable photographic equipment sales-
men in the business. And he loves his work.

Jason's original decision to change jobs was made hastily and emotionally. His second decision was well thought out, based on analysis of
the facts, study of future options, and trust in his decision-making capabilities.

Think of how many decisions you make in the course of a day. Some
of us are very good at it and make decisions with ease and assurance.
Many of us do not. Our ability to make decisions has to do with our
willingness to trust ourselves and our own judgment.

The more decisions you make, the better you get at it. Living as we
do with constant change and uncertainty, the need for strong decision-
making abilities is greater than ever. Aven Kerr, vice president of human
resources at The Prudential, says that decision making is a highly valued
skill because "everything about business is happening faster and faster.
Information comes flooding in and there just isn't as much time to make
a decision as there used to be."

Your market value will increase in direct proportion to your decision-
making abilities.

NINE STEPS TO MAKING A GOOD DECISION

Making a good decision involves taking risks. You can never be sure of
the outcome, but you can make the best decision possible at a given time.

1. *Pinpoint the decision that needs to be made.* Make sure you define
the problem so that it can be broken down into specific issues that determine the final decision.

2. *Try to get as much information as possible.* Realize, however, that
you can't get *all* the information there is; at some point you will just have
to do with what you have.

3. *Make sure your information is reliable.* Check facts and figures yourself whenever possible.

4. *Ask for suggestions and advice.* You don't have to follow it, but you
may find out some things you didn't know before.

5. *Make plus and minus columns (or pros and cons) and see which side
tips the scale.* When Benjamin Franklin had a problem to solve or a
decision to make, he would take out a piece of paper and draw a line
down the middle of it. To the left of the line he would write "Yes" and
to the right of the line he would write "No." In the "Yes" column, he
would list all the reasons to take a given action. In the "No" column, he
would list all the reasons not to. Then he would go with whichever list

was longer—the "Yes" list or the "No" list. His decision was made for him.

6. *Ask yourself what would be the best possible outcome of this decision.* And what would be the worst? What is most likely to happen? What will happen if you don't do it? List all possible solutions to your problem and their likely consequences.

7. *Determine the value of each of the previous six solutions and their consequences.* List the good and bad points of each one; then compare them all to find the best solution in its proper perspective. If you make this decision, where will you be six months from now? In a year? In five years?

8. *Trust your intuition.* Ask yourself why this "feels right" or "feels wrong." Learn to trust your deeper instincts instead of following your immediate impulse.

9. *Recognize errors and use them to improve your decision-making skills for the next time.*

When Jason chose to change careers, he made an emotional, hasty decision that led him to a job he was not well suited for. But the year and a half he spent in the jewelry business was not at all wasted. Jason discovered he was a natural salesman, and all his experience in the jewelry business led him to the work he now loves.

What positive actions can I take today to improve my decision-making skills? _____

_____

_____

9

Success Factor #6

Evaluation

Sales and Marketing Principle #9

The Best Sales Question You Can Ask Yourself Is,
"How Can I Do It Better Next Time?"

MAKING GOOD JUDGMENTS

If you were alone in the office working under a tight deadline and the computer went down, what would you do? Would you tell yourself there's nothing you can do about it? Would you panic, give in to fears that you'd lose your job, and start to cry? Or would you be able to look at the work load, set priorities, and find ways to solve the most immediate problems?

Obviously, employers are looking for people who fit into the last category. The ability to make reasonable judgments and assess unexpected situations is of great value on any job. This is the skill of evaluation, and it's one you use over and over again—in every area of your life.

A simple act like crossing the street requires an evaluation of the risks involved: Is a car coming? How fast is it going? Can you make it safely to the other side? You evaluate the risks, then make your decision. You use evaluation skills every time you make a purchase, every time you make a new acquaintance.

The same kinds of evaluation skills are needed at work. You may be asked to evaluate situations (such as the computer failure mentioned earlier), purchases (from office supplies to company mergers), and people (co-workers, staff, and supervisors).

MAKING BETTER JUDGMENTS

The evaluations you make in everyday life are often hastily formed subjective opinions and gut feelings. Making an evaluation at work, however, requires more than a gut feeling. It requires an *objective* opinion, based on a set of formal standards. Most people rely on surface impressions and instinct. A good evaluator listens to instinct, but doesn't rely on it.

Formal evaluation is a three-step process:

1. *Describe the object of your evaluation.* Is it a person, place, or situation? Is it the job someone is performing? Is it a purchase to be made?

2. *Set up a list of standards.* Suppose you're in charge of finding a new pencil supplier for your office. What standards will a vendor have to meet for you to make a positive decision? Your list might include:

- ■ Top quality
- ■ Low cost
- ■ Ability to deliver large quantities
- ■ Ability to deliver within a week of receiving the order
- ■ Good-quality erasers

3. *Compare the object of your evaluation to the list of standards.* You've found four pencil suppliers. Only one meets all six of the standards you set up. You choose that supplier, If two suppliers meet your criteria, you set up more standards to make a choice between them.

These three steps apply to any evaluation you're making. This process can be used for one-time decisions, such as choosing a vendor, or as an on-going process (such as assessing the performance level of your staff).

PERFORMANCE APPRAISAL:
A GOOD AND FAIR ASSESSMENT

Performance appraisal is not a new concept. Take a look at the following letter:

Executive Mansion
Washington
January 26, 1863

Major General Hooker:
General:

I have placed you at the head of the Army of the Potomac. Of course, I have done this upon what appear to me to be sufficient reasons. And yet I think it best for you to know that there are some things in regard to which, I am not quite satisfied with you. I believe you to be a brave and skillful soldier, which, of course, I like. . . . You have confidence in yourself, which is a valuable, if not an indispensable quality. You are ambitious, which, within reasonable bounds, does good rather than harm. But I think that during Gen. Burnside's command of the Army, you have taken counsel of your ambition, and thwarted him as much as you could, in which you did a great wrong to the country, and to a most meritorious and honorable brother officer . . . I much fear that the spirit which you have aided to infuse into the army, of criticizing their Commander, and withholding confidence from him, will now turn upon you. I shall assist you as far as I can, to put it down. . . .

And now, beware of rashness. Beware of rashness, but with energy, and sleepless vigilance, go forward, and give us victories.

Yours very truly
A. Lincoln

If you were General Hooker, how would you have reacted to this letter? It contains both praise and criticism, which is how most performance evaluations are structured. It takes practice to produce an evaluation that is a constructive balance of the two.

To make a fair assessment, follow the three steps outlined above. It's important to keep ongoing records of an employee's performance—i.e, if an employee is expected to complete monthly reports, are they being done well and on time? You might want to make a note each month so that you'll have a complete picture at the end of the year.

Out of five hundred participants in a management seminar, only 5% said they had ever received a "good and fair assessment" by their superiors. Many managers tell me that giving performance appraisals is the most difficult aspect of their job. So most people feel that they don't give or get a satisfactory evaluation of their job performance.

You can improve your own evaluation skills by using the three-step method in evaluating everyday situations. The next time you have to make a purchase, weigh a risk or an opportunity, or assess a person's or product's performance, practice describing the object of your evaluation, setting up a list of standards, and comparing the object to the list.

Before going on to the next chapter, make a list of the positive actions you can take today to improve your evaluation skills.

10

Success Factor #7

Foresight

Sales and Marketing Principle #10

Marketing must be consistently future-oriented for a product or service to survive in a rapidly changing world.

GOING FOR THE GOLD

Since the concept of "tomorrow" was discovered, man has been trying to look into the future. But foresight doesn't come from a crystal ball or a deck of cards. It comes from a careful analysis of present conditions, along with a realistic projection of future trends.

When you see new trends appearing at work, or unexpected problems or benefits new technologies will bring, think about how they will affect you tomorrow as well as today. The idea, in this age of constant change, is not only to keep up with the Joneses, but to stay ahead of them. Anticipating future changes is a must, both for individuals and the companies for which they work.

Every business believes in its own growth potential. So all employers are looking for people with foresight, go-getters who can think in terms of expanding their markets, creating new applications for established products, or finding variations on services now provided. If you can demonstrate to a potential employer that you accomplished any of these in the past, it will be a strong selling point in your favor.

In the medical field, for example, foresight is perhaps the most valuable quality a job seeker can possess. Biotechnology is a growing field where cutting-edge research and development leads to exciting medical breakthroughs almost daily. Employers in that area are searching for candidates who can see beyond tomorrow.

Not only high-tech industries depend on foresight to survive, however. The garment and fashion industries, for instance, have always relied on foresight to anticipate what the fickle buying public will be wearing "next season." Retail sales buyers have to look ahead constantly so they know how to stock their shelves to profit from sudden buying trends. Financial institutions try to predict economic trends, nationally and internationally; real estate developers look for areas where growth potential is greatest. Almost every occupation needs people with the ability to look ahead.

I SHOULD HAVE SEEN IT COMING

If you can foresee change, or the possibility of change, you can start preparing before it actually happens. Problem solving is not only an exercise in creativity; it's an exercise in foresight as well. Foresight serves the same function as preventive medicine. When you choose a diet or fitness program today, you look for the benefits you'll get farther down the road.

Foresight is valuable to you on many levels. As you're developing your career marketing plan, foresight will help you keep moving forward in a positive direction. You need foresight to look at your own interests, talents, and abilities and compare them with the opportunities in today's job market.

Have you ever been in a situation where you said to yourself, "I should have seen it coming"? Oftentimes we do see "it" coming, but we don't pay attention or we let fear and stubborness stand in our way.

For over a year there had been rumors that the plant was closing. Tony and Jeannette were both supervisors, Jeannette on the day shift and Tony on the night. Jeannette chose to ignore the rumors. She'd worked at the plant for twelve years and had an "it can't happen here" attitude.

Tony's outlook was different. As soon as the rumors started, Tony began making plans. He took courses at the community college to improve his business and communication skills and complete his degree. Tony didn't wait for the plant to close. He made a plan for himself and began a job search immediately.

When the doors finally closed, Jeannette was out of work—and Tony reported the following Monday to an even better job just in the next town.

THOUGH YOU CAN'T SEE THE FINISH LINE, THERE'S NO REASON TO STOP

Is it possible to develop foresight? Isn't it just something some people have and most don't? Not at all. Foresight, like the other nine most marketable skills, is a matter of attitude. It requires a mind open to all possibilities, a mind able to imagine the unknown. People with foresight can always envision themselves in more successful circumstances.

You can develop foresight by being enthusiastic about moving ahead, even if you're not quite sure where you're going. Charles Garfield, in his book *Peak Performers: The New Heroes of American Business,* describes those people who are consistently successful at always being able to see ahead. "Peak performers want more than merely to win the next game. They see all the way to the championship." So keep your mind open—and go for the gold.

What positive actions can I take today to improve my foresight skills?

_____

_____

11

Success Factor #8

Independence

Sales and Marketing Principle #11

The more we rely on our own sales and marketing abilities, the more self-assured we become.

ON YOUR OWN TWO FEET

As corporate America restructures itself, the ability to work on your own is an absolute necessity—especially if you decide, as more and more people do every day, that you would like to work at home as a free-lancer or consultant. Even in a more conventional job setting, however, you'll probably find yourself in a less structured atmosphere. Work is becoming project-oriented rather than task-oriented; you make a "contract" with your boss for a particular project and you decide how you want to go about it.

The standard workday used to consist (and in some cases still does consist) of coming in to the job, being told what to do and how to do it, doing it, and going home. Half of the future jobs in America will not impose this kind of rigid structure. You'll be given a specific job to do, but you'll have much more leeway in how to go about doing it. You will decide (by yourself or with a group of co-workers) the best way to accomplish a task in order to complete it within a certain time frame. How you break down your individual day's work will be up to you.

THE GHOST OF WORKING PAST

The old work scenario might go something like this: On Monday morning Kevin Stanley speeds into the parking lot. He pulls hurriedly into the first

59

available spot. He runs into the building, knowing that his supervisor is watching the clock and glancing at Kevin's empty cubicle. Kevin is hanging up his coat just as Mr. Price comes through.

"I need this report on delivery schedules done today," Mr. Price tells Kevin, "so I can send it over to trucking for their approval. They'll send it back up tomorrow for revisions and then we'll zip it over to production where it started. When you finish that, go and see James for your next assignment; he's got an overload."

"Sure thing, Mr. Price," Kevin mumbles, thinking that James doesn't know what overload is. He works on the report through the morning, goes out to lunch at exactly twelve-thirty, returns to his desk, and finishes his section of the report at three-thirty. He gets his next project from James and works until exactly five, when he clears off his desk and runs out to his car in order to beat the rush on the freeway.

THE SPIRIT OF WORKING FUTURE

The new scenario looks more like this: Kevin pulls into the parking lot Monday morning thinking about the report he'll begin working on today. Kevin will be meeting with two other people this morning, one from trucking and one from production, and they'll be working jointly on the new delivery schedules. Kevin called the meeting for this morning when he was given the task of coordinating the project, to be completed and delivered to the big boss by Thursday. The three men meet until one, order in lunch, and quit around three. Kevin goes down to the company gym in the basement and works out for a while, then hops in his car, picks up his son at school, and gets home in half an hour, having beat the afternoon rush. Driving home, he's thinking of how to implement some of the suggestions the other two had about rerouting some of the trucks. After dinner, Kevin works on the report for about an hour on his home computer and looks forward to sharing his solutions with the others tomorrow.

The "new" Kevin scenario is beginning to happen all over America.

If you want to become more independent, don't be afraid to ask questions. It's important to know all the relevant facts in order to understand the significance of the task you're doing and how it relates to the project as a whole.

You may even have to define your entire job for yourself, as traditional job descriptions become harder to compose. Jobs will be structured around key results. The job description will contain certain goals to be met through that position, but how you choose to meet these goals will be your decision. This is not to say help will not be available. Being independent doesn't mean doing everything alone; it means being able to seek out those individuals who can be of assistance and being able to enlist and utilize their talents in conjunction with your own.

Computer technicians, for example (a high-growth career), are expected to do most of their work on their own. They may work for a large computer service-contract firm that is responsible for maintenance and repair for many different clients. When a client calls, technicians are sent out alone to determine the problem with the system or hardware. They have to determine what's wrong, fix it, or know when to call for help. Employers in a field like that are hungry for people who can demonstrate their ability to work independently.

What positive actions can I take today to improve my independence skills? _____

_____

_____

12

Success Factor #9

Be a Team Player

Sales and Marketing Principle #12

Interdependence and trust are the essential relationship builders.

DOING YOUR FAIR SHARE

According to Casey Stengel, teamwork is trying to keep the five guys who hate your guts away from the four who are undecided. I see teamwork as a cooperative and coordinated effort on the part of a group, and the individuals in that group, in the interests of a common goal.

Whatever the definition, teamwork is a necessary requirement for many of today's "hot" career opportunities.

Evan, an aeronautical engineer, worked for a large international corporation with many different divisions. He was a brilliant engineer, and the fact that he spoke several languages made him doubly valuable to the firm. Work patterns in this organization (as in many other high-tech industries) were project-oriented: Each employee was assigned to a certain project, and when that was completed (or sometimes even before), the employee was assigned to a new one.

The problem was that Evan, although outstanding in his own specialty, was not a team player. He liked to work alone and didn't know how to help or accept help from others. He greatly diminished his worth to the organization by refusing to change his attitude toward working with others.

It's not only high-tech or large corporations that require team orientation today. Teamwork is the backbone of small businesses as well. Jana, a young woman I know, recently got a job as a secretary in a small organization with a staff of seven. All seven people share one large room.

How uncomfortable the workday would be if each of those seven people were not a team player!

TEAMING UP FOR BUSINESS SUCCESS

Wherever you go in today's business world, there are certain words and phrases you hear over and over again: *quality circle, task force, action committee, employee participation group, joint union/management leadership panel, project group, self-directed work team.*

What do all these buzzwords signify? They're indicative of the tide of change in the structure of the American workplace. This country rose to economic power on a hierarchical management style: One person sat on the management "throne" and issued directives to all the subordinate levels. Ideas came from above and were simply carried out below. This structure was viewed as the most efficient way to get things done.

Efficiency isn't enough, however, to compete with today's worldwide technological advances. In order to keep up with and get ahead of the competition, many companies are looking for innovative ideas and new ways to solve old problems. And most of these companies have discovered that small work groups, or teams, are the answer. The hierarchical pyramid is changing to a team-oriented structure to motivate and energize employees, allow them greater participation in the decision-making process, and regain the sense of "family" and commitment that once made American business strong.

Employees at all levels are being asked to make this kind of team commitment. The days when rival managers are pitted against each other in fierce battles for power and position are numbered. In an article in the February 1990 *Training and Development Journal,* Gregory E. Huszczo states that "individuals in management and other leadership positions are being asked to team up with their counterparts instead of competing in the typical political 'turf wars' within organizations." To succeed in the business world of tomorrow, you're going to have to team up to do it.

TIPS FOR TEAMING UP

What makes a successful team? A team is more than individuals working together. Take a football team, for example. Just because you have the eleven best individual players in the country doesn't mean you'll have the greatest team. The success of the team also depends on how the eleven players support and work with each other. A good football team is much more than a collection of individual skills. The whole is greater than the sum of its parts.

What does it take to be a successful team member? Here are eight suggestions:

1. Recognize that your personal contribution and the team contribution are of equal value.
2. Be willing to help others when asked; be willing to ask for help when you need it.
3. Make sure you understand the objectives of the team and your role in it.
4. Express your ideas, suggestions, disagreements, and questions openly with other team members.
5. Be willing to accept comments and proposals from other team members; try to understand their point of view.
6. Realize that every team experiences conflict; work to resolve conflicts quickly and constructively.
7. Participate in team decisions while understanding that the team leader has final authority.
8. Take pride in the success of your team as well as in your own accomplishments.

A team player gives his or her best to the team, at the same time allowing others to contribute. Teams can't succeed with star players who think only of themselves. Becoming a team player means developing your interpersonal skills.

- Do you know the difference between being authoritative and being authoritarian?
- Can you criticize others constructively?
- Can you take criticism without being devastated by it?
- Do you know how to be assertive without being aggressive?

These are all questions you'll need to answer for yourself as you analyze your aptitude as a team player.

WOULD YOU PICK YOU?

The best teams in any sport are those that respect and use the talents of all their players. Each team member has his or her own job to do—but each player also knows that winning depends on everyone working together. A star player can't win the game if no one else is playing.

The first step in building your own team skills is to look around and observe other people. Who has real team spirit? If you were forming a team, whom would you choose? Would you pick yourself to be on the team? Or are you like Groucho Marx, who said, "I don't want to belong to any club that would have me as a member"?

ASSESS YOUR T.Q.

Remember the category on your elementary school report card, "Works well with others"? It was important in kindergarten, and it's important again today. Like a football manager, an employer is looking for the players with the best skills—and the ones who will support and work with each other.

Here is a short quiz that will give you an idea of your "team quotient." There are no right or wrong answers.

1. How do I feel about teams in general?
    A. I like being part of a group
    B. I usually feel ambivalent about group activities—sometimes I like them, sometimes I don't
    C. I usually feel like an outsider, not part of the group
2. Am I comfortable in a team environment?
    A. Most of the time
    B. I often feel the need to be careful about what I say
    C. I never feel I can be myself in front of a group
3. Do I contribute to team efforts?
    A. I make my share of suggestions
    B. I give opinions when asked
    C. I express myself only when absolutely necessary
4. How do I feel about team leaders?
    A. I respect their authority but let them know when I disagree with their decisions
    B. Leaders intimidate me, and I often pretend to know things I should be asking questions about
    C. I resent their authority and go out of my way to make problems
5. How do I feel about team members?
    A. I am usually concerned about others' well-being
    B. I am sometimes concerned about others
    C. I seldom go out of my way for anyone else
6. How do I feel about other people's opinions?
    A. I respect their opinions, even if they differ from mine
    B. I usually listen to what others have to say
    C. I'm intolerant of the views of others
7. How do I feel about criticism?
    A. I welcome it
    B. It makes me nervous, but I'm willing to listen
    C. I avoid it as much as possible

8. How do I view conflicts within the group?
   A. I think they're healthy and try to use them constructively
   B. It makes me uncomfortable, but I'm able to deal with it
   C. I'll do anything to avoid "making waves"
9. How do I fit into the "group dynamic"?
   A. I'm an active participant, but I allow others to work the way they want to work
   B. I like things done certain ways, but I will listen to others' ideas and opinions
   C. I tend to manipulate others to do things my way
10. How does the team influence me personally?
    A. I am clear about my personal values
    B. I doubt my personal values when others disagree with me
    C. I am largely influenced by the views of others

Give yourself 5 points for every A answer, 2 points for every B answer, and 1 point for every C answer.

If you scored from 35 to 50, your team quotient is excellent. You have a good attitude toward team concepts, team leaders, and other group members. If you scored from 20 to 34, you need to improve your outlook toward groups and group dynamics and take a more active role in team efforts. If you scored below 20, you're probably very much of a loner. You may need to change your style somewhat to work within a team-oriented workplace.

Can you find any examples in your past where you worked as part of a team? Consider your experiences at previous jobs, on sports teams, in religious organizations, on student councils, or in choirs, clubs, and scout troops. Even your family constitutes a team. Here are some questions to ask yourself about your background as a team player:

What was your role on the team? _____

_____

_____

What were some of the things you enjoyed about being on a team? _____

_____

_____

How did you deal with people who were not living up to your expectations? _____

_____

Were you able to help other people on your team? _____

_____

_____

Were you able to accept help from others? _____

_____

_____

Keep this important success factor in mind when you go in to any interview. For every two or three individual accomplishments you mention, bring up one in which you were part of a team. Don't always talk in terms of "I, I, I." Be sure to use the words, *we, the team,* and *the company.* Employers want to know you can work on your own, but they also want to be sure you can fit in with the rest of the company "family."

What positive actions can I take today to improve my team player skills?

_____

_____

_____

13

Success Factor #10

Value-Added Marketing

Sales and Marketing Principle #13

The success of value-added marketing lies in knowing what people want and giving them more than they expect.

THE NEW CUSTOMER SERVICE REPRESENTATIVE

Although it may seem otherwise in this age of electronic telephone answering systems, computer-generated mail, and fax machines, companies are still made up of human beings. And many companies are finding, because of all the high-tech gadgetry that surrounds them, that maintaining the human touch is all the more important. You *are* the company. Employers are looking for people who will reflect and represent their company's image.

With more and more people in business today having direct contact with the public, every employee becomes a representative of the company. We've not only moved into the information age, we've also moved into the age of the customer service representative.

THAT LITTLE SOMETHING EXTRA

This new emphasis on customer service is leading employers to hire people who go beyond what is absolutely necessary to get the job done. Employers want people who give more than what's expected—to the company, to the customer, and to themselves.

I recently had the pleasure of being a sponsor in an exchange student internship program. For six weeks, Victoria, a lovely Finnish student, was a part-time office assistant. She is the kind of person any employer would be happy to hire. She came in every morning with a "let's get started" attitude, and as soon as one job was completed she would ask, "What is next for me to do?" She will get my strongest recommendation for any job she goes after.

We've all seen examples where exceptional service makes a difference. My neighborhood is well known for its abundance of Szechuan Chinese restaurants (and I don't live in Chinatown). I've tried them all, and they all have similar menus and high-quality cuisine. So why is one restaurant my favorite above the others? Because of the service. The waiters and waitresses are friendly, polite, and rush to welcome me at the door. I wasn't even going to try this place when it first opened, because it seemed just like all the others. But I was standing outside the restaurant one afternoon, checking out the menu taped to the window, when the hostess came outside and invited me in to try the lunch special and have a free glass of wine.

That kind of service makes me feel I'm getting more value for my money.

VALUE-ADDED MARKETING

Companies today are looking for people who:

1. Know what people want
2. Give them more than they expect

You might think that marketing involves zooming in on what's unusual and singular about your product and "selling" those features to the buying public. In reality, successful marketing is finding out the needs of the buying public and figuring out how your product can exceed them.

As we defined it in Chapter 1, marketing encompasses all the activity that gets a product or service from the seller to the buyer. But because there's so much competition out there, it's getting more and more difficult to make any product or service stand out from the crowd. That's why understanding the importance of value-added marketing should be your top priority, whether you're part of a large organization, own your own business, or are in the process of looking for a job.

Every company today, large or small, is on the lookout for employees who give that something extra, people who have a "sales attitude" and aren't content merely to meet the customers' most basic needs.

Successful salespeople are persuasive, persistent, enthusiastic—they're initiators and go-getters. They have the nine marketable skills we've discussed so far and know how to use them for the company's benefit as well as their own. But most importantly, they go above and beyond the call of duty in serving the customer.

This is the attitude of the service society of the 1990s: Your job is to represent your company, solve your customers' problems, and fulfill their needs. That is your ultimate job description, whether you're the receptionist or the CEO. And it's this attitude, along with a "sales personality," that employers want to see.

Understanding the concepts behind selling and marketing is absolutely necessary for every employee today—not just to get a new job, but also to be successful in the one you have.

THE VISIBILITY FACTOR

Being successful in the job you have requires more than just doing your work well. It requires marketing—just as any product or service must be out there to be seen above the competition.

Everyone wants to get ahead, but not everyone is willing to pay the price—which involves making yourself visible. People who do get ahead are constantly asking themselves this question: What can I do to make myself stand out?

You can use this question as a jumping-off place wherever you are right now—whether you're in management, in the mailroom, still in school, engaged in volunteer work, or looking for your first job. Keep the value-added concept in mind. You'll not only be giving more, you'll be adding value to yourself!

Take advantage of any opportunities you come across to make yourself more visible. That means getting out in front of other people. If you're asked to head a committee, join a team, or give a presentation, do it. If your organization needs a spokesperson, volunteer. If you've been given an award, earned a degree, or received an unusual honor, tell the local paper. Let people know. In order to be successful, you've got to be seen.

That doesn't mean you have to pull publicity stunts or get your name in the tabloids. It does mean that self-promotion and high visibility should be part of your overall plan for success.

You want to give potential employers the signal that you understand the importance of value-added marketing. According to Michael Le Boeuf, author of *How to Win Customers and Keep Them for Life,* the customer's perception of the business or service is what causes him to buy. If the customer perceives he's being given special attention, he'll return to get that attention again; he'll even pay a higher price for it. If a potential employer perceives that you take pride in your work and are willing to go that extra mile, he or she will be much more inclined to consider you for the job and pay a higher price to get you.

Everything about you is part of your marketing effort: the way you look, the way you speak on the phone, your business cards, the letters you write. As I wrote in my book *Smart Questions: A New Strategy for Successful Managers,* "Your image is an expression of your best self. It's not something you put on like a dress or a suit. Your image should reinforce all of your best qualities. A strong image almost always reflects certain constants: self-confidence, reliability, the unmistakable aura of success."

Here are some questions to ask yourself in order to work on improving your image:

How am I presently perceived? _____

_____

_____

How do I feel about those perceptions? _____

_____

_____

How would I like to be perceived? _____

_____

_____

When I speak on the telephone or write a letter, memo, or speech, how do I want others to feel about me? _____

_____

_____

If I were a potential employer, how would I describe me? _____

_____

_____

What do I have to offer that's unique and special? _____

_____

_____

What can I do to enhance my best qualities? _____

_____

_____

Our culture teaches us not to blow our own horns. You needn't be arrogant to be successful, but a certain degree of self-promotion is necessary. Don't be afraid to be proud of your accomplishments, to say "That was my idea," to present yourself with energy and enthusiasm. Remember the old rhyme that goes:

> The codfish lays 10,000 eggs, the homely hen lays one
> The codfish never cackles to tell us what she's done
> And so we scorn the codfish
> While the humble hen we prize
> It only goes to show, it pays to advertise!

I AM, THEREFORE I SELL

These ten success factors are the most important skills you will need to take with you through the job search process. The rest of this book will continue your journey of self-discovery, including your discovery of the tools you'll need to take you from your next job through the rest of your life.

You'll go through many career changes in your lifetime. You may decide to change jobs every two or three years, you may decide to switch from one field to another, you may decide to retire, you may decide to move to Tibet. But whatever your decisions are, you'll have the sales and marketing skills to make any possibility a reality.

What positive actions can I take today to improve my value-added marketing skills? _____

_____

_____

How many of these ten success factors do you already possess? Probably more than you think. Take the following quiz and find out.

12. You are a supervisor. You have just instituted a new work flow program for your staff which has increased production by 25 percent. Do you:
    A. Write up a report and send it to your department head
    B. Accept it as part of your job and make no mention of it
    C. Write up a report showing how this could apply to other departments as well and arrange a meeting with your boss and other department heads
13. What's the first question you ask at a job interview?
    A. "What are the benefits?"
    B. "What's my career path here?"
    C. "What is this job really like?"
14. Do you feel you work for:
    A. Security and money
    B. Recognition and moving up in the organization
    C. Building a professional career that will span a lifetime
15. If your boss criticizes your latest report that took three grueling months to finish, do you:
    A. Defend yourself loudly because you worked so hard on it
    B. "Yes" him or her, but feel lousy about it
    C. After thinking about it, realize that the criticisms are valid and make the changes
16. You planned a vacation with friends and they've decided to go somewhere else at the last minute. Do you:
    A. Go on the trip you've planned
    B. Go along with their new plans
    C. Look for other friends to go where you want to go
17. At a party, do you:
    A. Meet everyone
    B. Talk to one or two acquaintances who are familiar
    C. Chat with the bartender the entire evening
18. You're usually a casual dresser, but you've been invited to a business lunch at a fancy restaurant with a strict dress code. Do you:
    A. Decide that you don't want to conform and cancel the lunch
    B. Realize that it's a small price to pay
    C. Dress according to the rules but hate every minute of it
19. Your voting record shows:
    A. You vote for the candidate of your choice, regardless of party
    B. You follow your party line
    C. You don't vote
20. Your car has broken down and you were to pick up a friend at the airport. You can't get there on time. Do you:
    A. Call the airport and have your friend paged
    B. Leave your car with a tow truck and hitch a ride to the airport
    C. Figure your friend will manage, and take care of your car
21. If someone pushes ahead of you in line, do you:
    A. Speak up

    B. Move in front of the offending party

    C. Complain to your partner

22. You've been made part of an existing team or group project. Do you:

    A. Feel shy about asking the others for help

    B. Do your part alone, thinking your best contribution is to do your own work well

    C. Find out what the others' areas of expertise are and how you can exchange the information you need

23. You've been asked to create more work space in a crowded area. Do you:

    A. Bring in an interior designer

    B. Design a few sample floor plans

    C. Find someone who'd done something similar and copy his design

24. If you were in college, what kind of job would you look for in the summer?

    A. Anything you could get

    B. Something easy and relaxing

    C. Something related to a potential career

25. If your best friend, who is a sharp dresser, criticizes your choice of attire, do you:

    A. Get defensive and argue the merits of your own personal style

    B. Listen, but do what you want anyhow

    C. Realize that there's some truth in the comments and decide to change your outfit

RATE YOUR SUCCESS FACTORS

1. Decision making   A = 4   B = 0   C = 5

    The best way to make a decision is to take the time to look at several options and ask experts for advice (C). In the future it's going to be more important to seek expert help, because business functions are becoming so specialized. The answer also shows you're willing to bring other people into the decision-making process. Many times we have to make quick decisions (A). But it's a good idea to think about the possible consequences. You can't really avoid decisions by procrastinating (B)— they only come back to haunt you later.

2. Independence   A = 5   B = 4   C = 1

    Calling technical support (B) is not a bad idea when you're in trouble. While in question 1 asking for advice was the best choice, here a better choice is to go back to the manual (A). If you're really stuck, you can call for help. Going back to the old design (C) may be easier—but you must have had a reason for wanting to change the design in the first place. If you give up every time you hit an obstacle, you won't get very far.

3. Independence   A = 0   B = 3   C = 1
If you're working too many hours (B), it's probably because you enjoy what you're doing. But you have to be able to set limits for yourself. You don't want to work all the time. If you need support and find it very difficult to work without it (C), you may be better off not working at home—or you may have to be creative in finding ways to get the support you need. There are always going to be distractions working at home (A). If you find this a problem, working at home may not be suited to your personality.

4. Independence   A = 1   B = 3   C = 5
With people working more and more on their own, understanding and focusing on priorities (C) will be essential skills. Having a "to do" list is good (B), as long as you remember to check the list. Going with the flow (A) is fine for a vacation day, but if there's work to be done, you'll need to have the planning skills and initiative to get things done.

5. Communication skills   A = 0   B = 3   C = 5
If you are being described as a persuasive and interesting storyteller (C), you should get a 5+. That's exactly what a good salesperson needs to be. It's also good to be organized and have a lot of information (B), but remember that too much information is going to be boring and turn people off. If you're very shy and nervous (A), people won't listen to you, no matter how much you know. Practice your communication skills.

6. Communication skills   A = 0   B = 2   C = 5
You need to be clear and concise and get right to the point (C). Too many people write too much and too long and it becomes difficult to follow. It's important to be logical, but it's hard to see the logic if you are too wordy (B). If you're a "creative" speller (A), study on your own or take a course to help you correct your mistakes.

7. Communication skills   A = 5   B = 1   C = 3
In the information age, listening skills will be vital in order to get the information you need. Being attentive (A) will not only provide you with data: it also will show that you care about people's feelings. Listening only to the facts (C) means that you aren't paying attention to feelings or intent. You can learn to listen for clues in those areas as well as for the words. If you don't pay attention and you interrupt (B), you're going to have problems. Go back and study the difference between active and passive listening.

8. Evaluation skills   A = 0   B = 5   C = 2

Being open-minded (B) is going to be of major importance in building evaluation skills. You'll need to see all sides of the story, be objective, and rely on your own judgment in order to make the best decisions. Jumping to conclusions (C) is never a good idea and usually means you're trying to make a decision without having enough information. If you think you have no analytical skills (A), look into your own life and see how you evaluate people and situations during daily activities.

9. Sales and marketing skills   A = 0   B = 5   C = 3

Skill in negotiating is also a critical element of selling and marketing yourself. You have a lot of power when you've been offered a job—your future employer is delighted that the search is over. The hiring process is tough and time-consuming. In negotiating, it's important to pause after asking a closing question or making an important pronouncement (B). This kind of negotiating technique will be a big advantage. If your explanation of why you need the money is a sound one, you may get it (C); but by talking too much you may just talk yourself out of the job as well. Accepting the salary and hoping you'll get a raise later (A) is risky. You're in a strong position now—this is the time to ask for what you think you're worth.

10. Communication skills   A = 0   B = 3   C = 5

Communication skills include body language and other nonverbal signals—including how and where we place ourselves for a conversation. In an interview, you want to create a friendly atmosphere. People hire people they like and feel comfortable with. The couch is the most informal and the best choice (C). Sitting opposite the desk (A) creates a barrier between you and the boss and puts you in a less advantageous position. Sitting in a chair alongside the desk (B) doesn't create quite as open an atmosphere, but it's still better than having the desk between the two of you.

11. Communication skills   A = 5   B = 2   C = 3

Calling on a colleague you've met at a professional conference (A) is a good example of effective networking, one of the most potent marketing weapons in a job seeker's arsenal. Calling a headhunter or a placement agency (C) is good if you're just the kind of person they're looking for. It's better to take action on your own. There's no harm in looking in the newspapers (B), but everyone else is looking there too. Working on your networking skills will probably get you farther than looking in the classifieds.

12. Foresight   A = 3   B = 1   C = 5

You score extra points for seeing the possibilities in your project not only for yourself but for the company (C). People who can turn foresight into profitable action will have little trouble succeeding in almost any field. You are on the right track by showing your report to your boss (A). If your boss sees the possibilities too, you might get some recognition—but why not be more ambitious? If you just accept it as part of your job (B), you're missing out on a good opportunity to increase your value to your company.

13. Evaluation   A = 1   B = 3   C = 5
When you're looking for a job, you make choices that affect your future. You need the right information to make the best choice. Asking about the career path (B) might provide some insight into your future with the company. But many jobs, especially at smaller companies, may not have clear career paths. Benefits are important (A), but if that's your main concern, you're probably shortchanging yourself. What you're really looking for is an interesting and challenging job—which is why it's so important to ask questions and find out what the job is really like (C).

14. Commitment   A = 1   B = 3   C = 5
Working to build your career over the course of a lifetime is the best route to personal and professional happiness (C). If your main reason for working is just to move up in the organization (B), you may miss out on the deeper satisfaction of contributing meaningfully in a job you really enjoy. With the pace of mergers and acquisitions quickening, working for job security and money alone (A) could be frustrating.

15. Adaptability   A = 1   B = 0   C = 5
In your working lifetime, you'll probably be part of many teams and you'll need to be flexible and open to suggestions. If you're able to deal with criticism and not be defensive (C), you'll move ahead faster. Feeling angry is self-destructive (B). Why say yes if you disagree? Defending yourself (A) shows that you believe in your abilities, but you should determine if the criticism has any validity before you defend your work.

16. Independence   A = 5   B = 1   C = 4
Going by yourself (A) means you don't depend on other people for your enjoyment. You get full credit for being able to enjoy yourself despite the change in plans. There is nothing wrong with wanting to share your activity with others; looking for others to go with you is another good choice (C). You get one point for wanting to be with your friends (B), but what happened to your plans? Were you thinking independently, or did you give in to peer pressure?

17. Communication skills   A = 5   B = 3   C = 1
A party is a wonderful opportunity to practice your communication skills. If you make a conscious effort to meet and mingle (A), you may make social or business contacts you never dreamed possible. Building

a strong support base with only two or three acquaintances (B) can also be helpful, at least to get your networking started. If the bartender looks like Tom Cruise or Kim Basinger, you'll get extra points; otherwise this is not a good choice (C). Nothing against bartenders—it's just that staying in one place for the whole party is not the best way to make new friends and contacts.

18. Adaptability   A = 1   B = 5   C = 3

Corporate fit will still be an issue for some time to come, and if you're interested in moving ahead you may have to make some small compromises. It's one thing to stick up for your principles, but quite another to be stubborn and closed-minded. If you cancel the lunch (A), you may be cutting off your nose to spite your face. If you dress appropriately but resent it (C), you'll be uncomfortable during the whole lunch and unable to conduct the business at hand. Realizing it's a small price to pay (B) shows you're able to judge each situation as it comes up and make appropriate adjustments.

19. Independence   A = 5   B = 2   C = 0

You get two points for following your party line (B). It does show a certain degree of commitment and loyalty, but it means you're prone to letting others tell you what to do. Voting for the candidate of your choice (A) shows you make careful, thoughtful decisions on your own and don't take the easy way out. You get no points if you don't vote (C).

20. Reliability   A = 5   B = 3   C = 0

Accidents happen. The important thing is to make sure you don't leave your friend stranded and waiting at the airport. By having your friend paged (A), you can explain the difficulty and make arrangements to meet elsewhere. Since you're already too late to pick your friend up, hitching a ride to the airport (B) is not a practical solution. Then neither one of you will have a ride home. But it does show that you're concerned and don't want to leave your friend wondering what happened to you. Your friend will probably survive if you don't show up (C), but this is a very selfish and unreliable way to behave.

21. Communication skills   A = 5   B = 4   C = 2

Knowing how to communicate well even when angry is a valuable skill. If someone pushes ahead of you, you've got to let that person know—assertively, not aggressively—that you're aware of what he or she has done and are angry about it (A). Actions often speak louder than words (B) and moving ahead of the offending party can make you feel better about not just standing by and letting people push you around. If you complain to your partner (C), you can let off steam, but it won't get you back ahead in the line.

22. Team player   A = 1   B = 3   C = 5

It's difficult to fit right into an already existing group. But if you're shy about asking for help (A), it will be even harder to get into the swing of things. People like to help others, especially if you're asking about their areas of expertise. You always want to do your part well (B), but when you're working as part of a team everyone must contribute to the group effort in order to make it a success. The best way to become part of the team is to find out how you can help the others and let them know how they can help you (C).

23. Creativity   A = 3   B = 5   C = 3

This is a problem-solving question, and all problem-solving requires creative thinking. Designing a few sample floor plans (B) shows you can see problems from many different angles and come up with a solution. Answers (A) and (C) aren't bad choices, but they involve looking to others for solutions. Asking others for help is better than giving up, but only if you've made a strong effort on your own first.

24. Foresight   A = 2   B = 1   C = 5

You work hard at school all year, so during the summer you want something easy and relaxing (B). If the only thing you want out of a job is cash, this may be the right choice for you. But you're missing a chance to develop your professional skills. Choosing a job that's related to a potential career (C) means you're always looking for ways to grow and develop and that you have an eye to the future. Taking anything you can get may be the only choice you have (A); jobs for college students aren't always easy to find.

25. Adaptability   A = 0   B = 3   C = 5

How you react to criticism shows a lot about your adaptability. When people criticize you, it means they're asking you to change. If you see this as a threat, you'll be defensive (A) and unwilling to make any changes, even ones that would be to your benefit. Listening to suggestions without being defensive gets you three points (B), even if you decide to go with your original choice. If you admire your friend's taste in clothing and listen to the suggestions (C), it means you have an open mind and are willing to change when someone else makes a valid suggestion.

SCORING

96–120 points

Congratulations! You're an ideal job candidate. You possess most of the qualities employers are looking for and will enjoy adapting to a changing world. Now all you need is to develop your marketing plan and go after the career you want.

71–95 points

You have done very well, and with just a little improvement you should have no trouble achieving your goals. There is always room for improvement, of course—but you're the type who's willing to make that improvement.

46–70 points

You tend to be set in your ways and are less willing to explore new ground. If you want to succeed, you'll have to learn to be more open-minded and willing to learn new skills. That you are reading this book, however, means you're willing to give it a try. You'll need a little more practice, but don't be afraid to go for what you want.

45 points or less

To be successful in the years to come, you're going to have to put in some time doing the exercises in the success factors chapters. You tend to be a more passive person, allowing others to make choices for you. Starting now, you can make the choice to put this knowledge about yourself to good use. Using this book as a guide will help you on your way to future success.

You can see from this quiz that being prepared for success may not always be easy. There are few absolutely right or wrong answers. Nor is there a perfect response for all the intricate situations that crop up in day-to-day working and living. This book will help you develop the answers you'll need to get ahead in this increasingly complex world of ours.

PART THREE

Know Your Product

THE FUNDAMENTAL RULE OF SALES

During my Marketing Yourself seminars I often ask people to make a quick list of their proudest accomplishments. One woman, Angela, seemed to be having an especially difficult time making her list, so I asked her a few questions.

"What do you do?" I asked.

She said, "I'm a mechanical artist at a small design firm."

"Do you like what you do?" I asked.

"Most of the time. A lot of times I feel like they don't appreciate me very much, though."

"Tell me," I said, "can you think of a time when you did feel appreciated? Anything out of the ordinary?"

Angela thought for a while, and then described a time when the art director became ill in the middle of preparing a major presentation, and she stepped in and finished the project—on time. The client loved it and went on to recommend her company to three other clients.

After several more minutes of probing and questioning, Angela estimated that her company had received over $1,600,000 in new business because she was able to complete that project successfully. And she had almost forgotten about it!

Now, isn't that amazing? How can a person forget about $1,600,000?

Surprisingly, Angela's response isn't unique. Whenever I ask for a record of past accomplishments, most people come up with a very short list. This isn't due to a lack of accomplishments—it's because people often forget or undervalue their own achievements.

Angela would have a hard time selling herself to a potential employer because she doesn't know her product well enough, even though the product is her own self! The most basic rule of sales is that *you must know everything there is to know about your product.* Buyers all want to know the same thing: "Why should I buy *your* product? What does your product have to offer that another doesn't?"

Just how do you know what it is that makes you special, what it is that you are offering the "buying public"? You must know what it is about that product that someone else would need and want—even if they don't know it themselves.

15

Your Career and
Confidence Inventory

Sales and Marketing Principle #15

Success comes from building on your strengths, not from correcting your weaknesses.

TAKING STOCK OF YOURSELF

I'm going to ask you to do an assignment.

"What?" you say, "Homework? I hate homework! I know what I've done in the past—I have my résumé. I think I'll just skip to the chapter on interviewing skills. That's where I always mess up."

I know. I hate homework, too. But perhaps the reason you "mess up" at interviews is you haven't done enough homework. It's like taking a history exam without studying. You may have some general knowledge of the subject, but the specifics are going to trip you up. You may know *what* happened but you also need to know what difference those events made to the world—why they were important.

The same concept applies to you. You may know what you did, but a prospective employer will want to know what effect it had—on your company, or your schoolwork, or your personal life. And just as the history professor could tell when you hadn't studied, the interviewer will know when you are not thoroughly prepared.

You have to take stock of yourself. Go back and look at your past with new eyes. It doesn't matter if you have forty years of work experience or if you have none. Everything you've done in your life—everything you are—counts. Make a list of your life's achievements. Don't worry, you're not expected to include the Nobel Peace Prize. Perhaps you won an award for selling the most cookies in your Girl Scout troop. Or perhaps you designed a new brochure for your father's business, or maybe you were a champion swimmer in college. . . .

85

Taking stock of the merchandise is an essential step to beginning any new sales or marketing campaign. This chapter will help you catalog your personal accomplishments. I call this catalog your Career and Confidence Inventory.

HOW YOUR CCI WILL INCREASE YOUR SELLING POWER

Your CCI will enable you to find out exactly what you've done in the past in order to get a better price for your services in the future. *Your Career and Confidence Inventory is an organized list of all your accomplishments*. It will take time to compile, but it's time well spent. This is the key to your marketing plan. And it's something that you'll add to and expand for the rest of your life.

Here is what your CCI can do for you:

1. It's an indispensable reference guide for use in all your communications with prospective employers.
2. It will help you to get recognition and promotion in your present job.
3. It's the basis for your "sales" letters and telephone calls.
4. It will help build your confidence by reminding you what you've done and how good you are.

DISCOVERING WHAT MAKES YOU TICK

Your CCI will tell you a lot about yourself that employers would like to know. And you won't feel put on the spot trying to come up with impressive stories. Having done your homework, you'll be prepared for the "quiz." Susan Boren of Dayton Hudson Corporation says that when she interviews people, she tries to find out what makes them tick. She spends time "talking with individuals to determine how they've changed in their work and personal lives, and how they've made choices in their lives. . . . This is all done during the interviews."

Imagine that Angela (whom we met in the introduction to Part Three) is being interviewed for a new job and the prospective boss says, "I'm looking for a real team player. Can you tell me something about yourself that would demonstrate your ability to pitch in and help?"

If Angela hadn't done her homework, she might not have remembered her $1,600,000 emergency takeover story. She wouldn't have had anything to offer as proof of her abilities. But because she'd done her homework, the question didn't take her by surprise; she had a good answer and she made a good impression.

CAREER OBJECTIVES: THE HIDDEN BENEFIT OF YOUR CCI

There is another hidden benefit to putting in time on your CCI. In order to take full advantage of the marketing concepts in this book, you'll need to have a clear and specific career objective. In other words, you have to know what you want to do. Just as you can't make the general statement "I'm going to California" (you have to know where in California you want to go), you can't just "look for a job." You have to be more specific.

"Computers," you say. "I want to work with computers."

Good choice. Computer careers are hot right now; there are lots of opportunities. But take a look at this partial list of computer careers:

- Application programmer
- Computer consultant
- Computer scientist
- Computer security specialist
- Database programmer
- Computer engineer
- Hardware designer
- Office automation specialist
- Sales representative
- Systems programmer
- Technical writer
- Word processing operator

And this is just part of the list! There are many more categories and subcategories of computer careers from which to choose. The more specific you are about what you want to do, the easier it will be to target your marketing efforts to people who are looking for your special talents.

Don't be concerned if you don't have a specific job objective right now. Your CCI can help you develop your job objective; by taking a look back through your experiences and accomplishments, you'll be able to see exactly what you're good at.

BEGIN AT THE BEGINNING...

Take the time to think about the events in your life. Write them out in story form; they don't have to be in chronological order. You can go as far back as you like, all the way back to that paper route or the lemonade stand in front of your house. If you have no work experience, think about how you've organized your life, how you've managed on a limited budget and how you made decisions for major purchases or important life choices. Perhaps you're a young mother who organized a play group for the preschoolers in your neighborhood. Or maybe you volunteered as a Big Brother to a less fortunate family.

If you're still in school, think about how you organize your study time, how you balance sports and academics, how you decided on your school or course of study, and how you improved your study habits.

If you're working presently, think about ways in which you saved your company money, how you reorganized and raised productivity, how you get along with your boss and co-workers, and how you developed new systems or improved the old ones.

Don't place value judgments on anything. Don't worry about your writing style—this is a personal inventory, not a submittable résumé. Don't be shy. Include the small and the large, and don't be concerned about applicability. At the moment, you are concerned only with getting it all down on paper.

Here are some guidelines to help you get started, examples of questions you might ask yourself. Use these questions as springboards, then dive right in and keep going on your own:

What I accomplished in school
Courses:

How were my grades? _____

_____

Did I get any special comments or commendations from teachers?

_____

_____

What was my best subject? _____

_____

What made it special? _____

_____

Clubs or activities:

Did I hold any offices? _____

_____

Was I part of any club competitions? _____

_____

Did I have any special responsibilities? _____

_____

Did I receive any awards or commendations? _____

_____

Sports:

What position did I play? _____

_____

How did I do in competition? _____

_____

Were there any outstanding games I remember? _____

_____

How, when, and where did I practice? _____

_____

Did I receive any awards or commendations? _____

_____

Part-time work:

How, when, and where? _____

_____

How did I balance my job with schoolwork? _____

_____

What did I do with the money? _____

_____

Awards:

Academic? _____

_____

Athletic? _____

_____

Extracurricular activities? _____

_____

Community services? _____

_____

Special Interests:

What did I do outside of school? _____

_____

How, when, and where? _____

_____

How did I balance this with schoolwork? _____

_____

Other accomplishments? _____

_____

What I accomplished at home
Planning and scheduling:

How do I run my day? _____

_____

How do I get things done for myself and my family? _____

_____

How do I keep track of schedules, appointments, social events?

_____

_____

Part-time work:

How, when, and where? _____

_____

How did I balance my job with family life? _____

_____

What did I do with the money? _____

_____

Volunteer work:

How, when, and where? _____

_____

How did I balance my job with family life? _____

_____

Did I receive any awards or recognition? _____

_____

Budgeting:

How do I keep my "books" or record my spending? _____

_____

How have I been able to save money for myself and my family? _____

_____

How have I been able to make extra money? _____

_____

Prioritizing:

How do I decide what's most important in my day? Week? Month?

_____

_____

Do I set goals for myself? _____

_____

Do I accomplish them? _____

_____

Entertaining:

How do I plan social events? _____

_____

How do I organize my extra time, money? _____

_____

Do I do all the work? Do I delegate? _____

_____

Do I plan the menu, shop, cook, hire a caterer, decorate? _____

_____

Hobbies and interests:

What are my special interests? _____

_____

How do I spend my "spare" time? Do I read, travel, cook, sew, write, work out, build furniture, sing, etc? _____

_____

Other accomplishments? _____

_____

What I accomplished at work
Organization:

Have I set up systems to make my job more efficient? _____

_____

How do I organize my day's work? _____

_____

How have I helped others be more organized? _____

_____

New ideas:

What new ideas have I had for my work or company? Where did the ideas come from? _____

_____

How were they implemented? _____

_____

Saved company money:

What exactly did I do? _____

_____

How much money was involved? _____

_____

Was it an assigned task, or did I come up with the idea myself? _____

_____

Was it a one-shot deal or a continuing assignment? _____

_____

Teamwork:

How do I get along with colleagues? _____

How do I get along with bosses and supervisors? _____

Have I led any team projects? _____

Have I been involved in any collaborative efforts? _____

Improvements:

What suggestions have I had for my work or company? _____

Where did the idea come from? _____

Whom did I tell, and how did I tell them? _____

How was it implemented? _____

Affiliations, societies, associations:

What work-related organizations have I belonged to? _____

Were there requirements to join? _____

Did I participate or hold any office? _____

Did I contribute to any volunteer activities? _____

Have I written for, or been featured in, the newsletter? _____

SKILLED AND UNSKILLED LABOR

Many people today consider themselves unskilled labor because they don't have a lot of work experience or because they "don't know how to do anything else." What they don't realize is that they may already possess the most important skills they'll ever need—skills they use every day in their jobs and in their lives, and skills that are becoming more and more appreciated as the nature of work is changing. You'll be expected to work with less supervision, but you'll also be asked to make informed, important decisions.

Almost everyone's job is being affected by the demand for higher skill levels. It used to be that a gas station attendant was required to know how to pump gas, check the oil, and make correct change. Now the same attendant may never even touch the gas pump or step out of the glass-enclosed booth. But he or she needs to know how to handle credit cards, how to run a computer, even how to manage the mini–grocery store. One-stop shopping has made it easier on the customer, but more demanding for the employee.

"It's amazing to me," one manager told me recently. "These kids come out of school thinking they're so smart. But ask them to write up a simple report or memo—they don't know how to do it." I've heard other complaints, from "No one has any initiative these days" to "I don't know what to do with this guy. When it comes to computers, the kid's a genius, but he doesn't know how to relate to people." Assistant Secretary of Labor Roberts T. Jones says that there will be a definite lack of opportunity for unskilled labor in the future. "To obtain the growth jobs that every American wants," he says, "you'll have to invest more in basic skill attainment."

Skilled workers are traditionally defined as those who have technical expertise in a particular (and narrow) field. But there are other, more basic abilities that most people do not take into account in the search for their own job qualifications.

These abilities are universal; they apply no matter what job you are doing. They allow you to function responsibly and responsively in any work situation and are the skills that are becoming more and more valuable as the workplace continues to change.

Why? Because they are transferable skills—they go with you from promotion to promotion, from company to company, even from one career to another. They are now, and will continue to be, universally valued and applicable.

CHECK OFF YOUR SELLING POINTS

Although we looked at ten of the most universally marketable skills in Part Two, there are many more skills applicable to any job or career you may pursue.

Look for these basic, transferable skills when listing your CCI accomplishments. Check the ones that apply to you:

Analyze and edit written material _____

Do library and research work _____

Conduct surveys and interviews _____

Analyze and evaluate ideas and presentations _____

Travel: meet with colleagues, meet with the public _____

Identify problem areas _____

Develop new approaches to problems _____

Help people with their problems _____

Supervise and lead others _____

Evaluate and appraise others _____

Observe, inspect, review work of others _____

Plan, organize, systematize, revise _____

Work on long-term projects _____

Do detailed and accurate work _____

Meet work deadlines _____

Invent, imagine, create, design _____

Calculate, analyze, use computers _____

Motivate others _____

Think logically _____

Manage time _____

Set goals _____

Work on more than one thing at a time _____

Manage stress _____

Delegate _____

Teach or instruct _____

Have patience _____

Show assertiveness _____

Take risks _____

Have willingness to learn _____

Show enthusiasm _____

Coach   _____

Display a sense of humor   _____

A PORTABLE TOOLBOX OF SKILLS

Options is the key word here. If you have an array of tools before you and you know how to use them all, you can choose the ones best suited to the task at hand. If you know what a screwdriver is and how to use it, you won't waste time picking up a hammer. Having a portable "toolbox" of skills always available is what your working future is all about.

The skills you have checked off are your strongest selling points. Suppose an employer doesn't want to hire you because you don't have work experience that directly relates to the job opening. He or she says, "I'm looking for an experienced administrative assistant. You've never done this before." How would you answer?

It may be true that you don't have the experience, but if you've done your inventory, you know what skills you have. You know you can organize, prioritize, think logically and accurately. You're resourceful and detail-oriented; you have a willingness to learn. These are important skills in any job. You'll sell yourself by demonstrating how you have used these skills and abilities in your past accomplishments.

These are the skills that, separately and together, allow you to work confidently and effectively in any situation. They make you *valuable;* they enhance job satisfaction, increase productivity, and give you the competitive edge.

A *skill* is defined as anything you can learn to do competently, a developed aptitude or ability. Any of the skills on the list you've just examined can be taught, practiced, and mastered effectively. The more you use them, the easier they become. And you can practice most of them in all your daily activities.

Discovering abilities and skills that can be transferred from one job or career to another is the main reason you're writing your CCI.

Marshall, a political science major who had been an expert researcher in college, used that research skill to obtain a job as a research assistant with the American Civil Liberties Union. Kathryn is a single parent who created beautiful Christmas ornaments at home. She took this skill to a major women's magazine and became a contributing editor in their crafts department. And Dan, who for years had been a popular high school guidance counselor, used his knack for helping people to begin a career as a training and development executive in a large midwestern utility company. All these people discovered their portable skills after writing their CCIs.

Now that you have a good idea of the portable skills you possess, are you ready to go out and sell them to future employers? Not quite. You can't just go out and hand an employer a list of every single skill you've ever mastered. Remember the concepts of marketing: You have to know what he or she is looking for and how your product can help solve his or her problems. The next chapter will let you in on one of the surefire selling secrets used by all the top sales professionals: benefit selling.

16

Benefit Selling

The Real Reasons Employers Say Yes

Sales and Marketing Principle #16

People want to know the features, but they buy for the benefits.

"I have some swampland in Florida I want to sell you," I say.

"Not interested," you answer, wisely.

"It's more than fifty acres and filled with mosquitoes and alligators," I say.

"Not interested," you say.

"It's very cheap," I say.

"Still not interested," you say.

"It comes with a map," I say.

"So what?" you say.

"So," I say, "this map shows the way to the Fountain of Youth, which lies in the middle of the swamp."

"It does?" you say.

"Yes, it does," I say, "and not only will this Fountain of Youth keep you young and healthy, it will make you millions of dollars as well."

"It will?" you say.

"Guaranteed," I say. "Plus, you'll be the envy of everyone you know, be interviewed by Barbara Walters, and win the Nobel Peace Prize by allowing only those heads of state who sign a global peace treaty access to your fountain."

"I'll buy the swampland," you say.

Not an easy sale, but I did it. And what made you buy? It wasn't the fifty acres, I'm sure, or the mosquitoes or alligators. It wasn't the map.

It wasn't even the fountain itself. You bought this swampland because it holds the promise of health, wealth, fame, and power. You didn't buy because of what the swampland *is,* you bought because of what it could *do for you*.

THE "WHAT'S IN IT FOR ME" PRINCIPLE

The only reason you'd ever buy that swampland—or anything else, for that matter—is because *there's something in it for you*. The only reason an employer will hire you for a particular job is because *there's something in it for him*. You have to find out what that something is. That's how you make the sale.

The most successful salespeople rely on what is known in the sales trade as *benefit selling*. They know that all customers are asking themselves one simple question before they buy anything: "What's in it for me?" And they know they'll have to answer this question before they can make the sale. The secret of successful benefit selling is knowing the difference between features and benefits.

Features are used to describe what a product or service is. *The features of a product remain the same for everyone*. A green and blue plaid shirt that buttons down the front is always a green and blue plaid shirt that buttons down the front, no matter who buys it. If you hate plaid, or if you prefer pullovers, you probably won't buy this shirt. But if the green in this shirt brings out the green in your eyes and perfectly matches the new outfit you bought last week, the sale is made.

The benefits of a product change for each person who considers the purchase. People want to know the features, but they buy for the benefits. People don't buy an air conditioner because they love having a big brown box sticking out their window. They buy an air conditioner to be more comfortable during the hot summer months.

My husband loves to fish in his spare time; I enjoy jogging and bicycle riding. A few years ago, a travel agent was trying to convince us to go to a beautiful new resort that had just opened in the Bahamas. He described all of its best features: the rooms, the location, the casinos, and the reasonable price. But we'd already been to the Bahamas. We don't gamble, and for the same money we could have gone somewhere we hadn't been before.

"The fishing is really spectacular down there this time of year," the travel agent said, and my husband was ready to go. I still had my doubts. The travel agent made a phone call. "The beach is perfect for jogging," he said, "and the hotel rents bikes to guests for a very small fee." We went to that resort and both of us had a wonderful time, each for different reasons.

Here's a short list of a table's features and benefits. See if you can tell which is which:

	Feature	Benefit
1. The table has four legs	____	____
2. The table is lightweight so it can be moved easily	____	____
3. The table is white with black trim	____	____
4. The table has a formica top	____	____
5. The table can be cleaned easily with paper towels and glass cleaner	____	____

1, 3 and 4 are features, 2 is a benefit, and 5 is both a feature and benefit. Get the idea? Try it yourself. Take any familiar object around the house and see if you can describe its features and benefits.

FOCUS ON THE BUYER

Employers "buy" for their own reasons. Whether they hire you as a full-time employee, a free-lancer, or an outside consultant, prospective employers will be "buying" your services, and they will buy for *their* reasons, not yours.

Imagine that you are an importer of French perfumes and you're looking for an administrative assistant. You're out of the office frequently, you're slightly disorganized, and you need someone who can use the computer.

You see several candidates who all seem responsible, organized, and have good knowledge of the software you use. And they all *want the job*. What would make you hire one above the rest? As it turns out, two of the candidates speak French, a big benefit to you. That narrows the field. In the end, you go with the candidate who can start on Monday, because it's important that you get someone *now*. You didn't hire this person because he wanted the job more than the others. You hired him because he filled more of your needs than the other candidates did.

Translating your job search efforts into sales and marketing terms is the way to build your lifetime career strategy. Your reasons for wanting a new job or career are not important to a prospective employer. You'll be hired only if you fill the employer's requirements and satisfy his or her needs.

Any interviews you go on, any letters you send, any phone calls you make, must be focused on what your employer needs and what problems he needs to have solved. The more you can tap into this, the more he'll want to hire you.

Suppose you saw an advertisement that read:

COME IN AND BUY MY SHOES
THEY'RE EXPENSIVE, BUT I NEED TO MAKE
A LARGE PROFIT
IF YOU BUY THESE SHOES,
I'LL MAKE A MILLION DOLLARS

You would never buy shoes just so someone else could make a lot of money. You might, however, respond to an ad that read:

COME IN AND BUY MY SHOES
THEY'RE EXPENSIVE,
BUT THEY'RE THE MOST COMFORTABLE SHOES
YOU'LL EVER WEAR
IF YOU BUY THESE SHOES,
YOU'LL FEEL LIKE A MILLION DOLLARS

SECRET REASONS WHY WE GET HIRED

Do you know what makes employers "buy," or hire? They make this decision for their own emotional reasons. This has always been true and will remain true no matter how many technological advances the future holds. Emotional needs will not be changing, even if the world does. So while you may have to reshape your attitudes and learn new skills to remain a marketable "product," the tricks of the selling trade remain the same. Employers hire for the same emotional reasons they always have.

There are many reasons why people buy (or say yes, or make a commitment), but there are four major categories:

1. *Money.* People are always concerned with making a profit and/or avoiding losses. Everyone wants to make money or save money; this is why bargains were invented. More importantly, this is why, as I'll explain further in the next chapter, it's vital to link your past accomplishments to bottom-line dollar results. Can you show that you've been able to save money in the past, either for yourself or someone else? Can you apply that ability to a potential employer's needs?

2. *Recognition and acceptance by others.* We always search for ways to improve our relationships with others. Employers need to feel that hiring you will enhance their recognition and acceptance, because if you turn out to be a disappointment, it will reflect badly on them. Will the

decision to hire you be a popular one? Will you fit in with the rest of the team?

One of my consulting assignments brought me to the office of a mid-level manager in a large financial conglomerate. As we were talking, her supervisor walked by and poked his head in the door.

"Sorry to interrupt, Mary," he said, "but I just wanted to say that the new man you hired last month is doing a terrific job. Glad to have him with us. Congratulations—you picked a good one."

Needless to say, Mary was thrilled. And the next time her performance was evaluated, you can be sure that this hiring decision was rewarded.

3. *Feeling good.* Self-acceptance and physical and mental health are extremely important. People need to feel good about themselves, to take pride in what they do, their reputation, and their position. Can you assure an employer that he or she is making a smart decision by hiring you? Can you demonstrate that you will relieve some worry or solve some problem?

A colleague of mine, a time management consultant, is a very calm, soft-spoken gentleman with an aura of authority about him. Many highly stressed executives in the midst of chaos use his services because, they say, "Just having him around lessens the tension."

4. *Looking good.* We are, more in the last decade than ever before, concerned with how we look. We want to buy products that enhance our appearance and the way we feel about ourselves. People want to associate with other people who look good. Employers want to hire people who take pride in themselves and their appearance, and have a style that matches their company's. Do your looks and demeanor reflect the way you think about yourself and the way you'd like others to see you?

OUR EMOTIONAL NEEDS

Recently, I saw an ad in a magazine for biodegradable disposable diapers. The ad mentioned many of the features of the diapers—super absorbency, elastic legs, reusable tab closures—but the headline referred to a "concern for our babies' future." The advertising agency was betting that consumers would spend more money for these diapers for ecological reasons. But the real, emotional reason people will buy this brand is because it makes them *feel good* to be contributing to the baby's future by saving the environment.

Here is a list of eighteen of the most common reasons people are persuaded to buy or say yes to something or someone. When you are selling yourself, ask yourself if what you have to offer ties in with at least one of these emotional needs:

1. To make money
2. To save money
3. To save time
4. To avoid effort
5. To gain comfort
6. To be popular
7. To gain praise and recognition
8. To conserve our possessions
9. To increase our enjoyment
10. To be in style
11. To emulate others
12. To avoid criticism
13. To avoid trouble
14. To exploit opportunities
15. To enhance our individuality
16. To protect our reputation
17. To gain control over our lives
18. To be safe and secure

NEVER ASSUME

In order to appeal to a prospective employer's emotional needs, you need to know how to translate the features of your "product"—of yourself—into benefits. Never assume that she can figure it out for herself. Always make the connection between what you can do and how it will help the employer. A potential employer doesn't want (or need) to know exactly what you did in your previous job unless she also knows the *results* of what you did. She needs to see your past in relation to her future, to see the results of your accomplishments in terms of how you might be able to produce similar results for her.

Imagine you last worked for a toothbrush manufacturer in the design department. The company brought out a revolutionary new design that wasn't selling because the brushes wouldn't fit in standard toothbrush holders. You designed a plastic adapter that could be manufactured inexpensively and allowed the curved-handled brushes to fit into those little round holes. Suddenly these brushes (which had previously been bought only by a few novelty stores and the boss's mother) were selling like hotcakes in a new package that included your plastic handle adapter.

Your prospective employer asks you what was your most important contribution to your last job. You say, "I designed the little plastic adapters that make Acme Curved-Handled Brushes fit into the little round holes."

True, that's what you did. But the employer will probably say "Thank you very much, it's been a pleasure to meet you," and that will be that.

You make another attempt. "I'm a very good designer," you say. "My designs are aesthetically pleasing as well as practical and economical."

Better. But the prospective employer is still not impressed.

However, if you were to add, "My design for the plastic handle adapter enabled the company to repackage the item and *sell three times as many brushes* as they had before," the prospective employer would undoubtedly consider you strongly for the position.

It's not enough merely to describe what you did on the job—or even to try to convince someone how good you were at it. You must get to their bottom line—the reason why hiring you would benefit them.

Now that you're familiar with this important concept of the selling game, it's time to get specific. We're going to go back to your CCI, look for your most marketable skills and success factors, and package them into a formidable selling tool.

17

The AAAs of Selling Yourself

Sales and Marketing Principle #17

You sell a product best by selectively emphasizing features and customizing benefits.

You walk into a prospective employer's office. She offers you a seat. After a few minutes of small talk, she says, "Tell me about yourself." What are you going to say? Are you going to tell her your whole life story, from the lemonade stand to yesterday's achievements?

Not a good idea. You have to be selective.

If you were selling your life as a book, you'd have to highlight and summarize the important (and relevant) parts to put on the book jacket. This is essentially what you're going to do now: Go back through your CCI and pick out the parts that accentuate your strengths. Then you'll compose your "book jacket" copy, concentrating on features and benefits.

LEARNING YOUR AAAs

Go back to your CCI and find your first achievement listed there. You are now going to divide it into three distinct sections, creating an AAA:

- The Assignment to be dealt with;
- The Action you took;
- The Accomplishments that resulted.

Let's take a simple example. John was a scholarship student at a state university. He was required to maintain at least a 3.0 grade-point average in order to keep his scholarship. During his junior year, all of his midterm exams fell within a two-day period.

John's *Assignment* (the situation behind his actions, or *why* he did what he did) was to take and pass all his exams.

The *Action* John took (or *how* he resolved a conflict or solved a problem) was to design a prioritized study schedule that let him know exactly how much time he had for each course, which subjects required the most study, and what specific topics he needed to cover in each subject.

The *Accomplishment* (or *what* actually happened due to the actions he took) was that John not only passed all his exams, he achieved a 3.5 grade-point average for the semester.

Writing your AAAs takes practice. But before we go into that, let me share some other sample AAAs with you to give you an idea of how they work:

EXAMPLE 1.   Brad, a production manager at a large cosmetic firm, was faced with escalating prices on the plastic containers his company used. His *Assignment* was to find a way to cut these costs.

Brad's *Action* was to set up a negotiating session with the plastics people and in that session to propose a new long-term purchase agreement with a restructured pricing plan that reduced the price per container. This was a win–win solution, and the plastic supplier readily agreed.

The *Accomplishment:* Brad saved his company more than $250,000 in the next fiscal year.

EXAMPLE 2.   Donna, a sophomore at a small college in Michigan, was informed that funding for a grant she had been counting on was not available. Donna's *Assignment* was to raise the additional $5,000 she now needed for her tuition.

Donna already had a part-time job working in a small real estate office in town. Her *Action* was to negotiate a raise for her work in the office. She also made an agreement that for a nominal fee (to cover electric costs, etc.) she could use the office computer evenings and weekends to make extra money typing papers for students.

The *Accomplishment* was that she earned the $5,000 she needed, plus additional spending money.

EXAMPLE 3.   Gary's *Assignment*, as a supervising social worker, was to solve the problem of the necessary, but costly and time-consuming, in-person consultations.

His *Action* was to develop guidelines and to train his staff to use better questioning skills and more effective consulting techniques.

His *Accomplishment* was to reduce the time of each visit by about one-third, saving over 3,900 person-hours per year.

Continue on with your own AAAs. Keep listing your accomplishments: Think of all the different kinds of problems you have solved and how you came to the solutions.

Be on the lookout for transferable skills and salable success factors. To help you get started, here are fourteen important areas to consider:

1. *Money.* Employers are always looking for people who know how to save, or make, money. Think of a time when you saved money for your company, family, or organization.

How did you do it?_____

_____

When? _____

Where?_____

Was there a time when you made money for your company, family, or organization? How?_____

_____

When?_____

Where?_____

2. *Time.* Second only to money, time is of the essence to every prospective boss. Was there an action you took that increased productivity or saved time for your company, family, or organization?_____

_____

When? _____

Where?_____

3. *Efficiency.* Employers want to know they're hiring someone who can work speedily, logically, and accurately. Can you think of a problem you solved in such a manner?_____

_____

How did you go about it?_____

_____

4. *Organization.* Employers, especially those who are a bit disorganized themselves, want people who can see a job through from beginning to end and keep track of all the component parts. What event, activity, or project have you planned and implemented from beginning to end?

_____

_____

How did you organize it? _____

_____

How did it turn out?_____

_____

5. *Making improvements.* Just because something's "always been done" a certain way, doesn't mean it's the best way to do it. Employers want candidates who can recognize areas for improvement. Have you ever observed the way something was being done and figured out a better way to do it?_____

_____

What was the old way?_____

_____

How did you improve it?_____

_____

What were the results?_____

_____

6. *Teamwork.* This is one of the most salable success factors. Employers want to know that you can work well with others. Were you ever involved with any team projects, sports, or activities?_____

What was your position or function on the team?_____

_____

How did you and your team work to solve a particular problem?_____

_____

What were the results?_____

_____

7. *Innovation.* A creative spirit is a valuable commodity in a service society. The only way to keep up with competition is to keep coming up with new ideas. Have you ever come up with a new idea for your company, family, or organization?_____

_____

Where did the idea come from?_____

_____

Did it solve a particular problem?_____

_____

What were the results?_____

_____

8. *Hiring or recruiting.* As we discussed earlier, most people lack essential skills in this area. If you have experience here, it can be a strong selling point in your favor for managerial or supervisory positions. Have you ever hired people or recruited volunteers for your company or organization? _____

_____

How did you go about it?_____

_____

What were the results?_____

_____

9. *Public Speaking.* Good communications skills are a prized and salable success factor. Did you ever have occasion to speak in public?_____

_____

_____

For what reason?_____

_____

How did you prepare yourself?_____

_____

What were the results?_____

_____

10. *Writing skills.* Written communications skills are also highly valued. Many jobs require you to use writing skill, for instance, to write reports or send memos. Did you ever use this skill at school, on a previous job, or in any other setting?_____

_____

What was the purpose?_____

_____

What were the results?_____

_____

11. *Risk Taking.* This doesn't mean employers are looking for people willing to jump off cliffs at a moment's notice. Sometimes taking a risk can involve accepting a position at a small but growing firm rather than a large, established company. Employers at newer, smaller companies are looking for people willing to give them a chance. What was the last "risky" situation you were involved in?_____

_____

Why did you decide to do it?_____

_____

What were the results?_____

_____

12. *Adaptability.* Change is all around us these days, and employers need to know that you can handle various kinds of situations. Think of a time when you were called on to be flexible or adapt to a new situation:

_____

_____

How did you handle it?_____

_____

What were the results?_____

_____

13. *Helping others.* Growing career fields such as health services and legal and medical assistance need people who are concerned with others. Think of a time when you helped someone in your company, family, or organization: _____

_____

Why did they need assistance? _____

_____

How did you help them? _____

_____

What were the results? _____

_____

14. *Perseverance.* Prospective employers want to know that if you're handed an assignment, you'll be able to see it through until the end. Think of a time when you completed a particularly difficult task or assignment.

_____

_____

What were your challenges or obstacles?_____

_____

How did you handle them?_____

_____

What were the results?_____

_____

The Assignment: The Impossible Mission Force

In order to make a prospective employer aware of the value of your accomplishments, you've got to let him know what the original problem was—how you were presented with a Mission Impossible and how you rose to the challenge and tackled the assignment.

We take action because of a specific problem, need, or desire. Why does a company suddenly become aware of customer service? It's not because it wants all its customers to "have a nice day." It's because the company is losing business to inefficient service. Why does a secretary develop a new filing system for herself and her boss? It's not because she has no other work to do; it's because she's spending too much time searching for misfiled or lost documents. So when you write the assignment, relate it to a specific problem.

An assignment doesn't always come from someone else. Very often the assignment can be self-directed. It arises out of a situation, condition, or problem—something you've seen that no one else has seen, something that needs adding, correcting, or eliminating. Top corporate executives seek people who see needs no one else has spotted.

The Action: Take the Ball and Run with It

The purpose of the action step is to state concisely what steps you took to fulfill the assignment. The idea is to tempt your prospective employer to want to know more, to be interested enough to talk to you.

Use dynamic words and strong action verbs. Don't write, "I worked on this program." It's much better to say, "I implemented [or organized] this project." It's better to say "I analyzed" rather than "I saw," and "I designed and created" rather than "I wrote" or "I did." "I trained" is better than "I showed" or "I explained." Use a good dictionary and thesaurus to find the most potent action verbs. Here is a sample list of action-oriented verbs to use in your AAAs:

accelerated	enlarged	persuaded
adapted	established	planned
addressed	exceeded	presented
analyzed	executed	procured
arranged	expanded	proposed
assembled	expedited	provided
attracted		
authored	facilitated	recruited
	formulated	reduced
budgeted		refined
built	illuminated	renewed
	illustrated	reorganized
charted	implemented	replaced
collected	improved	reported
compiled	increased	researched
completed	initiated	restructured
conceived	innovated	revised
concluded	instructed	revitalized
constructed	invented	
contracted	investigated	shut down
contributed		simplified
controlled	managed	sold
coordinated	marketed	solved
corrected	maximized	started
created	minimized	strengthened
	motivated	stimulated
decreased		summarized
demonstrated	negotiated	supervised
designed		systematized
developed	obtained	
devised	operated	terminated
diagramed	optimized	took charge
directed	organized	took over
documented	originated	trained
	overhauled	transacted
eliminated		
enhanced		

Focus on your own effort and contributions. Your action must affect the situation: It should solve the problem, cure the disease, fix the inefficient system.

Do give credit where credit is due, however. If you were part of a team effort, include that information, but let the prospective employer know how you personally affected the accomplishment. Since being a team player is an essential success factor, you'll want to have at least one AAA that shows your team spirit.

The Accomplishment: It's the Bottom Line That Counts

Any company that hires you is making an investment in you. It's an investment in time and money and, as any potential investor would, this company will want to know just how good an investment it's making.

Since all companies watch the bottom line, try to show your accomplishments in dollars or percentages. It demonstrates your business sense and your concern for costs and expenses. Did you ever increase your company's profits? Decrease costs? Increase sales or productivity? Put it all down in writing.

Remember that time is also worth money, and good organizational abilities are a valuable commodity. My friend Nicole, a homemaker in Connecticut, volunteered to head a telephone campaign for a local politician, a Democrat running in a Republican county. She recruited a small group of friends and neighbors and set up an efficient, organized system covering the entire district. The candidate won—the first Democratic victory in fourteen years. The following year, when Nicole was about to reenter the workforce, she was able to use this Assignment–Action–Accomplishment as an important selling point. Nicole's AAA looked like this:

- *Assignment:* To contact by phone all eligible voters in my candidate's party.
- *Action:* Recruited a staff of dedicated volunteers and created a system for covering the entire district.
- *Accomplishment:* My staff and I increased contact with voters by more than 40 percent over previous campaigns. The candidate won by a 10 percent margin.

Larry is an ambitious college student who used his organizational and time-saving skills to secure two interesting summer job offers after his first year at college. While a senior in high school, Larry had worked as an assistant in the administrative office. His job was to program all the students' schedules for the following year. Larry created an easy, efficient system that eliminated duplication and errors and saved the high school many hours of additional work. The principal was extremely pleased with Larry's accomplishments and wrote him a glowing letter of recommendation, which resulted in Larry's two job offers. Larry's AAA would look like this:

- *Assignment:* To program all student schedules for the upcoming school year, within a limited budget and time frame.
- *Action:* Designed and implemented an efficient, error-free program for fall registration.
- *Accomplishment:* Saved school the cost of computer programmer, reduced the number of person-hours needed to work on this project by 50 percent, and completed the project a week ahead of schedule.

THINKING IN DOLLARS AND PERCENTS

You might find it difficult to think of your accomplishments in terms of dollars and percentages. It's easy for salespeople or fund-raisers to see the direct benefit of their effort. But all employees have a dollar and percentage impact, directly or indirectly. Find out how your efforts affect the bottom line. If possible, set up a system of measurement with the financial people in your company. This is important even if you are happily ensconced in a satisfying career: All raises, promotions, and salaries are tied to your bottom-line value.

Don't wait until tomorrow to start connecting your assignments to your company's profits. In jobs like public relations, advertising, training, and administration, it may be more difficult—but become a detective and find that connection. Samantha, an advertising copywriter, created a terrific new slogan for an old client and as a result the client signed on for two more years. Samantha discovered that signing this client for two years had improved the company's bottom line by $820,000.

This extra effort, this little bit of research, can make all the difference between an average AAA and a great one—one that not only gets you an interview but a job offer.

Make sure you have listed all your accomplishments in the strongest possible terms. You want to show yourself in the best light. I'm not suggesting you tell anything but the truth. I am only suggesting you pick out and emphasize the most positive aspects of your past experiences. You want to show employers that they would be getting more than their money's worth by hiring you.

Your accomplishments may involve a small number. For example, you may have saved yourself or your company only $100—but if your spending limit was $200, you saved 50 percent of your whole budget!

Fred has $200 to spend on books in college. He searched carefully through used books and books for trade and spent less than $100. His AAA might go like this:

- *Assignment:* Obtain needed research and background materials on a limited budget.
- *Action:* Instituted targeted search for least expensive materials.
- *Accomplishment:* Located and purchased all needed materials and came in 50 percent under budget.

Fred effectively used the percentage rather than the dollar amount in this case. As Mae West said, "It's not what you say but how you say it."

FIVE WAYS TO CREATE PERFECT AAAs

Here are five secrets to writing salable and marketable AAAs:

1. Have only one assignment, one accomplishment, and no more than two action verbs.
2. Use strong, potent, descriptive, tempting action verbs.
3. Your assignment and accomplishment must match and complement each other—the result must solve or resolve the assignment.
4. Arouse the would-be employer's curiosity by leaving out many of the details.
5. Tie in your accomplishment to the company's bottom line where you can, using percentages and dollar figures whenever possible.

THE WRONG STUFF

Avoid being judgmental when writing your AAAs. Get everything down on paper—brainstorm with yourself. No brainstorming session is successful if judgments are made. Judgments curtail the free flow of ideas. You can do your refining and prioritizing later.

Another common pitfall is having a great accomplishment with an unrelated assignment, so that the problem and the result don't connect at all. For example: Your assignment was to promote three consumer product lines with a minimal budget. Your action was to consolidate staff and restructure advertising schedules. Your accomplishment states that you increased sales. Although this is a fine accomplishment, it doesn't relate to the problem of dealing with a small budget. A better way to state the accomplishment would be to say you successfully promoted all three lines using only 80 percent of your usual budget—with a 15 percent increase in sales.

Many job seekers try to tell their professional life story in one AAA; they become too detailed and too wordy. Here's an example of what not to do, received during one of my workshops:

> Our company was understaffed and morale was very bad. No one had been able to solve the problem during the last year. People were leaving as well.
>
> I created and organized a series of employee problem-solving sessions where each employee could be heard. There were fifteen employees at each session. I also secured management's commitment that one vice president would attend these meetings and try to solve at least one problem at a time.
>
> This system helped improve morale, and no one left and work became more satisfying to the entire staff.

Try your hand at rewriting this AAA simply, clearly, and effectively. Remember to use action words and to relate the problem and the accomplishment:

Assignment: _____

_____

_____

Action: _____

_____

_____

Accomplishment: _____

_____

_____

Here is my solution to the AAA example just given:

- *Assignment:* For over a year, morale had been an escalating and unsolved problem, causing high turnover and absenteeism.
- *Action:* I organized and conducted a series of morale-building sessions between management and employees.
- *Accomplishment:* Within three weeks absenteeism was down by 25 percent. In six months, there was no turnover and absenteeism was down over 40 percent.

Compare this to your solution. Is yours short and concise? Did you include figures and percentages? Did you tell too much? Would it make an employer curious to know more? Keep it short and simple—don't overtell and overwrite.

This ties in to the last stumbling block in writing your AAAs: modesty —the reluctance to see yourself in the best light. John Kenneth Galbraith said, "Modesty is a much overrated virtue." In your job search you have to be your own public relations agent. Advertising mogul Stuart Henderson Britt says, "Doing business without advertising is like winking at a person in the dark. You know what you're doing but nobody else does."

CUSTOMIZING YOUR AAAs

If you were selling a sports car to a race driver, would you emphasize the car's fuel efficiency? Probably not. Since a race car driver is much more interested in speed and horsepower, you would concentrate on those benefits when selling him the car.

If you're applying for a job as a computer programmer, which requires skills like logic, patience, and analytical abilities, you wouldn't stress success factors such as teamwork and public speaking.

Whether you're writing your AAAs, sending out letters, or are in an interview situation, it's important to make the distinction between the features of your past experiences and the benefits for your prospective employer. The tendency for many people is to stop at the action they took and expect the benefits to be self-explanatory.

Pick the benefits that fit the job. You can restructure your AAAs to emphasize abilities that will be of value to a particular employer.

Let's go back to an AAA we used earlier in the chapter: Brad and the plastic jars. His company was faced with escalating prices on cosmetics containers. His assignment was to find a way to cut these costs. His action, or the feature, was twofold:

1. To set up a negotiating session with the container manufacturer
2. To propose a long-term agreement with a new pricing structure

These are the facts, and they remain constant. If Brad were looking for a new job as a production manager for a different company, he would be smart to state his accomplishment, or benefit, as having saved his company over $250,000. But let's suppose that Brad is looking to change his career and wants to move into labor relations. He might restructure his AAA by adding that his assignment was to reduce costs while maintaining good relations with suppliers. His accomplishment in this case would be that he was able to conduct a win–win negotiation, reducing costs while both his cosmetics company and the container manufacturer got a good deal. For this job, Brad would want to stress his negotiating abilities in his accomplishment. The feature, or action, remains the same, the benefits change.

Now, go back through your own AAAs and translate your actions into as many benefit statements as possible.

Benefits Worksheet

ASSIGNMENT: _____

_____

_____

ACTION: _____

_____

_____

BENEFITS (How did your action affect you and your company?)

1. _____

2. _____

3. _____

Use this format for each of your AAAs. It's important to know this list backward and forward, inside and out. You want to have as many benefit statements at your disposal as possible. You'll never know exactly what a potential employer is looking for until you are face to face. In the meantime, store up an inventory of benefit statements.

You should always keep a list of ten AAAs fresh in your mind so that you can choose what you need when you need it. Each different assignment and action results in an accomplishment that demonstrates your abilities in certain areas. One AAA may show your organizational abilities, while another may concentrate on creative problem solving.

Think of the confidence with which you can face any interview situation, knowing all the ways you have to solve this potential employer's problems!

PART FOUR

Know Your Market

Now that you know all about your product, you need to familiarize yourself with your buyer.

Who are the people out there who are doing the hiring, and how do you get to them?

You begin with your marketing plan. Every business has a plan, a guide for getting customers. Your marketing plan will help give your job search direction and a clear focus so that you can proceed straight toward your goals.

Knowing your market also means cultivating an awareness of what's happening in the economy as a whole—what trends and social factors are shaping our society today and tomorrow, and how those trends affect you and your job search.

No one can know what the future holds, but we do know that a new century is just around the corner and that it will be a century of choice and change. You can expect to hold several different jobs—even have several different careers—during your working lifetime. Technology is already giving you many new and unexpected choices about how, when, and where you choose to work.

Modern technologies have brought us from the industrial age to the information age, the age of the service society. According to *Workforce 2000: Work and Workers for the 21st Century* by William B. Johnston and Arnold H. Packer, a study commissioned by the U.S. Labor Department, "Service industries will create all of the new jobs, and most of the new wealth, over the next 13 years."

What is a service industry anyway? A service industry doesn't produce goods the way manufacturing or agriculture does. You don't end up with a solid object you can ride in, taste, or sleep on. Services create economic value without creating a tangible product.

Service industries can range from low-wage minimal skill jobs, such as fast food servers and supermarket cashiers, to high-wage jobs requiring knowledge of advanced technology, as in biological engineering and computer technology.

The mass production in the twentieth century has shifted from manufactured goods to information. From 1986 to 2000, manufacturing employment will have declined by more than 800,000 jobs, while industries such as finance, insurance, and real estate will create more than 1.6 million new jobs.

Technology has influenced changes in every conceivable industry and occupation—from agriculture to zoology, from fine arts to meat packing, from plumbing to worm farming. A teacher in rural North Dakota, for example, may now be using satellite technology to connect her students to specialized teachers in distant areas of the country. Technology is forcing us to retrain and restructure our ways of working and the tasks we perform on the job.

Technology may eliminate your job. If you're prepared for change, you'll study a different technology and be able to transfer your skills easily. "Job security, as we are used to defining it, may be a thing of the past," says Roberts T. Jones, assistant secretary of labor. "The only real security you have is your investment in yourself. Job skills are changing so rapidly that you need to be constantly involved in training and retraining. You've got to be adaptable."

If you refused to give up your horse and buggy when the car was invented, you never got to travel very far. But if you were farsighted, the first time you saw an automobile, you opened up a gas station. Keeping up with state-of-the-art technology will ensure that you and your talents are constantly marketable.

In this section you'll find a list of thirty "hot" job markets—career choices that are in demand for the 1990s and have great future potential. You'll find out where those jobs are and what it takes to get them.

But you don't have to go after a "hot" job to be successful. Any job can be hot if it's the one you really want. Gear your marketing plan toward your personal ambitions and interests, and success is sure to follow.

18

Your Marketing Plan

How to Position Yourself for Future Success

Sales and Marketing Principle #18

Effective marketing is the result of careful planning.

Once upon a time there lived a brother and sister named Jack and Jill. Jack and Jill went up the hill to fetch a pail of water. After sliding down the hill several times, spilling most of their water and almost breaking their necks in the process, Jack looked at Jill and said, "There must be a better way." So they invented nonskid shoes that would stop a tumble mid-fall and decided to open a retail store called "Kids' Skids."

"Boy, Humpty Dumpty's gonna love this!" said Jill.

They found a great spot right along the highway. And there they sat— skidless and kidless. No customers, except for Humpty and a few of the King's men. Jack and Jill thought of ways to attract customers, but nothing seemed to work. They wanted to mail out fliers, but Nurseryland was a big place and it was too expensive to mail to everyone. An ad they placed for nonskid snow boots in *The New Rhyme Times* came out on the sunniest day of the year, and nobody bought. They didn't know what to do.

One day Little Jack Horner, on his way to a pie-eating contest, passed the store and decided to stop in.

"Hey, this store's great!" he said to the two J's. "How come I never knew it was here?"

"Nobody knows it's here," Jill said sadly.

"Why not?" asked Little Jack. "Don't you guys have a marketing plan?"

"Well, no, we don't," said brother Jack. "Why do we need a marketing plan? We have a great product; everyone in Nurseryland should come to our store and buy our shoes.''

"They would if they knew about it," Horner said. "You've got to be more organized about this if you're going to run a business. You have to know what your purpose and objectives are. Of course, you have to know your product upside down and backward—then you'll know just what kind of people want and need what you have to sell. Last but not least, you have to know the best way to tell people your product exists. If you haven't thought all this out, you'll be stumbling around in the dark like a couple of blind mice. That's why you need a marketing plan.''

Jack and Jill took his advice, and Kids' Skids soon became the biggest thing to hit Nurseryland since Mary Mary's *Garden and Grow* seed catalog.

THE NEWEST SERVICE IN THE SERVICE INDUSTRY

"I'm very happy for Jack and Jill," you say, "but first of all, they live in Nurseryland, and second of all, they have a business. What's that got to do with me and the real world?''

To get the job of your choice in the real world, you're going to have to market yourself as if you were a small, growth-oriented business, with an eye to future potential as well as immediate sales. Creating a marketing plan will not only help you get a specific job, it will help you set and achieve long-range career goals.

You are the newest service in the service industry. You are the most important commodity in today's world. Technology doesn't replace the need for excellence; if you've acquired the essential skills for your chosen field, along with the success factors discussed earlier in this book, you'll be in great demand to meet the needs of America's business environment. But first you've got to let the buying public know you're out there. You need to do the same kind of careful study, research, and creative planning any business does.

Just what is a marketing plan? *Marketing* is a term usually applied to a product or business and is loosely defined as all the activities involved in getting a product or service from the seller to the buyer. In this case, you are the product as well as the seller. The buyers are the people you want to work for.

Effective marketing is the result of careful planning. A few very unusual products (such as the hula hoop) have been successful by being one-of-a-kind phenomena; another few (such as *Trivial Pursuit*) have become successful because of excellent word of mouth. You too can be successful by accident, but how much more satisfying (and likely) to be successful by design. Creating a marketing plan is the first order of business for any new enterprise.

Having a thoroughly researched, well-thought-out marketing plan will prepare you for any situation. Without one all you can do is react to those events that might come your way. You'll be counting on luck instead of creating your own future. Like the grasshopper who didn't listen to the ant's advice, you will have fiddled away the summer and be left without a job in the fall.

MARKETING: THE KEY TO BUSINESS SUCCESS

When I started my business as a speaker and consultant, I had no marketing strategy at all. I was leading seminars for the American Management Association, and they would send me out on "assignments." Occasionally someone in the audience who was in a position to hire me for his or her company would do so. Furthering my career was totally dependent on chance; I was always waiting for someone to come up and offer me the next job. It didn't take me long to realize I wouldn't get very far this way. I needed a plan. I worked on my own CCI. I created a brochure to let clients know how I could be of benefit to them; I made a targeted list of potential clients and set long-term goals for myself. Without a plan, I would have moved slowly and haphazardly along. Once I had a plan (which I still use and update constantly) my career moved along at a pace that surpassed anything I had ever imagined!

This may seem a little dramatic, but it's the truth. When you create your marketing plan, several things happen:

1. *You create order out of chaos.* Without a clear, well-defined plan, you'll be stumbling around in the dark. A plan helps you keep track of people and appointments and helps you set up a realistic timetable for yourself.

2. *You feel better about yourself.* You know you're standing on a solid base, not falling into quicksand. Remember how crucial confidence is to a successful job search.

3. *You focus yourself and your thinking.* When your plan begins to take shape you can put opportunities and problems in their proper perspective.

4. *You set up goals and measure your progress.* Your plan lets you know exactly what needs to be done and when, and allows you to keep track of what you've already accomplished. A plan helps you set up consistent, thoughtful guidelines to help you achieve your goals.

5. *You facilitate the ability to consider alternatives.* A marketing plan

allows you to set out alternate routes beforehand so that if one tactic doesn't pan out, another one is readily available and you can continue working toward your goals.

Developing a marketing plan means developing a sense of commitment. If your goals remain vague and ill-defined, you won't know if you're heading in the right direction. Create a plan and follow it, and you've made a real commitment to shaping your future the way you want.

THE FIVE-PART PLAN

Every business, large or small, has a marketing plan. Those fliers you see posted on bus stops and supermarket bulletin boards are as much a part of a marketing plan as is Michael Jackson endorsing Pepsi. Skywriting your product name over a crowded beach on a hot summer day (especially effective if your product is a cool summer drink), mailing out free samples, or sponsoring a charity event, all can be part of such a plan. Your career search marketing plan might include writing a letter to your uncle in the business, or handing out your business card at a party. Every business creates its own unique marketing plan, but almost all plans contain the same five major elements:

1. The statement of purpose (what it's all about)
2. The product description (who I am)
3. The big picture (my long-range career plans)
4. The immediate action plan (my short-range career plans)
5. The marketing tools and strategies (how I'll get where I need to go)

You begin your marketing plan by asking yourself five corresponding questions:

1. What are my main career objectives?
2. Who am I and what do I have to offer?
3. What is my basic field (or fields) of interest?
4. Who specifically do I want to work for?
5. Exactly how am I going to go about achieving my goals?

Your answers will be the foundation of your plan and will guide you toward future success. Just as any business would, you should review your marketing plan every six months or so. Are you on target in striving for the goals you set down? Have you used the tools and strategies you planned to use? Perhaps your goals have changed—in which case you should revise, update, or rewrite your plan to fit the new circumstances.

The Statement of Purpose: What It's All About

What are my main objectives? What do I want from my work? What would make me happy and fulfilled?

A statement of purpose should contain a brief summary of where you are today and where you want to be in the future. This section will help you clarify and define goals, and set up a reasonable timetable for their attainment.

> *Barry was a struggling actor and bartender in Chicago. He spent more time struggling than acting, however, and at the age of thirty-two decided to set new goals for himself. He enjoyed the restaurant atmosphere but didn't want to remain a bartender. Barry worked on his CCI and came up with a list of twenty AAAs he could apply toward his food-service ambitions. He then began to work on a marketing plan and wrote out his statement of purpose. First, he asked himself what he wanted and needed in his working life. He decided he really enjoyed the interaction with different kinds of people that working in a restaurant afforded him. He also felt energized by the constant activity and diverse responsibilities of this type of service industry. His objective was to become a manager of a small- to mid-sized food service establishment within the next two years. (Barry's completed marketed plan, along with a worksheet for one of your own, appears at the end of this chapter.)*

The Product Description: Who I Am

What are my strongest assets? What exactly am I offering to the "buying public"? What needs, real and emotional, does my "product" fill?

In order to market a product, you first have to be able to describe it in such a way that it becomes exciting and irresistible. Describe exactly what it is, and its purpose, so that someone who has never seen it before will know what it is.

If the product is similar to others on the market, the description must include those factors that distinguish this one from all the others. Since you are unique, and since most potential employers have never met you before, you'll need to provide a general description of who you are and how you can be of benefit to them. You also need to convince them that you are more desirable than the competition.

Your CCI and AAAs are the basis of your product description. All of those accomplishments describe who you are in active and positive terms. Analyze yourself thoroughly and honestly: What are your strengths and your weaknesses? What accomplishments give you marketing power? Everything and anything that would make you attractive to a potential employer should be carefully noted. The more specific and detailed you are, the more you'll be able to identify those qualities that make you "salable."

When you go to the supermarket looking for a breakfast cereal, you're confronted with dozens of different flavors and brands. But it's the one that says "calcium enriched" that you reach for, because that's what is important to you. Someone else may pass that one right by and go for the "rich fruity flavor" of another brand. It was part of one cereal company's marketing plan to emphasize the health aspect, and the other's to bring out the flavor.

The only way we can make a choice is to know what special characteristics make one product different from another. The same is true for you. Knowing what your strengths are, and presenting them in the most favorable light, is the only way to convince a prospective employer to choose you.

> *Barry's Career and Confidence Inventory gave him the personal insights he used to form his product description. He had done a lot of work over the years in several areas of food service, including being a bartender, a waiter, and a supervisor in a friend's catering business. He was able to use these experiences to build a storehouse of benefit-oriented AAAs.*

The Big Picture: My Long-Range Career Plans

What is my main field of interest (law, engineering, manufacturing, accounting, etc.)?

This part of your plan takes into consideration any and all factors that might influence your marketing tactics. What is required here is a study of the "market" or industry you wish to enter, knowledge of the companies you may wish to join, and familiarity with your competition. This section requires some thought and research—but you can't go forward without it. It's another area everyone is tempted to skip over, but you may miss a lot of opportunities if you do. If you want to make a career out of flying airplanes, for instance, you'll want to know what options are open for you. You decide you want to be an airline pilot. What if that doesn't work out? What if you miss the height requirement by three-quarters of an inch? Do you have to give up flying altogether? If the only position you know about is "commercial pilot," you might miss out on many other alternatives, such as flying for the Armed Forces, being a pilot for a freight delivery service, or flying in a corporate jet fleet.

You're limiting yourself by not taking advantage of what others have learned before you. Most people want to skip this step because it takes time and footwork. Make it into a game for yourself—the game of "Untrivial Pursuit." Go to the library, talk to other people, read newspapers and magazines. You don't have to do it all at once.

Become familiar with people currently working in your field and, if possible, those who are also trying to get in. This is a way to get to know the lay of the land, find out how you might fit in.

Study economic trends. Are you entering a "hot" field? If so, will it stay hot? In Chapter 20, I've included a list of thirty hot jobs with solid growth potential. Of course, there's no way of knowing if a new technology will suddenly make your job obsolete. The career you pursue should offer you enough transferable skills to be able to retrain easily and move into another position.

There are fads in the job market just as there are fads in the fashion world, and you should be sure you're going after a growth industry, not one that will disappear in five years. Assistant Secretary of Labor Roberts T. Jones advises job seekers to "be very careful of product (or service) life-cycle when looking for a job or career."

Study of the overall market is particularly helpful if you want to move up in the same or a related field. If you study your industry, you will find ways of becoming visible within it—and the more visible you are, the wider your network of contacts and the greater your chances for moving up and out. Your marketing plan should include a study of associations, industry trade shows, and conferences.

Keeping yourself out front means keeping yourself in front of the competition. Elane, my dental hygienist, has been working in that field for nineteen years. Burned out, she was looking to make a career move, but felt limited because she had such a technically specific background. She joined her local dental hygiene association and eventually became its president. One of her responsibilities was to coordinate the regional meeting for the entire state of New York. Using this experience, she is now examining the possibility of changing her career to meeting planning. Because of her visibility in the association, she was also offered a position selling dental equipment at trade shows around the country. She now has two interesting options, all because she stepped out of her office and let the dental world know she was around.

Other considerations in your overall marketing view are the personal factors. Do you want to travel in your job? Are you getting married or divorced, or moving from one part of the country to another? Anything at all that will influence your strategy belongs in this section.

At this point, Barry began a serious study of the restaurant and food service industry. His research told him that this was an area with good growth potential, a "hot" field that would be around for a long time. He subscribed to trade papers and joined a Chicago-area restaurant association. Since he knew a lot of people in the business, Barry was able to speak to other managers and restaurant owners. He considered buying a fast-food franchise or opening his own catering service. Barry also spoke to the Chambers of Commerce in nearby cities to find out what his competition was like in other areas of the country.

The Immediate Action Plan: My Short-Range Career Plans

Just who is it you want to be working with and for? Who would your ideal "buyer" be? What kind of job would you be willing to settle for if necessary?

Now narrow and refine your list of job opportunities until it includes only and exactly those that fit your criteria. If you desire a lot of structure and privacy in the workplace, for example, then you would pursue only those companies that provide this type of atmosphere. If you like a relaxed, friendly environment with a greater emphasis on teamwork, your research should be leading toward a looser, less hierarchical company structure.

This is where your plan starts to get specific. You can no longer say, "I'm looking for a job." Companies should now have individuals' names attached to them—your objective being to reach not only that firm but the particular person in that firm who has the power to hire you. Start off with a list of ten to twenty people. (The length of your list will depend on the industry and the area you're covering.) You'll need the name of the company, the name of the specific person with the power to hire you, his or her correct title, address, and telephone number.

Find out as much as you possibly can about each company. Companies have personalities just like people do: Your personality must be compatible with theirs; otherwise the relationship will never work.

Carol is a vivacious, outgoing person with a high energy level. She's one of those people who loves to be with people. When she interviewed for a telemarketing job in a two-person office, it seemed like a good opportunity. But Carol didn't think it through carefully. She didn't take her personality into consideration. She thought that talking to people on the phone would be enough interaction, but what she really needed was personal contact. Carol soon realized that she needed a larger office setting and a job that put her in personal contact with customers.

Some companies are extremely conservative and traditional; others are more aggressive and experimental. If you enjoy a more aggressive, innovative atmosphere, you probably won't be happy in a staid, conservative corporation. Go to the library and do some homework. Study recent annual or quarterly reports to get a general idea of the corporate style. Look for sources that will tell you how well the company is doing and who its top officers are. Some of those sources are:

- Standard and Poor's reports
- *Moody's Manuals*
- *Thomas' Register*
- *Ward's Business Directory*
- *Dun and Bradstreet's Million Dollar Directory*

You could also check out the *Encyclopedia of Associations* and the *National Trade and Professional Associations of the U.S. and Canada.* Write to the associations that interest you for a list of members in the industries in your area. Also check the Chambers of Commerce in other cities or towns where you would like to work. They will often be able to supply you with a list of local industries.

Barry decided he would look for work in Chicago, Detroit, St. Louis, and Indianapolis. He visited many restaurants and spoke to a large number of people in all the cities he had on his list. (It's not always possible to check out potential job sources in other cities—but if it is, it's a good way to get firsthand knowledge of the opportunities and atmosphere a company has to offer.) Barry drew up a list of eighteen promising restaurants. His criteria included establishments that had been in business five years or more, a semiformal or formal atmosphere, good location, quality service, and excellent food. He had names, addresses, and phone numbers of owners and/or managers and was ready to move into the action phase of his marketing plan.

The Marketing Tools and Strategies: How I'll Get Where I Need To Go

Exactly how am I going to go about achieving my goals? Where do I begin my search? How do I let people know I'm out there?

When Jack and Jill wanted to let people know about Kids' Skids, they had no idea how to do it. They wasted time and money on ideas that didn't work. It wasn't until they studied the market and found out exactly who was interested in their product that they were able to get the word out to *their* buying public.

When you have developed your product description, your big picture, and your immediate action plan, you can begin to select your marketing tools and develop your creative strategies. If you were developing a marketing plan for a small business—selling children's shoes, for example—your marketing tools might include radio and television advertising, newspapers, magazines, and direct mail. Your strategy would define which of those media you choose, how often you advertise, what percentage of your budget you spend on advertising. It would be based on all the knowledge you've accumulated about the market. In order to sell children's shoes, you might choose prime time television and the Sunday newspaper family section. If you were selling jeans for teenagers, you might want to advertise on MTV, or in *Seventeen* magazine.

The same goes for marketing yourself. You choose the marketing tools that are best suited to your "product." Do your homework—search out all the marketing tools available to you, analyze their potential for generating leads, and plan your marketing effort accordingly. Your purpose is not just to get a lot of leads; you want to get qualified leads that will move you forward to getting an interview.

Notice I said move you forward toward an interview, not to getting a job. Though employment is the ultimate goal, your marketing effort is designed to give you as many options as possible. The more interviews you go on, the more job offers are potentially yours.

Your strategy should also include a timetable. Plan out how much time during each day, week, or month you will devote to your search. Is your goal to go out on two interviews a day, or two a week? (This will depend on whether or not you are presently employed.) Make an action plan for yourself, such as:

- Sunday: Read the classified ads.
- Monday: Answer the ads and set up appointments; go to library.
- Tuesday: Write letters and/or go on appointments.
- Wednesday: Network via the telephone and/or appointments.
- Thursday: Go to employment agencies.
- Friday: Continue research in the library.

Your action plan will change from week to week as you progress in your search. Set up rules and deadlines for yourself. Remember, there are no losers in this game, only quitters.

Barry was still working when he decided to change careers, so he had to devise ways to structure his time. Most of his free time was in the morning, as his bartending duties didn't begin until midafternoon. He decided his two most effective marketing tools would be direct mail letters and personal contacts. He would also check the classified ads daily in Chi-

cago papers, and weekly in Sunday papers he subscribed to from the
other cities on his list.

Review your strategy periodically and keep a record of your progress.
Which marketing tools have yielded the most leads? Did any have better
results than you expected? Worse? Revise your strategy accordingly.

THE MARKETING TOOLS

Networking and Personal Contacts

Statistics show that up to 80 percent of all new jobs are found through
networking. James Clemence, director of management development at
Peat Marwick, says that in the future "getting a job will depend on your
networking skills. It's going to be more and more difficult for job seekers
to come face to face with the people who can actually hire them. You
must become visible within your profession—therefore networking
should be a major area of your job searching strategy."

The important thing to remember here is that *all leads are worth*
pursuing. Not every lead will turn out to be productive, but you'll never
know unless you take the time to find out.

Everyone has contacts. I don't mean that everybody knows somebody who will offer you a job. But somewhere along the line, a lead will
bring you to someone who knows of a job opening. The most farfetched
situations often turn out to be the most interesting.

There's no way to predict who among your contacts will produce the
best leads; therefore you should contact everyone. This includes family,
friends, old business acquaintances, college alumni or professors, your
doctor, your dentist, your lawyer, your hairdresser, members of clubs
you belong to . . . everyone you know.

Make sure you tell people specifically what you're looking for. Let
them know you appreciate any help they can give you. The next person
they speak to may just tell them about a job opening and you want your
contact to think of you immediately. And if someone says "Call me back
in a week," do it. It may not be the brush-off it seems to be.

Make a list of the different reasons you might have for networking,
and the people you know who might fit those needs.

Your networking notebook might look something like this:

Information Sources:

Who knows the most about my field? _____

_____

Who do I know who can put me in touch with that person? _____

_____

_____

Who has information I can use to build my skills at home or at work?

_____

_____

_____

Who can provide guidance in solving problems or help me figure out what my next action should be? _____

_____

_____

If I don't know that person, do I know someone who does? (Most people enjoy helping, as long as you call at a convenient time and have specific questions in mind.) _____

_____

_____

Additional names: _____

_____

_____

Support Groups:

Who are the people around me who are "in the same boat"? _____

_____

_____

Have I done any favors for friends? Who are they? _____

_____

_____

With which of my friends do I really enjoy exchanging ideas and experiences? _____

_____

_____

Which of my friends and colleagues recognize and appreciate my skills and accomplishments? (These are people you can use as sounding boards. For instance, why not try out that new idea before presenting it to top management? No need to give away all the details. Present it as a concept to a few people in your network and check the response. Use their feedback to help you determine your next move.) _____

_____

_____

Additional names: _____

_____

_____

Family, Friends, Acquaintances:

Who do I know (don't forget distant relatives) who works in the same or related field as I do? _____

_____

_____

Which of the people I know is the best networker? _____

_____

_____

(Get these people to help you network—they'll love it!)
Have I let everyone know I'm looking for a job? Did I tell my:
Friends _____   Family _____   Doctor _____   Lawyer _____
Dentist _____   Accountant _____   Neighbors _____
Former employers _____   Colleagues _____
Club members _____   Sports team members _____

Future Possibilities:

_____

_____

_____

Who are the people I'd most like to meet? (Someone I heard speak at a conference, someone a friend or colleague spoke highly of, etc.) _____

_____

How can I get in touch with those people? _____

Are there any clubs, organizations, or associations I can join that will put me in contact with the kinds of people I want to meet? _____

Do I know anyone, or is there anyone I want to know, who can make me think, who will challenge me to grow? _____

How can I find these people? (Networking is very much like solving a puzzle—finding one clue leads you on to the next and the next. One contact refers you to another, who refers you to another, until you find that one contact who will provide you with the solution you need.) _____

How can I do my own "public relations"? Is there a newsletter I can tell about my promotion, successful presentation, etc.? _____

A local newspaper? _____

A trade magazine or journal? _____

Additional publications: _____

The Information Interview

The information interview is one of the strongest marketing tools available to you. Information gives you power. If you're moving from one field to another—for instance, from dental hygiene to meeting planning—your disadvantage is that you probably don't know many details of the industry that is new to you. If you go on information interviews, where your object is not necessarily to get a job offer, you can concentrate on filling in the gaps in your knowledge.

People who would say no to a job interview will often be flattered and say yes when asked for their advice or opinion. However, be prepared in case it should turn into a job interview. I remember going on one information interview with a Mr. Stein. A friend had referred me to Stein knowing there were no jobs available in his firm, but also knowing he knew a lot about the advertising field. While I was sitting in his office, a colleague of Mr. Stein's happened to stop by. It turned out he was in need of an advertising sales rep, and he gave me a job interview on the spot. An opportunity would have been lost if I hadn't been prepared for the unexpected.

In an information interview, you'll want to ask questions like:

- What do you like about this industry?
- What don't you like?
- What do people look for when they hire in this field?
- What associations best represent this industry?
- Are there trade newspapers and magazines I should know about?
- How did you get into the industry?
- Is there a "normal" career path for people in this field?
- What qualifications are essential to succeed in this industry?

The more you know about any industry, the more you'll know about what people in that industry are looking for and what qualifications you already possess. You can then tailor your approach in a job interview so that you stress those particular qualifications. You can even quote your information sources as authorities in the industry: "Stan Philips at XYZ Corporation says you need patience and logic to succeed in this industry. These are two of my strongest qualities."

Information interviews also serve as practice for job interviews. You can practice your interpersonal and communication skills so that when you actually have a job offer at stake, you'll be prepared and confident of your interviewing abilities.

The Classifieds

The first marketing tool that comes to everyone's mind is the want ads. The advantage of want ads is that you can scan them quickly, covering a lot of territory in a little time. The disadvantage is that everyone else is doing the same thing and, especially in larger cities, the competition can be tremendous. Don't let that stop you. If the job sounds right up your alley, go for it.

Get hold of back issues of the papers if you can. Not all jobs get filled on the first go-round. Many times employers are waiting for just the right person to come along—and it could be you. Look through the entire classified section. Job titles can be deceptive, and a company (or the newspaper) may have placed the job you want under an unlikely heading. So don't limit yourself to looking only under the job title you think you want. For instance, the *New York Times* often has ads under the "A" section entitled "Accountancy—Tax", as well as ads under "T" for "Tax Accountants." If you want to get started in public relations, you might look under that heading—but you might also get a foot in the door by starting as a receptionist or an administrative assistance in a PR firm, and those jobs may be listed under different headings.

Subscribe to the *Wall Street Journal* and the *Sunday New York Times*. (If you're not from New York, make sure the classifieds are included with your subscription.) Be sure also to check the business and finance sections. Try the *National Business Employment Weekly*, put out by the *Wall Street Journal*. Read the business pages of your local paper and research any people or companies that seem interesting. Then make contact—call or write.

Although want ads are often a good source, keep the odds in mind. Not only is the competition the greatest here, but the truth is that the majority of job openings never even appear in the paper.

Business Publications, Trade Journals, and Job Fairs

Business publications and trade journals usually have very good classified sections, and they are geared to specific industries. These are usually ads for "insiders"—people who are already in the industry and are looking to change jobs.

Keep the odds in mind here too. There will probably be a large number of people with similar qualifications applying for these positions. That doesn't mean you shouldn't go for it; just don't be surprised if you get a rejection or no response at all.

Job fairs are a better source of leads. Usually held at a local hotel or convention center, they give you a chance to talk to an actual human being. These fairs are often geared to entry-level jobs, so they aren't for everyone. They can be a good source for information interviews, however, and may give you a feel for the kinds of people you're likely to encounter in a particular industry.

Personnel, Employment Agencies, and Headhunters

Employment agencies can be a very good source of job opportunities. The problem is that there are so many around, choosing a good one can be difficult. Don't be afraid to ask questions. Go to an established agency with a good reputation.

Headhunters usually work on executive-level positions and can also be a good source. The problem with both employment agencies and headhunters is that you're not dealing directly with the people doing the hiring.

Headhunters may be armed with your résumé, but if they just send it over to personnel, you're twice removed from the potential employer! You're the only one who can really sell yourself to the employer, and the best way to do that is to contact him or her directly. (We'll discuss this in detail in Part Five.)

Most employment agencies and headhunters collect their fees from the company, so the service to you is free. But make sure you understand any payment obligation before you sign anything, and certainly before you give anyone money. Be wary of any agency that requires money up front, before they have connected you with a job.

Direct Mail

Direct mail is the newest growth area in the advertising and marketing fields. All those letters you get at home urging you to buy new products, subscribe to a magazine, or donate to a charity are direct mail campaigns.

Direct mail is also one of the best and fastest growing methods available for your career campaign. It is so important that Chapter 23 is entirely devoted to your direct mail effort.

SAMPLE MARKETING PLAN

A marketing plan is a tool to clarify and focus your job search and long-term career strategy. The document is for your eyes only, so don't be concerned with style or format. Make it a plan that works for you.

Here is a sample of Barry's marketing plan:

1. Statement of Purpose

I, Barry, am currently bartending full time at Sullivan's Steak House in Chicago. I want to stay in the restaurant business or food service industry in a small- to mid-sized establishment. My goal is to be in a managerial position within two years.

2. Product Description

(This section consists of Barry's list of twenty AAAs. Here is one example):

My assignment, as a supervisor for "Fine Feasts to Go" Catering Service, was to revise scheduling procedures to avoid no-shows among the temporary catering staff. These no-shows were often the cause of inefficient service.

My action was to implement a networking system among employees, making each person responsible for finding his own replacement.

My accomplishment decreased no-shows by 65 percent, thereby improving service and efficiency and generating 30 percent more repeat business.

3. The Big Picture

1. I will remain in the food service industry.
2. I will subscribe to trade journals and join associations, including the National Bartenders Association and the National Restaurant Association.
3. I will write to the Chambers of Commerce in Indianapolis, Minneapolis, Detroit, and St. Louis.
4. I will also look at franchising possibilities in these other cities. Since I have contacts in the catering business, this is another area of exploration.

4. Immediate Action Plan

My first order of business is to go to the library to find addresses for the Chambers of Commerce and look up the restaurant trade journals, and then to make a list of personal contacts.

I have chosen eighteen restaurants to contact for assistant manager positions. There are five in Chicago, four in Minneapolis, two in Detroit, five in St. Louis, and two in Indianapolis. They've all been in business five years or more, have excellent locations, have a somewhat conservative atmosphere, and have a reputation for excellent cuisine. I also have the names of three catering services in Chicago and Minneapolis. (Here Barry would list names, addresses, and phone numbers.)

5. Marketing Tools and Strategies

My main marketing tools will be:

1. Networking
2. Direct mail
3. Classified ads in trade journals
4. Classified ads in newspapers

I'll do most of my marketing in the mornings. I'll have to make some calls from my present job, however, in order to reach people who come in later in the day or work in the evening.

I'll take a week off from my job and go to interviews in other cities I've targeted (all appointments arranged beforehand via phone).

I'll set up a special area at home where I keep all my notes and research, and create an organized follow-up system to keep track of all appointments, phone calls, and interviews.

Weekly action plan: (Here Barry would set up a day-to-day action plan, a week at a time, so that he would know exactly what he will do each day to reach his goal.)

Your Marketing Plan Worksheet (include timetables for each step)

Statement of Purpose

_____

_____

_____

Production Description (AAAs—list at least 10)

ASSIGNMENT: _____

_____

_____

ACTION: _____

_____

_____

ACCOMPLISHMENT (include benefit statements): _____

_____

_____

The Big Picture

_____

_____

_____

Immediate Action Plan

_____

_____

_____

Marketing Tools

_____

_____

_____

Marketing Strategies

_____

_____

_____

The next three chapters will help you develop your marketing plan. Before you can make any final decisions in planning your job search process, you need to study the market. The following chapters will give you an idea of current economic trends, some of the hot, growth-oriented jobs that are in demand right now, where those jobs are, and how to get them.

19

You've Got to Know the Territory

Trends in the New Economy

Sales and Marketing Principle #19

A successful marketing plan is based on understanding current economic trends.

Congratulations! You've just been hired by Kids' Skids to handle their new line of Jack B. Nimble athletic footwear to the entire Northwest Territory.

You feel pretty good about yourself, and you know a lot about the Jack B. line, but you don't know anything about the Northwest Territory. Which of the following is the first thing to do?

A. Get out there and start knocking on doors.
B. Get a map.
C. Call the Chamber of Commerce for a list of businesses that currently stock Nimbles and study who they are, where they're located, and how they're doing.
D. Go through old company files and look for concentrated areas of past Nimble purchasers and study who they were and why they no longer stock Nimbles.

B, C, and D are all logical and practical answers. If your answer was A, which is what we all tend to do in the rush of enthusism, you'll be spending a lot of time accomplishing nothing.

You have to know the territory.

Every sales effort requires background information that includes past, present, and future market trends for the product or service you're selling.

Your job search sales and marketing effort is no exception. Before you just "go out there" and start looking for a job, you should be able to answer these questions:

- Who's hiring whom?
- What are the available jobs in your field of interest?
- Where are these jobs located?
- What kind of background, education, and/or training do you need to get these jobs?

By understanding some basic facts about today's economy—where it's been and where it's going—you'll have a better chance of making choices toward a successful, secure, and satisfying future.

MARKETING YOURSELF IN THE NEW ECONOMY

Why are the facts, figures, and statistics of our changing workforce important to you? How will they help your marketing efforts? They can help you turn factors that were once seen as a disadvantage (such as age, race, or ethnic background) into an advantage.

Take the advertising industry, for example. Not so long ago, ads were geared for one generic "American" market. Now many companies have different segments of advertising, each focusing on a different ethnic market. Maria Hernandez, starting out now as an advertising copywriter, has discovered that she has an advantage over other entry-level applicants because of her Hispanic background.

Leonard Kolberg, a sixty-nine-year-old retired insurance claims adjuster, is now in great demand as a part-time private investigator for several small law firms. The firm gets someone with the perfect background and professional experience they need (to photograph accident sites, interview witnesses, serve subpoenas, etc.). And Leonard remains an active member of the workforce on a schedule that's convenient to his age and lifestyle.

Both Leonard and Maria used their knowledge of their own particular talents and abilities, along with their knowledge of changes in today's workplaces, and marketed themselves to employers who needed their skills and expertise.

But it's impossible to sell yourself in today's changing job market without knowing the trends and influences shaping our nation's economy —and determining the who, when, and where of today's workplaces.

THE CHANGING FACE OF THE AMERICAN WORKFORCE

The American workforce looks very different than it did even twenty years ago. According to *Workforce 2000*, "For companies that have previously hired mostly young white men, the years ahead will require major changes. Organizations from the military service to the trucking industry will be forced to look beyond their traditional sources of personnel."

John Doe, a bank manager in Chicago in the late 1950s, could look around him and see a dozen other Joe Doe's just like him in various positions all around the bank. He knew just how to handle them and their problems because they were a homogeneous group.

Forty years later, John Doe, Jr., manages a different Chicago bank. He looks around him and sees an ethnic variety his father never could have imagined. His managerial duties now require him to know and understand people of wide cultural differences. This situation is a typical reflection of the five major influences on our workforce today.

1. *The foreign influx.* Immigrants represent the largest increase in our population and our workforce since World War I. Previous immigrant populations, mainly European, have been replaced by those from countries as distant as China, Japan, Vietnam, Korea, and Iran, and as close as Mexico and Latin America. Both legal and illegal immigrants are having a great impact in the workplace. It's estimated that by the year 2000, immigrants will add anywhere from 4 to 7 million people to the labor force.

John Doe's bank, like most of the other financial institutions in this country, deals with many foreign corporations. Many of its new employees are brought in specifically to deal with those firms, so the bank is now actively recruiting ethnic personnel.

The immigrant population is affecting the workforce at both ends of the scale, due to the diversity of the population, both in social and educational backgrounds. While a large percentage of the immigrant population has less than five years of schooling, an equal percentage are college graduates.

The foreign influx affects various parts of the country differently: More than half of all foreign-born residents live in California, Texas, and New York. Outside of New York, most new immigrants can be found in the South and West, with a fifth of all recent immigrants living in Los Angeles.

If you are foreign-born, take advantage of your knowledge of your mother country. Market yourself to businesses that deal with your native land or that are in need of people who speak a language you speak. Sell your adaptability and communications skills, having made all the adjustments necessary to live in a country foreign to you.

2. *The minority factor.* At the bank, John Doe, Jr., relies heavily on his Hispanic employees to provide necessary services to the Spanish-speaking clientele. When his father was a bank manager, there were very few minorities employed at the bank at all. Today, a large portion of the staff, at every level, is minority-based.

Blacks, Hispanics, and other minorities are steadily increasing their share of the labor force. Minorities will make up about 15 percent of the American workforce by the year 2000. Black women make up the largest share of that increase and will soon outnumber black men in the workforce.

You can take advantage of your ethnic background the same way Maria Hernandez did. Knowledge is power. Find out which companies in your field of interest have a high percentage of minority employees in entry-level, management, and executive positions.

3. *Women in the workforce.* In the past two decades, women have joined America's workforce in unprecedented numbers. Thirty years ago, in the early 1960s, only 11 percent of women who had children under the age of six went to work. By 1988, that number had increased to 52 percent. According to *Working Mother* magazine "65% of all mothers work outside the home; more than 50% of new mothers enter or reenter the workforce before their child's first birthday." That pattern is continuing, although the rate of entry is beginning to slow somewhat.

The kind of work women do has changed rapidly as well, as women move into traditionally male occupations, from factory work to computer science.

Forty years ago, the only women employed at John Doe, Sr.'s bank were secretaries and cleaning women. Now more than half the bank's employees are women, including several vice presidents and the assistant manager.

The prevalence of women in the workforce has strongly influenced day care, and preschool education, wage rates (and, to some degree, the inequity between men's and women's pay scales), tax reforms for two-income families, part-time, flextime, and at-home job opportunities, and benefits packages.

Once again, knowledge is power. Knowing that other women have already asked for, and gotten, help coping with family and business responsibilities means that you too can find work that accommodates your needs. Women have demonstrated their value in the workplace and should now have higher expectations about what they can achieve.

4. *The end of the baby boom.* Even at mid-size companies, a slowing rate of population growth is having its effect. In the late 1970s, there was an overflow of applicants for mid- and high-level executive positions. That overflow has ceased and employers have to work harder to find qualified candidates. They also have to pay competitive salaries to draw people away from the larger banking and financial institutions.

The baby-boom generation (born between 1946 and 1964) accounted for much of the rapid growth rates in the labor force up until the 1970s. Now, the "birth dearth" generation (born between 1965 and 1978) is causing the workforce to increase at a slower rate than at any time since the 1930s.

This could be good news for job seekers. Employers will have to offer better salaries to attract the best people. According to *Workforce 2000,* "Labor markets will be tighter due to the slower growth of the workforce and the small reservoir of well-qualified workers. . . . Fewer well-educated workers will be available than during the 1960s and 1970s, and employees may bid up their prices." Armed with this knowledge, you'll be able to ask for more—and get it.

5. *America grows up.* America is maturing. The baby-boom generation is growing up and the number of young people is declining. In 1984 the median age of the American worker was thirty-five. By 2000, the median age will be thirty-nine.

The impact of an older America has both positive and negative influences on our economy and employment market. Some of the negative results will be:

- Industries that traditionally depend on young people for growth and survival (higher education, housing construction, home furnishings, etc.) may suffer.
- The decline in the number of younger workers may make it harder to start up new companies or for established companies to grow or change rapidly. Older workers are usually less willing to relocate or retrain in response to changing conditions.
- Many companies are looking for ways to scale down and reduce middle management. Competition for jobs at this level and age range will be great.

But there are positive effects as well:

- An aging labor force represents experience, reliability, and stability, which translates into improved productivity.
- The national savings rate will rise as the population gets older, which is good for the overall economy. Younger consumers are more likely to spend and borrow, while people over forty tend to save and invest.
- Companies that used to hire young people for little pay may have to raise wages and offer better incentives to entry-level workers.

The impact of an "older" America is good for both older and younger job seekers. Many companies are starving for qualified entry-level employees. If you are just starting out and show (from your AAAs) that you have the success factors employers are looking for, you'll be a very valuable commodity. And if you are in the older age bracket and are looking to reenter the workforce, you can use your experience and reliability to sell yourself to employers who are in need of people with exactly those qualities.

COMMUTERS VS. COMPUTERS

Not everyone is looking for a nine-to-five job in a traditional office setting. If the job of your choice involves an alternative lifestyle or flexible schedule, use your market research to learn how other people have made these nontraditional choices work for them.

Many people are now choosing to work at home in offices set up in spare rooms, basements, or garages. Advances in technology have made it possible to compute instead of commute—to work from home and tap into a company's resources across town or across the world via a remote computer terminal.

Having this option proved to be a perfect solution for a young New Jersey couple, Ellen and Larry Schneider. Ellen is a regional section manager at The Equitable, a large insurance company. Larry is a computer programmer for an accounting firm. When Ellen and Larry decided to start a family, they wanted to find a way to raise a child while they both continued to work.

"Larry's company was just beginning to revamp its human resources program," Ellen told me. "They were making a conscious effort to improve their benefits, including child care. We proposed a work-at-home plan for Larry. We sold them on the advantages for the company of keeping a valued employee, and they accepted the idea. I'm going back to my office after the baby is born, and Larry's going to be working from home.

"Since Larry now has twenty-four-hour access to his home computer, he can do full-time work on his own schedule. He's doing the same work he did at the office—it's just in a different setting."

There are drawbacks to this arrangement. Larry may not be promoted as quickly as someone else who is more visible at the office. And spur of the moment meetings with co-workers are no longer possible, so Larry will need to coordinate schedules and go into the office once a week for meetings. But both Ellen and Larry feel their "sales strategy" enabled them to find a way that works well for both the company and for their family.

"I couldn't really work at home," says Ellen. "My job isn't suited for it. And besides, I enjoy the daily interaction with other people. Larry is fine without it."

You may not choose to work at home either. Human beings are social creatures. We like being with people. We learn from them, we laugh with them. We enjoy seeing new faces now and again. But the operative word here is choice. Advances in technology have given us freedom of choice —and the choices we make will in turn help determine future technological advances.

THE TEMPORARY LIFE

One choice that many people are now making is to join the growing ranks of temporary workers. The part-time workforce is becoming a major factor in this country. In 1960, only one in ten workers was employed part time. In 1970, one in eight workers was part time. And by 1981 the figure was one in five. Companies will continue to institute broader part-time and flexible schedule plans and will hire more and more temporary workers.

William Olsten, chairman and chief executive officer of the Olsten Corporation, one of the country's largest suppliers of temporary workers, told me that "in 1987 we supplied over 272,000 people and grossed over $650 million. It appears that without temporary help, some corporations would be out of business—they succeed by maintaining a core of permanent workers and an outer layer of temporaries."

Many temporary workers are offered permanent positions once they've proven themselves on the job.

Being a temporary worker has its down side—you don't usually get any company benefits such as insurance, sick leave, or vacation pay. But even that is changing, as many temporary agencies are offering benefits of their own. The advantage of this kind of work is that it gives you near total freedom about when and where you work. If you have school-age children, for example, you can work when they're in school and stay at home when they're on vacation. That is just how Jane, a mother of two, manages to bring in extra income and still have time off when her children are at home.

A DIFFERENT WORLD

In the 1950s people faced an America quite unlike the one we currently know. They pledged allegiance every morning to a country that was the dominant economic force in the world. The U.S. dollar was the international medium of exchange. No other country could come close to American industry and technology.

Since the 1960s, however, improvements and innovations in transportation and communication have created a world where one country no longer dominates. The strength of the dollar is now measured against the yen—and the mark and the pound. World markets, not just the United States, determine prices of wheat, coal, oil, computers, clothing, and cars. In order to keep up and be a major contributor to this interdependent world economy, the United States has shifted from a manufacturing economy to a service economy. The chart that follows will show you the nine largest service industries in the country.

As you can see, retail trade tops the list. Many of the retail trade jobs (which include such categories as waiters and waitresses, sales clerks, cashiers, and retail buyers) are entry-level positions with high turnover rates. In the 1950s people might have been happy to secure a retail trade position and hang on to it, perhaps working their way up to managerial positions after many years with the company.

Today's workers are more likely to use retail trade jobs as part-time or summer employment, then go on to higher education—and better-paying opportunities in the service sector.

Virtually all of the new jobs being created today are in service indus-

The Nine Largest Service Industries
(1986)

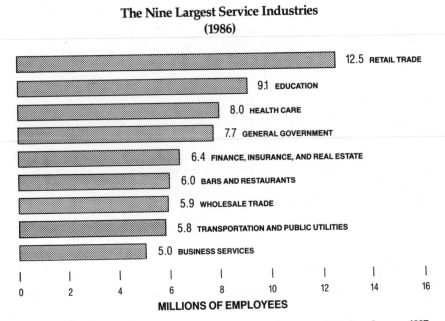

	Millions of Employees
12.5	RETAIL TRADE
9.1	EDUCATION
8.0	HEALTH CARE
7.7	GENERAL GOVERNMENT
6.4	FINANCE, INSURANCE, AND REAL ESTATE
6.0	BARS AND RESTAURANTS
5.9	WHOLESALE TRADE
5.8	TRANSPORTATION AND PUBLIC UTILITIES
5.0	BUSINESS SERVICES

Source: Derived from U.S. Bureau of Labor Statistics, *Employment and Earnings*, January 1987

tries. More than 20 million new jobs are projected to be added to the service industries between 1986 and 2000.

KEEPING UP AND LOOKING AHEAD

The way to make sure you remain a marketable commodity in the rapidly changing workplace is to keep looking forward. If you're already in the workforce and are looking to make a change, consider going back to school or enrolling in a vocational program. If you're still in school and are trying to choose a career, try to match your interests with the direction in which you see technology progressing.

Can you imagine our world without the technologies we take for granted? What if you, like Rip van Winkle, fell asleep under a tree one bright sunny day at the turn of the century? Only you slept for more than twenty years—you slept for almost a hundred. Think of all the changes you'd see around you when you awoke: electricity, telephones, cars, and airplanes—not to mention television, computers, and rockets to the moon! All in less than 100 years!

Today more than ever, choosing an occupation is a risky business. Many jobs have disappeared when technology rendered them obsolete. A graphic illustration of this occurred not long ago in the newspaper industry. Linotype machines, which used hot type formed from molten lead, were the workhorses of almost every large newspaper in the country until the 1970s. Linotype operators were vital to these newspapers. By the 1980s, however, cold type (set by computers) became standard in the newspaper industry. Linotype operator was an obsolete occupation within a decade.

That doesn't mean all of these people remained unemployed or unemployable. It means they had to learn new skills to keep up with advancing technology. Many operators were retrained to run the computers that set cold type.

It's impossible to predict the exact impact of each new technology that comes down the pike. Scientific progress also depends on social, political, and cultural attitudes. Even an invention as important as the telephone took more than fifty years to be widely accepted. Yet within a single decade of their invention, televisions were in a majority of American homes.

All we can say for sure is that as we move toward a new century, technological advances will continue to change the way we live and work. The more you know about the world in which you live, the more effective will be your campaign to sell and market yourself.

20

Hot Markets

Thirty Jobs with a Future

Sales and Marketing Principle #20

You increase the odds of making a sale by knowing what the buying public wants and needs.

I presume that you're reading this book for one of two reasons: because you're just starting out in life (career-wise), or because you're dissatisfied with your present situation and feel it's time to make a change. Either way, it's your future we're talking about.

Twenty years ago, money took a backseat to the meaning and relevance of work in the hippie generation. But the "money's not important" attitude of the 1960s eroded as yuppies in the 1980s turned the pursuit of wealth and power into an obsession. In the 1990s, a healthier, more balanced viewpoint of life and work is emerging. We're less willing to sacrifice everything for the almighty dollar, but we do want to be paid well for what we do well. We want jobs that will give us satisfaction, time to pursue other important interests, and time to be with our family and friends.

It's in your best interest to pursue a line of work that gives you a good sense of yourself along with a good salary. Using the principles of sales and marketing we've discussed so far, and the specific selling tools you'll discover in Part Five, you'll find it is possible to do satisfying work and be well paid for it.

This chapter contains an inventory of the thirty hottest job opportunities of the 1990s. According to information put out by the U.S. Department of Labor's Bureau of Labor Statistics, each of these areas of employment is "expected to grow much faster than average for all occupations through the year 2000."

150

Before you begin reading this list, consider these important factors:

▪ A high growth rate doesn't always mean a large number of jobs available. The percentage of growth is measured against how many people were working in this field in the mid-1980s. The total number of new jobs depends on the total size of the workforce in that area.

The Bureau of Labor Statistics says, for example, that in terms of percentages, legal assistants will increase by almost 100 percent from 1984 to 1995! Translated into real numbers, that means about 50,000 job openings. But there will be 275,000 job openings for secretaries, a field that's only going to grow by about 10 percent.

So just because an occupation that attracts you isn't in this group doesn't necessarily mean there are no jobs available.

▪ Don't rush into an occupation just because it's included in this list. Right now being a legal assistant is extremely hot. But suppose a new technology is invented tomorrow that enables the tasks legal assistants perform to be fully automated. There are no absolute guarantees that what's hot today will be around tomorrow.

▪ Most important of all: This list is based on statistical information. Statistics apply to the occupation as a whole—not to you as an individual. For instance, professional sports and most of the fine arts are not in the top thirty list. But that won't stop great talents from succeeding in these professions. Your success in whatever job you choose depends on your own interests, abilities, motivation, and marketing techniques.

THE BEST-SELLER LIST

The "best-seller" list of the thirty fastest-growing occupations in the country today was compiled from information in the *Occupations Outlook Handbook,* 1990–91 edition. The occupations are listed here alphabetically, not in any ranked order. The list includes a brief description of the occupation, the type of training usually required, and at least one source for obtaining additional information about that field.

You'll also find information on the success factors you'll need to sell yourself most effectively to employers in each field.

1. Accountants and auditors. Accountants prepare and analyze financial reports for many different purposes. They may specialize in such areas as taxes, budgeting, or control. Auditors review a client's financial records and reports on behalf of insurance companies or government agencies like the IRS.

How to sell yourself: If you have an aptitude for mathematics, are a stickler for detail, and are able to compare, analyze, and interpret facts and figures quickly, you'll enjoy being an accountant. Sell your adaptability (you'll have to go from client to client), your independence (you'll often be working on your own), your responsibility (you'll be working with limited supervision), your reliability, and integrity.

Training: At least a bachelor's degree in accounting or a master's in business administration with a concentration in accounting. Many employers require familiarity with computers and accounting and database applications.

Information source: National Association of Accountants, 10 Paragon Drive, Montvale, New Jersey, 07645.

2. Actuary.   Actuaries assemble and analyze insurance statistics to calculate probabilities of such occurrences as death, sickness, injury, unemployment, retirement, and disability. This information is then used to anticipate insurance losses. Actuaries design insurance and pension plans and make sure they're maintained on a sound financial basis.

How to sell yourself: People who love statistics are perfect for this job, which can be very lucrative. A strong aptitude for math is once again essential. Your strongest selling point will be your evaluation skills, as you'll be called upon to integrate and analyze information from many different sources. Decision making and foresight (the ability to project the results of your decisions) are important as well.

Training: At least a BA with a major in statistics or actuarial science.

Information source: American Academy of Actuaries, 1720 I Street, N.W., Washington, DC, 20006.

3. Architect, landscape architect.   An architect designs buildings and public areas. A landscape architect plans landscaping, for example, for parks, golf courses, recreational areas, building sites. Employment in this field is increasing due to the need to refurbish existing sites, and to growing budgets for city planning and historical preservation.

How to sell yourself: The best architects combine mathematical ability and a flair for solving technical problems with their artistic sensibilities. If you can easily visualize spatial relationships, this is a good field for you. Develop your AAAs to emphasize your creativity and communication skills. And don't forget the team player success factor—architects usually work in teams.

Training: You'll need a BA, preferably in landscape architecture, from a program accredited by the National Architecture Accrediting Board, plus three years of experience in an architect's office. A background in art, botany, and mechanical drawing is also useful. Thirty-nine states now require licensing.

Information sources: Director, Education Programs, American Institute of Architects, 1735 New York Avenue, N.W., Washington, DC, 20006.

American Society of Landscape Architects, 1733 Connecticut Avenue, N.W., Washington, DC, 20009.

4. Cashier. Cashiers handle payments, for example, from customers in supermarkets, department stores, movies, or restaurants.

How to sell yourself: This is one of those occupations that's suffering from the decline in population growth and the aging of America. Employers are searching for entry-level people with a sense of commitment to their work. (For many people, this will be their first job; it's also a good opportunity for retired older people.) Sell your reliability, responsibility, honesty, and ability to relate well to customers.

Training: This is an entry level position that requires little or no training or work experience. Most companies prefer a high school diploma and will provide training.

Information sources: Local businesses for information, state employment offices for job listings.

5. Chefs, cooks, and kitchen workers. People in these fields prepare meals that are tasty and attractively presented. There are opportunities for institutional chefs, cooks and kitchen workers, restaurant chefs and cooks, bread and pastry bakers, short-order cooks, and fast food cooks.

How to sell yourself: Besides needing a keen sense of smell and taste, you'll do well to market your creativity in this field. Another important success factor is being a team player. A pastry chef, for example, has to work with the head chef and the rest of the staff. A kitchen staff can be a close-knit group, so this is a sought-after quality in this field. Chefs also need managerial, hiring, and supervisory skills, the ability to work well under pressure, and a readiness to adapt to changing and unorthodox schedules.

Training: Training varies from learning on the job for fast food and short-order cooks to world-famous gourmet cooking schools for chefs in fancy restaurants.

Information source: Educational Foundation of the National Restaurant Association, 20 North Wacker Drive, Suite 2620, Chicago, IL, 60606.

6. Chiropractors.   Chiropractors practice a system of treatment based on the principle that a person's health is determined largely by the nervous system. They use manipulation of the spine to alleviate pain, relieve pressure, and reduce tension in the nervous system.

How to sell yourself: Chiropractors, like everyone in a health field, need a strong sense of commitment and a desire to help people. The most salable skills include energy and enthusiasm, office organization, independence, responsibility, and excellent public relation skills.

Training: Chiropractors are licensed by the state. Most states require at least two years of undergraduate college education plus a four-year accredited chiropractic course.

Information source: American Chiropractic Association, 1701 Clarendon Boulevard, Arlington, VA, 22209.

7. Computer operator, computer programmer, service technician, systems analyst.   Computers are now used in almost every conceivable business situation—stores, banks, colleges, government agencies, hospitals, factories. Their usefulness depends on the skill of the people who run them. Computer programming is one of the fastest-growing occupations of them all. Programmers write detailed instructions (called programs or software) that list in logical order the steps the computer must follow to organize data, solve a problem, or do an assigned task. Computer systems analysts plan and develop methods for computerizing business and scientific tasks or for improving computer systems already in use. Technicians are responsible for keeping intricate computer systems in good working order and repairing faulty systems. Technicians usually have several different clients and go from job to job. They must be familiar with technical manuals and diagnostic programs for each piece of equipment.

How to sell yourself: Projected increases in the fields of computer programmers and systems analysts for the year 1986 through 2000 average over 70 percent. All computer fields are hot now, but that means they're also competitive. To market yourself effectively, sell potential employers on your ability to think logically and analytically, your reliability, your problem-solving and decision-making skills, your oral and written communication skills, and your ability to work independently.

Training: Computer basics are taught in high schools, colleges, and vocational schools. Most businesses then provide on-the-job training in the particular system they use. Programming courses are available at many public and private vocational schools, community and junior colleges, and universities. Computer service technician training includes one to two years post–high school training in basic electronics, data processing, equipment maintenance, or electrical engineering.

Information sources: Local schools and businesses, personnel departments of computer manufacturers, and maintenance firms and state employment offices for job listings. For systems analysts: Association for Systems Management, 24587 Bagley Road, Cleveland, OH, 44138.

8. Dentist.   Dentists diagnose and treat problems of the teeth and tissues of the mouth.

How to sell yourself: Dentists need manual dexterity and strong diagnostic abilities. Many dentists open private practices where the ability to work independently is essential. If you're looking to join an established practice, however, market your commitment, managerial and hiring skills, communication skills, reliability, and your team player success factors.

Training: A college degree plus two to four years of education from an accredited dental school are necessary. Dentists are licensed by the state.

Information source: American Dental Association, Council on Dental Education, 211 East Chicago Avenue, Chicago, IL, 60611.

9. Dental assistant, dental hygienist.   Assistants work at chairside as dentists examine patients. They perform clerical and some laboratory duties. Hygienists provide preventive dental care, promote oral hygiene, and may develop and promote community dental health programs.

How to sell yourself: Communication skills and your ability to follow instructions will be your strongest selling points for dental assistant positions. You also need to be a team player, as you work closely with the dentist and office staff. Besides technical skills, hygienists should have an interest and background in biology, chemistry, health, and psychology. Hygienists also need excellent communication skills, along with sales and marketing abilities (hygienists can contribute greatly to the expansion of a dentist's practice), as well as independence and reliability.

Training: Assistant is an entry level job with on-the-job training. Hygienists need one to two years of college education. Hygienists are licensed by the state after graduating from an accredited dental hygiene school and passing a written and clinical examination.

Information sources: American Dental Assistant Association, 666 North Lake Drive, Suite 1130, Chicago, IL, 60611.

Division of Professional Development, American Dental Hygienists Association, 444 North Michigan Avenue, Suite 3400, Chicago, IL, 60611.

10. Dieticians and nutritionists. These are professionals trained in applying principles of nutrition to food selection and meal preparation. They counsel individuals and groups, set up and supervise institutional food systems, and promote sound eating habits through education and research.

How to sell yourself: Being a team player is one of your most marketable skills if you're interested in this area of the burgeoning health services industry. You'll also need organizational and administrative abilities. You'll increase your marketability if you use your AAAs to demonstrate decision-making and evaluation abilities as well.

Training: A BA with a major in food and nutrition is needed.

Information source: American Dietetic Association, 208 South LaSalle Street, Chicago, IL, 60604–1003.

11. EEG technician. These highly trained specialist run electroencephalographs, which measure electrical activity in the brain. A basic diagnostic tool in neurology, the EEG diagnoses, for example, the extent of brain tumors, strokes, epilepsy, and Alzheimer's disease.

How to sell yourself: For this growing field you need manual dexterity, good vision, and an aptitude for working with electronic equipment. You must be a team player and be able to demonstrate your ability to work well with patients and medical personnel. An essential success factor is communication skills.

Training: Some EEG technicians receive on-the-job training. There are also formal one- and two-year training programs at some vocational schools, community colleges, and junior colleges.

Information source: American Society of Electroneurodiagnostic Technologists, Inc., Executive Office, Sixth at Quint, Carroll, Iowa, 51401.

12. Employment interviewer. Employment interviewers help job seekers find employment and help employers find qualified staff. Most new jobs in this area will be with temporary help or personnel consulting firms.

How to sell yourself: For this kind of job you need excellent communication and "people" skills. You'll market yourself effectively with your adaptability (to work with a variety of clients) reliability, and evaluation skills.

Training: A college degree is usually required. Courses in psychology, sociology, or business administration would be helpful.

Information source: National Association of Temporary Services, 119 South Saint Asaph Street, Alexandria, VA, 22314.

13. Engineer—civil, metallurgic, ceramic, and materials. Civil engineers design and supervise construction of roads, airports, tunnels, bridges, and water supply and sewage systems. Metallurgic, ceramic, and materials engineers develop new types of metals and other materials to meet specific requirements (for example, metals that are lightweight and heat resistant). Engineers will be needed to develop new materials and alloys and to adapt current ones to new applications.

How to sell yourself: Technical ability is important here; you need mathematical skills, mechanical drawing skills, precision, and accuracy; you'll also need foresight, good communication skills, decision making skills, the ability to be a team player, and problem-solving capabilities.

Training: Entry-level jobs in engineering require a BA in engineering from an accredited engineering program.

Information sources: American Society of Civil Engineers, 345 East 47th Street, New York, NY, 10017.
National Engineering Council for Guidance, 1420 King Street, Suite 405, Alexandria, VA, 22314.

14. Engineering technicians. Engineering technicians assist engineers and scientists in research and development, preparing specifications, running tests, and studying ways to improve efficiency.

How to sell yourself: This is an exciting field for people who don't have or don't want the formal education and training necessary to be an engineer. You need an aptitude for math and science. And since you'll have to work well with others, you'll need to market your team player success factor, your oral and written communication skills, and your reliability.

Training: Training for these positions is a combination of formal education and on-the-job experience. Some companies have apprenticeship programs. Formal education is available at technical and vocational schools.

Information source: National Engineering Council for Guidance, 1420 King Street, Suite 405, Alexandria, VA 22314.

15. Financial Services.   Practically every type of company has a financial manager: a treasurer, controller, or cash manager who prepares financial reports required by the firm to conduct its operations and to satisfy tax and regulatory requirements. This broad category also includes careers in commercial and investment banking, personal credit institutions, and other financial services industries.

How to sell yourself: Financial institutions look for people who are bright and well rounded. They look for leadership qualities as well as decision-making skills, independence, oral and written communication skills, good judgment, and managerial talent.

Training: You need a BA, usually in accounting or finance, although commercial banks accept people from all majors. Most financial institutions also require an MBA and have their own highly structured training programs.

Information sources: American Financial Services Association, 4th Floor, 1101 14th Street, N.W., Washington, DC, 20005.

Institute of Financial Education, 60 Gould Center, Rolling Meadows, IL, 60008.

16. Health Services Manager.   The demand for good managers at health services organizations is expected to grow rapidly as the baby boomers age and force health care facilities and services to expand. Hospitals will provide some jobs, but most are expected to be in such places as HMOs (Health Maintenance Organizations), medical group practices, and nursing homes.

How to sell yourself: For any job in the health services field it's essential that you enjoy working with people and have good communication skills. You'll also need to sell your sense of commitment, responsibility, decision making and management skills, and hiring and staffing skills. You may also need public speaking skills.

Training: A graduate degree in health services administration, nursing administration, or business administration is usually required. Some employers also seek people with clinical experience, such as nurses or therapists.

Information sources: National Health Council, Health Careers Program, 622 Third Avenue, New York, NY, 10017–6765.

17. Hotel managers and assistants. Hotel staffers are responsible for the efficiency and profitable operation of their establishments. Positions include general manager, assistant manager, executive housekeeper (responsible for guest and meeting rooms and staff), front office manager (reservations and room assignments), food and beverage manager (restaurants, lounges, room service, banquets), and convention services manager (meetings, conventions, special events).

How to sell yourself. Adaptability is a key success factor for this kind of career. Your AAAs should demonstrate your ability to get along with a variety of customers and staff, as well as your ability to handle stress. Market your decision-making, problem-solving, and customer service skills as well as your reliability, responsibility, and organizational abilities.

Training: Most employers now prefer a BA in hotel and restaurant administration, although some people still advance through the ranks of the hotel staff. Part-time or summer work in hotels is encouraged.

Information source: American Hotel and Motel Association, 888 Seventh Avenue, New York, NY, 10106.

18. Human services workers. "Human services worker" is a generic term for people who hold professional and paraprofessional jobs in such diverse settings as group homes; halfway houses; correctional institutions; community mental health centers; family, child, and youth services agencies; and drug abuse and alcoholism centers.

How to sell yourself: You'll need a background in social work or behavioral science for this career choice. Your selling points are your commitment and desire to help others. Patience, understanding, sympathy, and a cheerful disposition are also pluses. Good communication skills and a strong sense of responsibility are other highly marketable qualities in this field.

Training: College graduates are preferred, with emphasis on human services, social work, behavioral science, or special education, though on-the-job training is available.

Information source: National Organization for Human Services Education, National College of Education, 2840 Sheridan Road, Evanston, IL, 60201.

19. Lawyers. Lawyers will always be in demand because they are involved in so many different aspects of our society. Since the legal profession has so many specialties—such as corporate law, real estate law, divorce law, environmental law, and tax law—it offers ample stimulation and challenge to people of varying interests and talents.

How to sell yourself: Being a lawyer is not always as exciting or glamorous as it appears on TV, but law can be a very interesting and satisfying career choice. You need integrity, honesty, and the ability to work with others. Selling points are decision-making and problem-solving skills, foresight, independence, and excellent communication skills.

Training: Undergraduate preparation should include proficiency in writing, reading and analyzing, thinking logically, and communicating verbally. Majors in social sciences, natural sciences, and humanities are all suitable. A law degree requires three years of schooling after college, in a school approved by the American Bar Association or the proper state authorities. You must pass the bar exam and be licensed by the state.

Information source: Information Services, American Bar Association, 750 North Lake Shore Drive, Chicago, IL, 60611.

20. Legal assistant. Legal assistants help lawyers investigate cases and gather information about legal precedents and judicial decisions. You may also be asked to assist at trials or help draft legal arguments.

How to sell yourself: This is another exciting and interesting career choice—but realize that there's also a lot of legwork and drudgery involved, especially at entry level. Market yourself as reliable and responsible, full of initiative and creativity, and as someone with excellent decision-making, problem-solving, and communication skills.

Training: Training usually takes about two years. Requirements vary from state to state. Some states have certified legal assistant programs, after which you're required to pass a two-day standardized test.

Information source: National Association of Legal Assistants, Inc., 1601 South Main Street, Suite 300, Tulsa, OK, 74119.

21. Marketing. Of course you know by now that marketing entails all the activities involved in getting a product from the seller to the buyer. Marketing experts are involved in studies of who buys what, when, where, and how.

How to sell yourself: Your AAAs should reflect a heavy emphasis on communication skills, creativity, evaluation, decision making, and foresight.

Training: Marketing usually requires a broad liberal arts background and a BA in sociology, psychology, literature or philosophy. You may also need an MA in business administration with an emphasis in marketing.

Information source: American Association of Advertising Agencies, 666 Third Avenue, 13th Floor, New York, NY, 10017.

22. Management analysis and consulting. Management consultants are called in to solve organizational problems; to collect, review, and analyze data; to make recommendations; and to assist in implementation of their proposals.

How to sell yourself: Many consultants work on their own and create their own small businesses. Larger consulting firms have staffs of several consultants, each an expert in a different area. If you're interested in this kind of work, you must have strong interpersonal skills and be able to work on a variety of projects at once. Excellent probing and questioning skills and a customer service orientation will be your best selling points, along with evaluation, decision-making, and problem-solving skills, foresight, independence, and creativity.

Training: There are no universal educational requirements for consultants, although most have college degrees. Many are former managers and executives from large corporations.

Information source: Association of Management Consulting Firms, 230 Park Avenue, New York, NY, 10169.

23. Medical assistant, nurses' aides. These auxiliary health professionals help physicians examine and treat patients and perform routine tasks to keep medical offices running smoothly. Nurses' aides work in such places as hospitals, nursing homes, and mental health clinics.

How to sell yourself: You need a strong commitment and desire to help others. Develop your AAAs to show your sense of responsibility and reliability, your "bedside manner," your willingness to listen and follow directions, and your ability to handle stress.

Training: Medical assistants usually receive on-the-job training; high school graduates are preferred. Nurses' aides also receive on-the-job training, but there are some formal training programs available at community colleges and vocational schools.

Information sources: American Association of Medical Assistants, 20 North Wacker Driver, Suite 1575, Chicago, IL, 60606.

American Hospital Association, Division of Nursing, 840 North Lake Shore Drive, Chicago, IL, 60611.

24. Property and real estate manager. These people control income-producing commercial and residential properties and condominium and community real estate associations. They may also plan and direct the purchase, development, and disposal of real estate for businesses. Or they may be involved in the day-to-day management of property for owners. A large portion of new jobs in this area will be in office and retail space, as well as rental housing.

How to sell yourself: If you're going to market yourself in this field, you'll have to demonstrate your responsibility and your decision-making and problem-solving abilities. You should possess excellent communication skills. You should be a real "people person," as you'll be dealing with a wide variety of clients on a daily basis.

Training: Previous employment as a real estate agent is an asset. Formal training is not essential, but degrees in business administration, finance, real estate, or public administration are helpful.

Information source: Institute of Real Estate Management, 430 North Michigan Avenue, Chicago, IL, 60611.

25. Public relations specialist. PR specialists help businesses, governments, hospitals, universities, and other organizations to build and maintain positive relations with the public.

How to sell yourself: You need an outgoing personality and excellent communication skills for this career choice. Many PR professionals start their own business. Others join a public relations firm or work in the PR department of a large corporation. (This is where the highest paying jobs are located.) Selling points are persistence, rapport-building skills, creativity, enthusiasm, adaptability, initiative, and an ability to function well as part of a team.

Training: You'll need a college education with a degree in communications, advertising, journalism, or English.

Information source: Public Relations Society of America, 33 Irving Place, New York, NY, 10003.

26. Physical therapist. This job helps the disabled become physically functional. It may involve stretching and manipulating the patient's arms and legs, using exercise equipment, or working closely with a medical team.

How to sell yourself: Develop your AAA's to emphasize your sense of commitment and responsibility. Also your team-player skills, as well as your ability to relate and explain procedures to patients. Decision-making and evaluation skills are other strong selling points.

Training: You'll need a bachelor's degree in physical therapy. Certification is required in some states.

Information source: National Therapeutic Recreation Society, 3101 Park Center Drive, Alexandria, VA, 22302.

27. Receptionist. Every business wants to make a good first impression. The receptionist plays a key role in that area, which is why this job will always be in demand. Duties vary, but most receptionists greet customers and visitors, determine their needs, and refer callers to the person who can help them.

How to sell yourself: Since you're the first person visitors and clients may see, being neat and well-groomed is vital to the company. Sell your other strong points, such as communication skills (especially your telephone voice and manners), your customer service orientation, and your reliability.

Training: This is an entry-level job for many people, and a good opportunity for part-time work. A high school diploma is the usual requirement.

Information source: Local businesses, or state employment office for job listings.

28. Registered nurse. Registered nurses work in hospitals, nursing homes, and mental health clinics observing, assessing, and recording symptoms, reactions, and patients' progress. They also assist in convalescence, administering medication, and in short do everything necessary to help people maintain good health.

How to sell yourself: A strong sense of commitment is a must in this field, along with a sincere desire to help others. Other success factors include decision-making skills, responsibility, evaluation, and being a team player.

Training: You must graduate from an approved school of nursing and pass a state exam. Training takes two to five years after high school.

Information source: National League for Nursing, Communications Department, 10 Columbus Circle, New York, NY 10019.

29. Retail sales and service sales. The job of a retail salesperson is to sell merchandise to customers. Service sales representatives sell a wide variety of services, from linen supplies to cable TV to telephone communications systems. They also sell services such as payroll processing, temporary help, consulting, and advertising.

How to sell yourself: Retail sales will provide more job openings than almost any other occupation through the year 2000. This field is especially appealing for part-time and temporary workers. To market yourself effectively for these positions, you need strong communication skills, high energy, follow-through skills, reliability, and independence. You also need the ability to work under pressure.

Training: Most training is on-the-job.

Information source: State employment agencies.

30. Writers and editors. This career involves communications through the written word. Writers develop original fiction and nonfiction for books, magazine, trade journals, newspapers, technical studies, radio, film, TV, and advertising. Editors supervise writers and select and prepare material for publication or broadcast.

How to sell yourself: Writing and editing are both highly competitive fields. Many people do one or the other part-time while holding down nine-to-five jobs. The fastest-growing areas for writers and editors are the technical fields. With the increasing complexity of industrial and scientific equipment and inventions, there is a high demand for people with a talent for writing and editing simple explanations and instructions. To market yourself in this field you'll have to demonstrate your writing or editorial skills. But you can also emphasize your reliability, creativity, independence, and commitment to getting the job done on deadline.

Training: Training is mostly on the job, although some editorial positions require degrees in communications, English, or journalism.

Information source: Society for Technical Communications, Inc., 815 15th Street, N.W., Suite 516, Washington, DC, 20005.

THE JOB SEARCH TIMETABLE

How long will it take you to find the job of your choice? There is no hard and fast answer to that question. There are two important factors to keep in mind, however:

1. *More money, more time.* An article in *Executive Female* magazine in November 1989 says that according to a survey taken by Right Associates, a Philadelphia-based outplacement consulting firm, "the length of time it takes to find a job is proportionate to salary requirements: the lower the salary, the shorter the search." This is both good news and bad news for women—good news because women usually find jobs faster, but bad news because that is due to the fact that women are still usually paid less than men in the same level jobs. Right Associates found that it takes women managers an average of sixteen weeks to find a new job, while it takes men about twenty.

2. *Less specific, more time.* The more specific your field of interest, the faster you can usually find employment. For example, if you go to law school and specialize in admiralty law or insurance law, you'll probably find a job before your classmate whose goal is to be a general trial lawyer. When your interests and background are more specialized, it's easier to focus your job search. If your interests are more general, or if you're changing from one field to another, it may take you longer to find the job of your choice.

AMERICA LOOKS FOR THE BEST—AND SO SHOULD YOU

Don't be concerned if your area of interest isn't included in this list. You can apply the sales and marketing principles to *any* career you choose to pursue. Just be sure to do your homework: Research the requirements of the field, the training you'll need, and the marketable skills you have to offer.

In addition to researching the overall market, you'll need to investigate specific companies. You want to work for people you trust and respect, in a company that treats its employees with a similar trust and respect.

During the early 1980s a great deal of research was done to determine the "best" companies in America. Here are the common denominators of all the chosen companies:

- Workers are being given more responsibility at lower management levels.
- A "team" or "family" atmosphere is encouraged.

- Quality of work produced is stressed.
- Profit-sharing plans are made available.
- There is concern about employees' health and physical fitness.
- The environment is pleasant.
- Promotion is from within.
- In-house training is provided, or reimbursement is made for outside tuition costs.

The "best" job for you is the one that makes you the happiest, gives you financial and personal satisfaction, and is compatible with your chosen lifestyle. The next chapter will help you put it all together and explore the one aspect of your marketing plan left to discuss: *where* to find your ideal job.

21

The Lay of the Land

Locating Your Ideal Job

Sales and Marketing Principle #21

*The odds continue to increase by knowing specifically
where your buyers are located.*

Meg had been a reader all her life. She loved books: the stories themselves, the printing and the paper, the quiet comfort of the library, the
crowded shelves of the bookstore. From an early age, Meg knew she
wanted to work in publishing.

"New York is the only place to go if you want to get into publishing,"
Meg was told over and over again by friends and counselors. Coming
from Bloomington, Indiana, Meg wasn't sure if she wanted to live in New
York, but she felt that her advisors knew what they were talking about.
So off she went, and landed an entry-level position at a large New York
publishing firm.

After two years, Meg's career was progressing, but she was increasingly unhappy. Feeling stuck, she thought the only way to solve her
dilemma was to change careers.

Meg was very depressed when she first attended one of my Marketing
Yourself seminars. As we worked through her CCI and AAAs, however,
Meg realized that *what* she was doing wasn't the problem. It was *where*
she was doing it.

Meg saw that she hadn't really explored all her options. There are
many excellent publishing houses located all across the United States.
Most are in large cities, but there are some in smaller towns where Meg
would feel more comfortable. By networking and using her present publishing contacts, as well as searching through industry trade publications,
Meg soon found a job in a mid-sized publishing house in Maryland. She's
flourishing and is very happy that she made the move.

LIFESTYLES OF THE HIRED AND HAPPY

You don't work in a vacuum. You can't make a blanket statement such as "I want to be in publishing" and expect to be happy with whatever you get. Finding the job that's ideal for you takes a combination of knowing yourself and knowing your market.

Any sales effort has the same requirements: You have to know your product and its benefits, and you also have to know where the markets for your products are located. For instance, if you're selling acne medication, you probably wouldn't do very well moving your business to Sun City, Arizona—a senior citizen retirement community. The product and the market must complement each other in order to make the sale possible.

Meg found the right job, but in the wrong place. How did she end up in that situation? First of all, she listened to what other people told her ("You *have* to go to New York") without making her own inquiries. Second, she didn't trust her own feelings. Deep down, Meg knew she didn't want to live in a mega-city, but she never asked herself where she would really like to live.

It takes preparation to explore all the options and make a suitable choice. Your ideal work location should suit your personality, your lifestyle, your interests, and your ambitions.

Whether you're looking for your first job or are changing careers after twenty years, there are priorities to be set and questions to ask yourself. Before you look for a job in another city or accept one that's been offered to you, make out a lifestyle compatability worksheet concerning that city similar to the one that follows. Add any other questions or categories that are important to you.

Available Support Service
Transportation

Do I need a car? _____

Public transportation: _____

Cost: _____

Taxi or car service: _____

Cost: _____

Nearest airport: _____

Nearest long-distance bus or train: _____
Family

Affordable child-care facilities: _____

_____

Nonemergency medical facilities: _____

_____

Hospital system: _____

_____

School system: _____

_____

Career and Education

Other job opportunities if this doesn't work out: _____

_____

Employment agencies, job or career counseling
    services: _____

_____

Adult education opportunities or facilities: _____

_____

Recreation

Facilities for my own interests: _____

_____

Facilities for my family's interests: _____

_____

Special Considerations

Is this a good place for a single person? _____

To raise a family? _____

Support services for minority groups: _____

For the handicapped: _____

Religious facilities: _____

Other considerations: _____

_____

Real Estate

Can I find affordable housing? _____

Within reasonable commuting distance to work? _____

How safe is it (if I have to work late, etc.)? _____

How far is it from family, friends? _____

_____

How often would I be able to visit, and what would it cost? _____

_____

General Lifestyle

Is nightlife important to me? _____

What is nightlife like in this city? _____

_____

Are there restaurants, clubs open at night? _____

Are there sports facilities? _____

Museums, theaters, bookstores, concerts, etc.: _____

_____

What do I like most about location? _____

_____

What do I like least? _____

_____

THE "LIFESTYLE FIRST" PHILOSOPHY

Finding a job has its own "chicken or the egg" dilemma: Which comes first, the kind of work you want to do or where you want to live while doing it?

There are two ways to look at the question of where you're going to find work. The first is to examine your lifestyle and your personal interests and to make a decision on that basis. In other words, you decide where you want to live first and then set about finding a job in that location.

However, it's not a good idea to move to a new location before you've done any research. Several years ago, some friends of mine met and married while living in California. Tired of the Los Angeles smog and the crowded freeways, they decided to relocate in Santa Fe. Tracy and Jim packed up everything they owned (including two guitars and five cats) and set out in a van to begin their new lives.

They arrived in Santa Fe knowing nothing about the local economy. To their surprise, they had a difficult time finding affordable housing and an even harder time finding employment. They started their trip thinking "We'll find some kind of job when we get out there," but they had no clear idea of what they wanted to do or what would be available. The move was not a success. After only a few months, Tracy and Jim, the two guitars, and the five cats returned to L.A.

If you're looking for work using the lifestyle-first philosophy, you'll need to make a marketing plan for each city under your consideration. Suppose you decide you'd like to live in either Phoenix, Arizona, or Reno, Nevada. Once you've filled out the lifestyle worksheet for each city, you'll need to make marketing plans specific to each city.

Write out your statement of purpose. Your goal is to meet your lifestyle requirements, but you'll have to give extensive thought to the kind of work you want and will be able to find in each of these cities.

Tailor your AAAs to specific job opportunities in your targeted locations. For the big picture, you should gather information on job opportunities in these cities from any available source, such as employment bureaus, trade journals, and Chamber of Commerce publications.

As part of your immediate action plan make a trial visit to the city. Perhaps take a vacation there; try to set up a few information interviews while you're visiting. Even better, visit the city more than once—in different seasons, or during special annual occasions (New Orleans during Mardi Gras, for example).

If you're unable to visit your targeted city, subscribe to a local newspaper or find one in a library. Research everything about the location (not just the help wanted section): housing, politics, society, lifestyle, business, culture, and recreation. Write to the Chamber of Commerce and get as much information as you can about the city.

Decide on your marketing tools and strategies and set up a weekly action plan. Use your networking skills. Tell everyone you know you're considering relocating, and ask if they have any contacts for you in that city. The contacts don't have to be work-related; you want to get an overall picture of the community before you make any final decisions.

How you choose where you want to live and work depends on your individual priorities. Some people want or need specific climates. Some look for special recreational or cultural settings. Some prefer to stay within a certain distance of family and friends. There are endless reasons why you might target a particular location as ideal for you.

THE "PURSUE THE MARKET" PHILOSOPHY

The second manner of deciding where to live is the "job first" philosophy: You are pursuing a particular job or career and will go wherever that job is located.

The same kind of preparation, research, and detailed marketing plan is needed for this philosophy as for the lifestyle-first scenario. Instead of subscribing to local newspapers, for example, you would subscribe to industry-related trade publications that have national help wanted classified ads. Directories such as the *Encyclopedia of Associations,* the *National Trade and Professional Associations of the U.S. and Canada, Ward's Business Directory,* and *Dun and Bradstreet's Million Dollar Directory* will help you locate and target the best markets for your skills and abilities.

Networking is once again essential. Trade associations and professional organizations often have job counseling services and/or nationwide chapters that can give you information about jobs in your field in different locations.

WHERE THE HOT JOBS ARE

Hot jobs can be found everywhere in the United States: The hottest job is the one that's best for you. However, certain generalizations can be made.

The Sun Belt and the Rocky Mountain regions of this country are the ''hot spots'' for the 1990s. The fastest-growing states are:

- Arizona
- Colorado
- Idaho
- Florida
- Montana
- New Mexico
- Utah
- Wyoming

Some of the fastest-growing cities (in terms of employment opportunities) are:

- Albuquerque, NM
- Austin, TX
- Anaheim, CA
- Columbia, SC
- Ft. Lauderdale, FL
- Las Vegas, NV
- Oklahoma City, OK
- Orlando, FL
- Phoenix, AZ

- Portland, OR
- Salt Lake City, UT
- San Diego, CA
- Tucson, AZ
- Tulsa, OK
- West Palm Beach, FL

The largest cities in the United States, like New York, Chicago, Philadelphia, Boston, and Los Angeles, will always have a great variety of jobs to offer. Many other places are built around a particular industry.

If you're interested in high-tech careers (computer hardware and software development, biomedical technology, defense contracting, etc.), for example, these areas will offer you the best marketing possibilities:

- *Silicon Valley.* One of the original high-tech regions in the country, Silicon Valley is made up of several California communities, including Sunnyvale, Santa Clara, Palo Alto, Mountain View, and San Jose. Its technologies include semiconductors, guided missiles, electronic components, and computer equipment. You can find out more about this area by contacting the San Jose Chamber of Commerce, P.O. Box 6178, San Jose, CA, 95150.

- *Silicon Prairie.* One of the newer high-tech regions to spring up, Austin, Texas, and its surrounding areas offers opportunities in engineering, computer design, and technical writing. Contact the Chamber of Commerce, P.O. Box 1967, Austin, TX, 78767.

- *Raleigh/Durham/Chapel Hill.* This green and beautiful area of North Carolina offers opportunities in electrical engineering, software design, data processing, technical writing, public relations, and medical technology. Contact the Chamber of Commerce, P.O. Box 2978, Raleigh, NC, 27602.

- *Colorado Springs, CO.* This is a fairly new and rapidly growing center for high technology, with opportunities in electrical engineering, and research and development in computers, electronics, defense, and aerospace. Contact the Chamber of Commerce, P.O. Drawer "B", Colorado Springs, CO, 80901.

- *Ann Arbor, MI.* Besides being a great college town, Ann Arbor is also home to the burgeoning robotics industry, as well as computer software design. Contact the Chamber of Commerce, 207 E. Washington, Ann Arbor, MI, 48104.

■ *Knoxville/Oak Ridge.* These two Tennessee communities offer many opportunities in engineering, nuclear and biotechnical research, data processing, systems analysis, and technical writing. Contact the Greater Knoxville Chamber of Commerce, P.O. Box 2688, Knoxville, TN, 37901.

Here are some other industries and cities that offer a wide range of opportunities for employment in various career areas.

■ *Accounting:* Chicago; New York; Philadelphia; San Francisco; Washington, DC.

■ *Banking:* Atlanta; Baltimore; Boston; Charlotte, NC; Dallas; Los Angeles; Minneapolis/St. Paul; New York; Pittsburgh; Philadelphia; San Francisco.

■ *Communications (journalism, publishing, telecommunciations):* Atlanta; Boston; Chicago; Detroit; Los Angeles; Miami; New York; Syracuse, NY; Washington, DC; White Plains, NY.

■ *Insurance:* Boston; Dallas, Hartford, CT; Indianapolis; Jacksonville, FL; Los Angeles; Minneapolis/St. Paul; Philadelphia.

■ *Management consulting and financial planning:* Boston; Chicago; Los Angeles; New York; San Francisco; Washington, DC.

■ *Public relations and market research:* Chicago; Cincinnati; Indianapolis; Los Angeles; Minneapolis; New York; Philadelphia; St. Louis; San Francisco; White Plains, NY.

■ *Retail sales, buying, sales management:* Boston; Chicago; Cincinnati; Los Angeles; Louisville, KY; Minneapolis; New York; Philadelphia; St. Louis; San Francisco.

If you want to pursue any of these careers but don't see anywhere you'd like to live among the cities listed, don't be discouraged. I make the same provisio here that I did in the chapter on hot job markets: These cities have been ranked by raw statistics. Remember, there is an exception to every rule; with determination and an efficient marketing plan, you can find an opportunity most anywhere you choose.

IT ALL COMES DOWN TO PREPARATION

Continued expansion of the service-producing sector conjures up an image of a work force dominated by cashiers, retail sales workers, and waiters. However, although service sector growth will undeniably create millions of clerical, sales, and service jobs, it will also create jobs for engineers, accountants, lawyers, nurses and many other managerial, professional and technical workers. *In fact, the fastest growing occupations will be those that require the most educational preparation* (emphasis added).

Occupational Outlook Handbook,
1988–89 edition

If you visit a college or university campus these days, you never know who you'll see there. Alongside the regular students, you're likely to find their parents and grandparents getting their first degrees or going back to school for advanced education.

One such story is that of Doc Gribble. An optometrist for more than thirty years, Doc Gribble loved to work with the soil. Ten years ago, he opened a part-time landscaping business with his son. During his last few years as an optometrist, Doc Gribble went back to school part-time. Two and a half years ago, Doc Gribble entered Purdue University full-time to get his degree in landscape architecture.

Though it wasn't an easy transition, it was worth every minute of it, according to Gribble. He was popular with the other students, and with the faculty as well. In fact, several of the forty-year-old professors took him aside and began to question him about what it was like to change careers after so many years in one field.

Doc Gribble is now successfully launched in his new career, taught one semester at the university, and has received several offers to plan and design golf courses. And he is just one example of how education and training and retraining are becoming more and more important to finding your ideal job.

HOW TO GET THE TRAINING YOU NEED

Training means something different to everyone. When my assistant left, she stayed on for two weeks with her replacement in order to show her the basics of running my office. That's on-the-job training.

If you choose to be a doctor or lawyer, you'll have to spend many years at school completing your training. But you can learn to be a travel agent in a few weeks at the local community college. How, when, and where you get your tutelage depends on the requirements of the job, along with such factors as what's available in your area, whether you're going to train full- or part-time, and whether you're at a beginning or advanced level.

The U.S. Department of Labor groups training into nine types of structure programs:

1. *Public vocational education.* Everyone remembers vocational school from their high school days—subjects like wood shop, home economics, and automotive repair. It often had negative connotations and was thought of as a place for students who couldn't handle traditional high school academics. But vocational schools and the people who attend them have changed. They now include high school, post–high school, and adult education training in a rapidly expanding variety of trade, industrial, health, home economics, office, and technical occupations.

2. *Private vocational education.* Most private vocational schools are fairly small and specialize in one or two skill areas, such as real estate, nursing, auto work, commercial art, cosmetology, and business and office skills.

3. *Employer training.* Some companies have more formal, structured on-the-job training programs than others. Some offer training manuals or computer- or videotape-based orientation programs. Other companies offer tuition aid or reimbursement programs to allow you to get necessary skills for the particular assignment.

4. *Apprenticeship programs.* These programs are used mainly in trade occupations, such as construction, metalworking, and printing. This is a required amount of time during which you work under supervision, learning the trade until you've mastered the necessary skills.

5. *Federal employment and training programs.* These programs are available through state and local governments and are geared primarily toward helping the unemployed and economically disadvantaged.

6. *Armed forces training.* Enlisted personnel receive a great deal of mechanical and technical training which may or may not be transferable to the civilian work world.

7. *Home study or correspondence courses.* These courses provide a variety of training options. Since some programs are better than others, they need to be carefully checked out beforehand. Many, however, are convenient, inexpensive, and effective.

8. *Community and junior colleges.* Community and junior colleges used to prepare people to pursue a university degree. Now the emphasis is on preparing students for the job market. Many programs are vocational or occupational in nature, offering, for instance, data processing or dental hygiene programs. The typical program lasts two years and provides an associate degree.

9. *Colleges and universities.* These institutions offer the traditional four-year undergraduate and graduate degree programs. The relationship of the program to the job market varies with different disciplines. Graduates of some programs have difficulty finding jobs in their chosen fields, especially graduates with liberal arts degrees. Colleges are now responding to declining enrollments by offering nontraditional, occupation-related courses and programs. They're also offering a variety of continuing

education courses, short workshops, and seminars. Many universities have internship programs that give students work experience related to their academic programs.

SMART QUESTIONS TO ASK ABOUT TRAINING PROGRAMS

Part of your market research is to determine the kind of training you might need and to find out about training programs available in your field of interest. How do you know if a college or university, vocational school, or training program is right for you? Or if it has the qualifications you're looking for? The only way you can find out is to do research and to ask questions.

Here are some smart questions to ask about a college or university you're considering:

- Does the major you choose demand a balance between technical and academic skills?
- Does the faculty include a mix of academic and practicing professionals?
- Are there internship programs available?
- Do the school and the business community work closely together?
- Does the school provide a placement service for graduates?
- Do you know any graduates you could speak to about how their education helped them in the job market?
- Is there a large library? Does it have access to databases and computerized information sources?
- If you had to transfer schools, would your credits be accepted at another school?
- Does the school provide financial aid and assistance?

Here are some smart questions to ask about vocational schools and training programs:

- What is the mix of vocational and academic training?
- Are courses regularly updated and reviewed?
- Do instructors have actual work experience in the courses they teach?
- How long has the school been in existence?
- What is the average size of classes?
- Does the school have strict admission standards? Does it test applicants in any way?
- How much is theoretical training and how much is hands-on?
- Can you learn at your own pace? How individualized is the training?

- Are there evening and weekend classes available?
- What are the total costs—including tuition, books, equipment, additional fees?
- What are the terms of payment? Is there a refund policy?
- Is the school accredited? Is it licensed by the state?
- Is financial aid or assistance available? Is government help available?
- What percentage of the students graduate?
- Is there a placement service for students? What percentage of students get jobs in the field after graduation?

For further information on training and educational programs available to you, there are several sources you can use. For information on educational institutions, write:

Association of Independent Colleges and Schools
Dupont Circle, N.W.
Suite 350
Washington, DC 20036

For information on trade and technical schools, write:

National Association of Trade and Technical Schools
Department OOH
PO Box 10429
Rockville, MD 20850

For information on home study and correspondence schools, write:

National Home Study Council
1601 18th Street N.W.
Washington, DC 20009

For information on apprenticeship programs, write:

National Apprenticeship Program
Bureau of Apprenticeship and Training
U.S. Dept. of Labor
200 Constitution Avenue, N.W.
Washington, DC 20210

For women in apprenticeship programs, write:

A Woman's Guide to Apprenticeship
Women's Bureau
U.S. Dept. of Labor
200 Constitution Avenue, N.W.
Washington, DC 20210

For programs for handicapped workers, write:

President's Committee on Employment of the Handicapped
1111 20th Street, N.W.
Room 636
Washington, DC 20036

This brings us to the end of Part Four. You now have a very strong foundation on which to build your marketing campaign. What you're missing are the specific sales techniques you'll need to put your knowlege into positive action. Read on, and by the end of the book, you'll know enough about selling to make employers the offers they can't resist, get through to the real decision makers, eliminate the stress and anxiety of the job interview, handle objections like a pro, negotiate for more than money, and get the job you really want.

PART FIVE

Closing the Sale

GOING AFTER SUCCESS

This is what you've been waiting for—the culmination of all the research, all the hard work you've put into determining your sales personality and attitudes, your marketable skills, and your own achievements and accomplishments. You've drawn up your marketing plan and set down your goals.

Now the real fun begins.

Now you're ready to go out and sell yourself.

This is where you put these newly acquired skills to work for you. In the final section of this book, we'll draw on two of the fastest rising industries of the 1990s to push your success into the twenty-first century. Direct mail and telemarketing have both seen phenomenal growth in the past twenty years and show no sign of slowing down. Both of these tools will be mainstays of your marketing effort.

Once you have successfully mastered those skills, you'll move on to the secrets of successful interviewing and negotiation. Perfecting these skills will help you reach the salesperson's ultimate goal: to close a sale so that all parties benefit equally. You get the job. The employer gets someone who can solve his problems, someone who has the ability to do the job, and who is eager to do it well.

You will no longer have to settle for whatever you can get. You will be able to get what you want. You will know that whether or not you're employed by someone else, you are working for yourself. Work will cease to be drudgery. It will bring you pleasure, satisfaction—and financial reward.

22

Sales Techniques 101

How to Use Sales Basics to Get the Job of Your Choice

Sales and Marketing Principle #22

The art of closing a sale is the ability to sell to the right person in the right way at the right time.

It's time for an anatomy lesson. This one isn't about hip bones, thigh bones, and knee bones, however. This one is about the anatomy of a sale.

A sale isn't a single action or a straight line from beginning to end. It's a complex operation made up of many smaller components.

Each component is vitally important to the process as a whole. You might be tempted to skip one or two of the steps and go right to "Closing the Sale." It won't work. You'll be wondering why you're not getting the job offers you want. You can't construct a building on a shaky foundation, and you can't get the job you want without going through all the necessary steps.

These are the five parts of the sale that make up the foundation for your job search effort:

1. Prospecting
2. Building rapport
3. Qualifying
4. Handling objections
5. Closing the sale

PROSPECTING: THE SEARCH FOR POTENTIAL CUSTOMERS

The term *prospect* applies to anyone who is a potential customer for your product or service. Before you begin your sales effort (or in this case, your job search), you need to have a rough idea of who those prospective customers (or potential employers) might be.

Prospecting begins with the lead. A *lead* is nothing more than a piece of information that directs you to a person or to a company where someone is likely to see you or speak to you.

Once you start talking to a live person, you've got yourself a *prospect*.

Picture Your Ideal Prospect

Does every employer in the world represent a potential job for you? Not really. In sales, no one product or service is right for everyone; in the same way, your skills and talents don't apply to every job that's out there. Nor is every available job right for you. You want to be selective with your time and energy. To find out what kinds of employers you should be actively seeking, paint a mental picture of your ideal prospect.

This is a picture of a person who:

1. Has the need for your talents and abilities
2. Has the necessary budget to meet your salary requirements
3. Has the authority to make the hiring decision

In my business as a speaker, for example, my ideal prospect would be someone who is planning a meeting for next month and must find a speaker immediately, who has read one of my books and/or seen me speak, who is looking for a female expert in sales techniques, who has the appropriate budget, and who has the authority to sign a contract on the spot.

Of course, you will have other criteria that are particular to your individual job search. Your ideal prospect may have to be within a limited commuting distance, for instance, or be able to offer you work on a flexible schedule.

Keith is a young family man with two school-age children. He's looking for a job on a newspaper so that he can work a flexible schedule and be at home after school while his wife is at work. His ideal prospect would be a publisher who's just lost his city editor, needs someone who can work nights, and has the authority to hire him.

There are very few real-life ideal prospects. But if your potential employers have no resemblance at all to the ideal, you're going to be wasting both your time and theirs.

A good salesperson is continually on the lookout for new prospects.

The most creative salespeople find prospects in unlikely places, opening new areas for sales. When IBM first monopolized the computer market big business was basically the only place computers were used. But the people who developed the Apple computer saw a whole new area for computer sales. They saw everyone in America as a prospective customer and introduced the concept of the personal computer.

Creative prospecting is a basic concept in planning your immediate job search or your long-term career strategy. The more potential employers you can reach, the more options you will have. When it comes to prospecting, more is better. You would never expect to hit a home run every time you go to bat. The more times you get up and swing, the better your chances of hitting the ball. So it is with job offers. You can't expect to get a job offer every time you go to an interview, but the more interviews you go on, the more job offers you'll get.

Leading the Way

It all starts with the lead. There are two basic types of leads: referred leads and nonreferred leads. You get *nonreferred leads* from sources such as newspaper ads, trade journals, and association or industry directories.

Referred leads come to you from another person. A referral can come from a prospect who doesn't hire you but who knows someone else who might be interested, or from former employers, acquaintances, friends, or family—anyone who knows someone else. There's no way to predict who among your contacts will product the best leads. Therefore, you should ask everyone you speak to for referrals.

If a referral doesn't work out, ask *that* person for a referral. Keep the chain going so you always have another lead to follow. Use the networking notebook set up in your marketing plan.

That's what Theo did. Theo came to my How to Market Yourself seminar as a newcomer to New York City. Divorced and with two grown children, Theo had moved to the city with a few personal belongings, a computer, a lot of determination, and a well-worn tape of Frank Sinatra singing "New York, New York." Like Frank, Theo believed that, paraphrasing the song, if "he could make it there, he'd make it anywhere." He knew very few people in New York, however, and none in his chosen field of desktop publishing. He had been a chemistry teacher for twenty years but was determined to make a successful career change.

Through a friend, he heard of a special interest group (or SIG, as these groups are called) for Apple Macintosh users and went to check it out. He met many people who had interests similar to his and continued to attend meetings and swap ideas with other members. A few weeks later, when the group needed a new art director for its monthly newsletter (a nonpaying, volunteer position), several people suggested Theo. Theo accepted the job and worked very hard to make it a success. SIG members were so impressed by his talent and his diligence that they began referring him to clients and to other desktop publishers who needed extra help. Within three months, Theo was offered a full-time position at a well-known advertising firm.

As we discussed in Chapter 18, networking is your most important marketing tool. It's the basis for the old saying, "It's not what you know, it's who you know that counts." Anyone can be "well connected." The numbers are staggering—your network consists of the number of people you know, plus the number of people they know, plus the number of people *they* know, and so on. With these kinds of numbers behind you, how can you lose?

Adventures in Networking

Perhaps the most valuable asset of networking is that it is by nature an *active* process. It helps you to help yourself; nobody else can network for you. Has the following ever happened to you? A friend says, "Oh, I met someone yesterday who has a widget manufacturing company. I know you've always been interested in widgets, so I told him about you. Here's his number. He said to give him a call." What is your reaction? Do you pick up the phone immediately? Or do you think, "Well, I'll call next week," or "I'll call when I have more time," or "I'll call when I get my life together"? Or do you think the guy was just being polite and would only be annoyed if you called?

If your reaction is not to call, think again. If you are sincerely interested in widgets, chances are this person would be happy to speak with you. He may not be able to help you advance in your career or offer you a new job, but you may find out some fascinating facts about widgets.

Networking is an adventure. You never know where it will lead. My staff always kids me because I'm constantly networking—sometimes in unlikely places. Every time I travel (they started the "frequent flyer" program just for me), I make friends with the people sitting next to me. I've gotten consulting assignments from several people, sold products, and learned many new and interesting facts about my business and theirs. I've networked in department stores, while getting a manicure, and during intermission at the theater. I never let an opportunity slip by. Follow up on every lead you get and you never know what surprises life has in store for you!

BUILDING RAPPORT: THE GOLDEN RULE OF SELLING

Building rapport is one of the most important steps in the sales process, because *people buy from people they like, trust, and respect.*

People like you when you're on the same wavelength as they are—when they feel you're concerned about their needs as well as your own.

People trust you when you're forthright and honest—when you're upfront and confident about who you are and what your goals are.

People respect you when you treat them with respect. People sense a bad attitude a mile away. The Golden Rule applies to everyone, including prospective employers.

My husband was once interviewing candidates for a new secretarial position in his office. Sheila arrived fifteen minutes late for her appointment. She rushed in without apology, said, "Hi. I'm Sheila," and stuffed her résumé into my husband's hand. She answered his questions crisply and abruptly, repeatedly pointing to the sheet of paper she'd thrust at my husband and saying, "It's all on my résumé."

Sheila had come highly recommended and her qualifications were perfect. But her attitude was not. "She acted as if I were imposing on her by asking questions," my husband told me. "I knew right away that she was able to do the job. I also knew immediately that she wouldn't fit in with the rest of the team."

Your first contact with a potential employer, whether it's through a letter, a telephone conversation, or a face-to-face meeting, can determine your success or failure to close the sale. "You can never go back and remeet someone for the first time," says Joe Gandolfo, the world's largest seller of insurance and number one financial and estate planner, in his book *How to Make Big Money Selling*. "A successful salesperson knows how important first impressions are in sales."

The purpose of this first contact is to establish a positive business relationship. Once that is accomplished, you can move ahead with the next step of the sales process.

QUALIFYING: SELLING TO THE RIGHT PERSON

Would you try to sell eyeglasses to a person with 20/20 vision? No matter how good a salesperson you are, a person with perfect sight won't need your product. You can waste a lot of time pursuing fruitless leads. A prospect is "qualified" when he or she has the need or desire for what you have to offer, has the necessary budget, and has the authority to buy—when he or she closely matches the picture of your ideal prospect.

How do you know if a buyer is qualified? You have to ask questions to find out how well this buyer measures up to your ideal. Sales trainer Tom Hopkins, in his book *How to Master the Art of Selling*, estimates that a sale to a qualified prospect can be closed 50 percent of the time, while unqualified ones will buy only 10 percent of the time. The more you know about a potential customer, the more likely your chances of making the sale.

HANDLING OBJECTIONS: TURNING "NO" INTO "YES"

An objection is what you hear when a buyer hasn't yet made a positive decision. The most important lesson a salesperson can learn, however, is that an objection is not equal to a rejection. It's a very rare sale that goes along smoothly from beginning to end.

You're with a customer who's very interested in purchasing the cameras you're selling. But when you mention the price, the customer says, "Sorry. I don't have the money right now." You could just say "Oh, I'm sorry to hear that" and lose the sale. Or you could say, "If you had the money, would you buy the camera?" When the customer says yes, you could then work out a time-payment plan or some other mutually beneficial arrangement.

Remember this: An objection is simply a request for more information.

If at a job interview an interviewer says she's looking for someone who's had a little more experience in the field, you can let her know about related experience you have and how your enthusiasm for learning new skills will more than make up for what you lack.

Objections are usually perceived as roadblocks to a sale. The truth is that objections are the gateways to moving a sale forward.

Do you know why canned or memorized sales pitches don't work? Because the prospect doesn't get a chance to object. Now, you may be thinking, "I don't want this prospect to object. If the prospect objects, that means he doesn't want to hire me." But all he did was object. When prospects raise objections, they are offering you the reasons they can't make a yes decision right now. When someone tells you "The price is too high," it means the terms of the sale, *the way this person currently understands them,* are not yet acceptable. There has been some miscommunication somewhere along the line.

Once that objection is voiced, you have the opportunity to clear up the misunderstanding. An objection isn't a rejection, it's a question or concern that hasn't been answered yet.

If the prospect doesn't ask any questions or raise any objections, it could be a sign that she's simply not interested. She may not realize that you have a variety of skills that will meet her needs. So you should welcome the chance to handle the objection. It's another chance to sell yourself. I'll go into detail about handling objections in Chapter 28.

CLOSING THE SALE: REMEMBERING YOUR ABCs

When a sale is closed, it means that the buyer has come to a favorable decision. Every salesperson's ultimate goal is to close the sale so that all parties benefit. The salesperson gets rewarded financially, and the buyer finds a solution to a problem.

In order to close the sale, you have to do three things: show the customer why purchasing your product will be of benefit to him, handle any objections that may arise, and ask for the order.

Our camera salesman, presented with the objection that the customer doesn't have the money right now, asked a trial closing question. "If you had the money, would you buy the camera?" The customer said yes. Then the salesman went on to say, "If I can show you how you can pay for this camera on an easy installment plan, would that be of interest to you?" Again, the customer said yes. All along, the salesman used his ABCs: Always Be Closing.

Remembering your ABCs is an important lesson to learn. Throughout your marketing effort, you'll be using these sales techniques to present yourself to qualified buyers. You'll use these skills to show potential employers how hiring you can fill their needs, to answer any objections, and to confidently "ask for the order." If the interview has gone well and you think this is a job you would like, don't walk out with just a smile and a handshake. You want to be offered the job, even if you ultimately decide not to take it. Your interview should end with a closing question, such as, "I'm very interested in working with you and your company. Can I call you tomorrow at noon to get your answer?"

Prospecting, building rapport, qualifying, handling objections, and closing the sale are the basic skills you'll use throughout your job search. These are skills that can be learned and practiced; the more you use them, the better you'll get.

23

The Direct Mail Approach

How to Make an Irresistible Offer

Sales and Marketing Principle #23

The secret desire of every prospective buyer is, "make me an offer I can't refuse."

THE MARKETING TOOL OF THE 1990s

"You may have already won a million dollars!"

Have you ever received this teaser from Ed McMahon? It's a direct mail letter. So are most of the letters you get from credit card companies, public television, magazine publishers, and most "initialed" organizations, such as ASPCA, NOW, and the NRA. Thousands of businesses, large and small, are taking advantage of what is proving to be one of the most effective marketing tools around—direct mail.

You too can take advantage of this very successful marketing tool. More and more small business owners are choosing the direct mail approach as the most effective and economical means of getting their product known.

Where your job search is concerned, you have to have some way of letting people know you're around. How will you go about it? Radio? TV? Newspapers? Direct mail?

Radio and television are much too expensive to be practical "advertising" choices. Even a fifteen- or thirty-second commercial spot can be way out of reach, especially if you're unemployed. Most newspapers have a column called "Situations Wanted," where people seeking employment place ads. Nine out of ten employers I asked said they very rarely thought of looking under Situations Wanted, however. One employer said he frequently read the column, but only because he was one of those methodical readers who pores over every word. One woman I

190

know did secure a job that way when she put an ad in the paper that read, "Bright, energetic secretary with a passion for baseball and football seeks position with sports-minded employer." A "sports-minded" lawyer with a private practice happened to see her ad, and they turned out to be a perfect match.

Financial considerations aside, radio, TV, and newspapers aren't useful marketing tools for you because with them you have no idea of who your "audience" will be. You may be reaching millions of uninterested people.

That's why direct mail is so effective. It gives you a chance to reach a very specific group of potential buyers—buyers you already know have an interest in what you have to sell. When you created your marketing plan in Chapter 18, you came up with a list of specific individuals to contact. Your job is to convince them it is to their benefit to hire you. This process begins with your introductory letter—the direct mail piece.

In order to create an irresistible mailing piece, familiarize yourself with the concept of marketing by specific objective. The clearer your understanding of each phase of your marketing campaign, the more effective it will be. You have to know the exact purpose of your letter or you'll have a hard time knowing what to include.

YOUR FIRST OBJECTIVE: BAITING THE HOOK

What is the objective of the letter? When I ask this question at seminars, the usual answers are "To get a job" or "To get an interview." That may be your eventual goal, but the specific objective of the letter is to arouse your prospective employer's interest enough so that when you call, he or she will want to talk to you. That's all the letter needs to do. It is bait.

Your goal at this step of your marketing strategy is to pique someone's interest—to convince this person that you are someone worth seeing. You want this letter to put you at the top of the potential candidate list. The only way you can accomplish this is by getting the right letter to the right person.

THE ONE-TWO MARKETING PUNCH:
THE LIST AND THE OFFER

The secret to success in direct mail marketing is the combination of the list and the offer. The list consists of the people you have targeted to receive your mailing. A good, well-researched list provides you with a group of customers who have reasons to be interested in what you're trying to sell. If you send a mediocre letter to the right list, you still have a fair chance at success. But even a great letter sent to the wrong list won't get you anywhere. It's like offering a vegetarian a juicy steak dinner. No matter how gourmet the meal, the vegetarian won't be interested. Last week I got a mailer from a publication called *Golf* magazine. I don't play golf. I don't like golf. I'm sure it's a wonderful sport, and a good magazine—but it's of no interest to me. I was on the wrong list. And where did the letter go? Into the "circular file."

No single product, service, or person appeals to everyone. That's why General Motors makes Cadillacs, Pontiacs, Oldsmobiles, and Chevrolets. Only a very specific group of people will be interested in you—and the more specific the group, the more they'll be interested. For instance, if you were going after a job as a researcher in an oil company, the person who would be *most* interested in you would be a head researcher who just lost two of his three best people and is in a rush to meet a deadline. The person who would be least interested would be someone who is overstaffed and has no new projects on the horizon.

You made up your list in the immediate action plan section of your marketing plan. You now have a list of ten or twenty individual names at companies where you'll be seeking employment. This is what's known as a *targeted list*—it's not just a random sampling of names, but a carefully considered group of people who all have an interest in the product or service you have to "sell." These are *hot prospects!*

The offer is the interest-getter. It's the answer to the customer's question, "What's in it for me?" It might be a "low, low discounted price." Or "Buy one, get one free," or "Subscribe now and get this beautiful hand-painted giant tote bag." It's your proposition to the client or customer: "Use my service and . . ." or "Buy my product and . . ."

The offer to your "buyer" is that you will do for him what you have done for others—"Hire me and I'll solve your distribution problem . . ." or "Make me a part of your team and I'll increase your productivity." One or two of your most relevant accomplishments, presented in terms of clearly applicable benefit to the reader, will often make the prospective employer want to see you even if there is no immediate opening.

Cara, an experienced legal assistant specializing in tax law, lived and worked in Chicago for twelve years. When her husband was transferred to Los Angeles, she began to look for work there. She wanted to remain in tax law. Cara wrote a well-thought-out, benefit-oriented direct mail letter. She didn't target her list, however, and sent the letter to dozens of law firms that had no tax departments. Once she realized that she wasn't getting the response she'd hoped for, Cara went back to her list and targeted it at forty tax attorneys in the L.A. area.

She set up seven interviews within a two-week period and eventually was offered three different jobs. By sending the right letter to the right people, Cara ended up having her choice of several offers.

PERSONALIZE YOUR OFFER

It might be easier to send out one mass mailing (using exactly the same letter) to all the people on your list. But a good direct mail letter makes the reader feel special for having received it, as if the person who wrote the letter took the time and effort to get to know something about him (which is what you have done). In this way, direct mail gets the reader emotionally involved with the sale. Remember: People buy for emotional reasons. In fact, a primary value of personalized direct mail is that it allows you to appeal both to the business (or intellectual) and personal (or emotional) sides of the "buyer" at one time.

Suppose you run a fence repair service. You pass a beautiful house surrounded by a lovely white picket fence. You notice that one section is beginning to fall over and the paint is starting to peel. How effective a salesperson would you be if you mailed that homeowner one of your standard brochures:

> Dear Homeowner:
> Don't despair over disrepair
> We repair with loving care.
> For quality service call
> Sherri Smith, Fencemenders, Inc.

You might get a response. The homeowner might call. But more likely he'd say "Cute card" and throw it on the pile with all the other junk mail.

But what if you wrote a letter like this?

Dear Jones Family:

As I walked by your beautiful home the other day, I noticed that your white picket fence was just beginning to need looking after. I've been in the fence-mending business for twenty years, and I know how to make your fence sturdy, bright, and beautiful once again.

Just ask the Bradley family down the street. The value of their house increased by one-third because of the fence work we did on their property. And if we start work on your fence before October thirtieth, we'll repair your driveway at no additional cost.

I'll call you next week to see how I may be of service.

Sincerely,
Sherry Smith
Fencemenders, Inc.

This letter has obviously been sent specifically to the Jones family and not to a hundred anonymous homeowners. Mr. Jones can't help but feel that if you took the time and effort to write him a personal letter, you would also take time and effort to fix his fence. The letter was targeted, the offer irresistible. Mr. Jones may still have several questions to ask you—he isn't necessarily going to hire you on the spot—but in all likelihood he will speak with you when you call. And that's all your letter was intended to do.

THE FASTEST-GROWING MARKETING SKILL

Writing successful direct mail copy is a branch of the advertising industry that is just now coming into full bloom. It stands to reason, then, that in creating a marketing strategy that is part of a lifelong career plan, we should utilize direct mail—the major marketing method of the future.

ATTENTION TO DETAIL

First and foremost, a direct mail piece is a personal letter, so be sure you have the right person. You want to reach the decision maker, the person who has direct responsibility for hiring you. So if you're contacting a fairly small company, you would write directly to the president. For a large organization, you would go to the head of the department or the division vice president.

Be sure you have the *correct spelling* and *proper title*. If you didn't call when you made up your list, call now. Since people are changing jobs more often, you're always better off to call and make sure the person is still there and that the title hasn't changed.

You don't have to identify yourself when you call. You can simply say, "I'm sending some information to Mr. Tompkins, and I'd like to have the correct spelling of his full name and his full title." Once again, this shows a sense of caring and attention to detail that may be taken for granted if all is in order—but will surely be noticed and held against you if you make an error.

HAVE I GOT A PROPOSITION FOR YOU ...

Now that you know who you're writing to, you want to make a business proposition: You will apply your knowledge, experience, expertise, and energy toward solving this individual's (and this company's) problems. In return you'll receive a salary, benefits, and job satisfaction. You're not pleading for the job out of desperation, nor demanding the position because you feel you deserve it; you're suggesting a mutually beneficial arrangement. You know the benefits to you. Your letter must demonstrate the benefits to the other party.

Your opening paragraph has three objectives:

1. To gain attention
2. To refer specifically to the needs of the person and the organization to whom you are writing
3. To establish the value of the product—you

Your research should have told you something about the successes and failures, the strengths and weaknesses of the companies you are contacting. Here's the opportunity to use what you've learned. You should at least know the special interests of each organization, so that you can point out just how hiring you would solve a problem or further an interest.

Take, for example, the letter from Fencemenders, Inc., to the Jones family. It begins: "As I walked by your beautiful home the other day, I noticed that your white picket fence was just beginning to need looking after." This says (after complimenting the family's home) that Fencemenders is aware that a problem exists and that it might be able to help. You don't necessarily have to point out the problem (no one likes to be told they're not doing a good job), but you do want to make it clear you know what is needed. You also want to make it clear that you are bottom-line-oriented. Fencemenders included the statement about the Bradley family: "The value of their house increased by one-third because of the fence work we did on their property."

Your letter might include a statement like: "Having had five years experience as a quality control analyst, I know I can reduce costs and increase production for you and your company." This lets the individual know that your interests and the company's are the same.

REDUCE THE RISK FACTOR

You also want to substantiate your value by including samples of how your abilities have previously benefited others. Employers want to know what you've done for competitors and colleagues. The natural assumption is that if you've done something well for someone else, you can do so for them. You know that the hiring process is just as hard on prospective employers as it is on you, that employers are often taking a large risk, sometimes putting their careers on the line, when they hire someone new. If you can show that you have successfully solved problems for others, you reduce the risk factor.

So here you would include two (or at the most three) of your

AAAs—carefully chosen and worded so that they are relevant to the needs of this particular company.

Would you respond to a letter like the following?

August 9, 1989

Ms. Rachael A. Miller
Vice President of Design
Happyface Health Care, Inc.
Sullivan Street
Chicago, IL 60606

Dear Ms. Miller:

I am a research and design expert. My research has been in personal dental hygiene and my designs are very successful.

Recently I was told that you have a job opening in your department. I'll be in Chicago the first two weeks in September. If you have an interest in discussing our working together, please call me before then so that we can set up a meeting for that time.

Very truly yours,
Jack Washington

There's nothing in this letter that distinguishes Jack Washington from the crowd. Judging from this letter alone, Ms. Miller wouldn't have any reason to call. It's not a terrible letter; it's just innocuous. That's the trouble. I've received many letters like this. I never give them a second glance.

Just telling an employer you're an expert proves nothing. Why should she believe you, a total stranger? Jack didn't list any of his accomplishments, and he didn't bring up any benefits for the reader. And finally, he's leaving the next step up to the potential employer, asking her to call to set up an appointment. There isn't sufficient bait in this letter to get her to call.

SET UP POSITIVE EXPECTATIONS

To close the letter, set up a specific date on which you'll be calling to schedule an appointment. Write this date down in your calendar and stick to it. If your letter is sufficiently intriguing, the reader will be very curious about you and will be waiting to hear from you. He or she will be expecting someone who actively pursues the company's goals, a person who has energy and initiative, not someone who is passively sitting by the phone waiting for a call.

Finally, creating an effective direct mail letter is a skill that must be learned and practiced. Don't send your first efforts to the people you'd most like to work for. Have friends or family look at the letter and ask them if they would want to see you. Have them explain why or why not. Then send your letter to someone at the bottom of your list of prospective employers. Do your practicing with the jobs that appeal to you least and by the time you get to your top choices, you'll be a pro.

DISSECTING A SUCCESSFUL LETTER

Now, let's go through the direct mail letter step by step:

1. *Be sure to call the company and verify that the prospective employer is still there* and to verify the correct spelling of his or her name and proper title.

2. *Open with a statement about the reader.* Let the reader know that this is a personal letter, not a mass mailing, and that you know something about him or her and/or the company. This paragraph should grab the reader's attention and convince him or her to go on reading even if there is no immediate job opening. It should imply that you're compatible with the company's aims and values—that you'll "fit in" with the organization and his or her department. It should make you stand out from the rest of the letter writers who haven't done their research as well.

Most introductory letters are formulaic and unimaginative. They don't say much more than, "I need a job. Please hire me. I'll wait for your call." So if you send a well-written, carefully researched letter, you'll be well ahead of the game—and you'll be remembered.

3. *Give the reader a glimpse of your abilities.* Pique his or her curiosity with a hint that hiring you will solve certain problems, such as increasing profits, improving efficiency, or generating creative ideas. Focus on benefits. Let the prospective employer know what line of work you are in, a general idea of your experience, and how you could apply that experience to the company. You don't necessarily have to state experience in number of years. You can use dollar figures, or the number of fund-raisers you have chaired, or projects you've completed, or any other number that would give an indication that your background is compatible to this company's immediate and future concerns.

4. *List two of your most relevant AAAs.* This is your *irresistible offer.* This is what makes someone sit up, take notice, and say, "We could sure use someone like that around here!" Make sure your accomplishments relate to this particular company's interests. Keep descriptions brief and to the point; you don't want to give everything away in the letter—you can always elaborate in the interview. Stress the results. It's not necessary to mention the name of the company for whom you achieved these results. Keep the employer on the hook. Also, you don't want someone to look at your letter and say, "Oh, yeah, Acme. I know them. We don't do the same thing they do." You don't want to give the employer the chance to make such a rash judgment. You can always be more specific and give the name of the company when you get to the interview.

5. *Let the reader know you want to work for him or her and that you'll call on a specific date to set up a meeting.* Use the word *meeting* or *appointment,* or even *a time to see you;* avoid using the word *interview.* You're only asking for an opportunity for yourself and the reader to discuss business. If a job offer comes out of this meeting, so much the better for both of you. And write with confidence, as if you're expecting the meeting to take place.

6. *You might want to include a P.S.* An inside secret of the direct mail industry says that people read the salutation first (hence the importance of correct spelling), and the P.S. next. If you want to make a more formal first impression, put this information in the body of the letter and leave out the P.S. If the company is not as conservative, a P.S. can be very effective. If you use a P.S., it should include an additional incentive for this person to speak with you when you call. They'll be waiting, or maybe even call you first.

Here's an example of a successful direct mail letter:

August 9, 1988

Ms. Rachael A. Miller
Vice President, Research & Design
Happyface Health Care, Inc.
Sullivan Street
Chicago, IL 60606

Dear Ms. Miller:

Your new design innovations in tooth care products tell me you are interested in improving dental health as well as expanding your market. As a research and design expert with ten years experience in personal hygiene products, I am continually discovering new and better methods of personal health care, and I do so in practical, profitable ways:

- Last year I increased sales of my company's curved-handled toothbrushes 300 percent by designing an inexpensive plastic adapter that allowed these brushes to fit standard bathroom holders.
- My suggestion for, and subsequent design of, better packaging for my company's "Little Brusher" children's toothpaste moved this product from a 2 percent share of the market to a 22 percent share in just six months.

I can bring the same kind of success to you and your fine organization. I will be in Chicago the first two weeks in September. I'll call you on Tuesday, August 16th, to set up a meeting.

Very truly yours,
Jack Washington

P.S. I was particularly impressed with your new floss dispenser and would like to discuss a plan I've devised for a profitable line of coordinated products.

MAKE A GOOD IMPRESSION

I was in a client's office once when he received a letter inquiring about a job opening. The letter was rumpled, torn, and was obviously a copy. My client said, "I don't care how skilled or talented this person is. I would never hire anyone who cared so little about the impression this letter would make. If he thinks I didn't notice, he's dead wrong. I'm looking for a professional. No professional would send me a letter like this."

Go over your letter and make sure it's perfectly and professionally typed. No typos or grammatical errors. No ripped, torn, or mutilated paper. Before mailing your letter, take the following important steps:

1. Copy the letter for your files.
2. Note the date and the person to call in your daily calendar.
3. Write the phone number on your copy of the letter.
4. File the copy of the letter in a clearly designated place.

TIMING IS EVERYTHING

One final but important consideration in direct mail is when to send the letter. You want to try to time the letter's arrival so that it will get the attention it deserves.

Call your local post office and find out how many days it will take your letter to reach its destination. The best time to mail it is so that it arrives on a Tuesday or Wednesday. Monday is too heavy a mail day and it might get lost in the shuffle; Friday is a day when many people are wrapping up and trying to get out early.

Your letter will be the first impression you make on a prospective employer. Make it a good one. This letter should be more than an introduction to one individual; it should be part of a lifetime plan of searching out opportunity. You are building connections with every letter and résumé you send. Did I say résumé? A résumé wouldn't be my first choice as a connection-builder, but sometimes a résumé is what's required. If you have to write a résumé, the next chapter will show you the best way to do it.

24

If You Have to Write a Résumé . . .

Sales and Marketing Principle #24

In the age of customer service, mass marketing is not as effective as an individually customized sales approach.

MAKING IT PAST THE FIRST CUT

When I was an actress "making the rounds" and going out on auditions, I always had at least two sets of photographs with me. If I was auditioning for a more dramatic role, I would hand the director the straight-ahead, no-smile, dark-background picture. If I was up for a comedy or a musical role, I'd use the brightly lit, shining-eyed, big-smile photograph. It wasn't that the director didn't have the imagination to see beyond my photograph—it's just that I needed all the help I could get.

At some point in his or her career, every actor or actress goes to a "cattle call," a pre-audition screening process where a director will usually line up ten or twelve people in a room, take a quick look down the line, and tell most of the people to go home. They just aren't what he's looking for. It's got nothing to do with their talent or past experience. Once this quick weeding-out period is over, the real auditions begin.

Some smart actors and actresses have learned to increase their chances of making it past the first cut. Before they go to a cattle call, they do some research and find out as much as they can about the play, the film, and/or the director. They change the way they dress, or comb their hair differently—small adjustments to make it easier for the director to picture them in the context of the play or movie.

Sending "blind" résumés—when you don't know anything about the job or the company—is the job market cattle call. Many employers will take a quick glance down the line of résumés they receive and reject most

201

of them. That's because most of the résumés they receive tell them very little about the people who send them, and nothing at all about why those people should be considered for this job.

That's why I don't like résumés. They are used to screen people out after only a cursory glance or two. That's also why the direct mail approach is a much better sales tool. In your letter, you're making a targeted offer with the benefits to the buyer clearly spelled out for him. Résumés never have the same impact.

I would like to tell you not to use a résumé at all. In the real world, however, we have to deal with the way things are. Most employers will insist on seeing a résumé. When that happens, my advice is to study the "role" and the "director" carefully beforehand—find out as much about the job and employer as possible—and present the employer with an image of yourself tailored to his needs and expectations (a customized résumé, which I'll explain later in the chapter).

THE PROBLEM WITH RÉSUMÉS

You walk into an elegant restaurant. You sit down at a table, open the menu, and read:

MENU
5 Chicken Dishes
3 Beef Dishes
4 Seafood Dishes
3 Vegetable Dishes
And Really Good Desserts

You wouldn't even know what kind of restaurant you were in! A menu has to be more than just a list of main ingredients. Many people write their résumés as if that's all they needed—a list of main ingredients. They say:

I WORKED AT:
Macy's
Gimbel's
Sears
K-Mart

An employer will look at that résumé and say, "So what?" The secret behind writing a good résumé is to follow the same principles you do for your direct mail letter: It must be benefit-oriented, value-added, and targeted to the specific job you're going after.

ATTRACTING THEIR ATTENTION: BREAK THE PREOCCUPATION

Like your direct mail letter, the résumé is intended to attract attention, not to get you the job. Its purpose is to get your foot in the door. Once you're in, you use your selling skills to land the job.

It's like sending out a flyer or placing an ad in the paper. You want to get the customer interested. The ad must concentrate on benefits to the customer. An ad placed in a newspaper crowded with similar ads has to attract attention, be easy to read, and be full of benefits to the reader. Otherwise the typical preoccupied reader will pass right over it. If the ad is good, the reader will pay attention and probably decide to go to the store to check it out.

An employer is like a preoccupied newspaper reader. She's not reading every word; she's skimming through reams of similar résumés. So the easier it is for her to see a potential match between you and the job, the more likely she'll stop skimming and start reading.

The employer should be able to read your résumé and determine just how your past experiences will benefit her future. This means you have to tailor your résumé to fit the job.

ONE RÉSUMÉ DOESN'T FIT ALL

"Just a minute," you say. "Do you mean that every time I go to a different interview I have to redo my résumé? I don't have that kind of time!"

I know. I don't expect you to. My daughter Laura now has three different résumés she uses when looking for work, updating each as necessary. They cover her three areas of interest: child abuse assessment and counseling, research and writing, and translating and interpreting. Laura has had experience in all of these areas, but to include everything on one résumé would be foolish—if not impossible. Because she has the three résumés, Laura is prepared to follow any unexpected leads that may arise.

You don't need a separate résumé for each and every interview you go on. But you do need a résumé that's relevant to the type of job you're pursuing, one that will emphasize your potential benefit to the employer and the company. Your résumé should make it easy for the employer to relate your past experience to the position now available.

Word processors, of course, make it fairly easy to update or personalize your résumé. If you don't have access to a word processor yourself, you can use a local service. Prices vary around the country, but most services will keep your information on file (usually for six months to a year), and revising the original is relatively inexpensive.

CHOOSING YOUR SALES APPROACH: WHICH TYPE OF RÉSUMÉ WILL SELL YOU BEST?

Like the direct mail letter, the résumé is a marketing tool to get you in the door. Your résumé should emphasize your strong points and de-emphasize your weaknesses.

You've already done the preliminary work you need to create a good résumé. Your CCI and AAAs will be your foundation. What you need to do now is put that information in résumé form, in the style best suited to your own experience.

There are three basic types of résumé: chronological, functional, and customized.

The Chronological Résumé

The chronological résumé is the most traditional type, used about 60 percent of the time. It is just what it sounds like: a chronological job history, starting with your most recent experience and working your way backward. A chronological résumé is best used to *emphasize job continuity* (either from one company to another, or steady advancement within one organization). If your job history is pretty straightforward and demonstrates growth and development, you'll probably want to use a chronological résumé.

However, this is the résumé that presents the most pitfalls, because we tend to think that all listing our experience means is stating the company name and job title. But even when writing a straightforward chronological résumé, you must remember the concepts of sales and marketing and the difference between features and benefits. The features of your résumé are those company names and job titles. But the benefits are what will get an employer's attention.

This is a sample of a typical chronological résumé that doesn't list any benefits:

Fred Wright
34 Elmwood Plaza
Wildwood, New Jersey 07886
(609) 555-1234

Work Experience:

ABC SCHOOL SUPPLIES, INC. (1982–present)

Dept. Controller, Furniture Division
Responsibilities included coordinating four other department controllers, preparing monthly sales analysis reports, supervising staff of four.

WALTERS ELECTRONICS CORPORATION (1978–1982)

Assistant Dept. Controller
Helped conduct financial audits, wrote reports, put in a new computerized cost accounting system.

Sr. Accounts Receivable Clerk
Analayzed accounts receivable systems, revised old system, improved collections system.

Education
B.A. Pace College

An employer looking at this résumé would learn where this person worked, for how long, and what his main responsibilities were. Not much there to tempt an employer. No bait. Now look at the work experience the way I've rewritten it:

Fred Wright
34 Elmwood Plaza
Wildwood, New Jersey 07886
(609) 555-1234

Work Experience:

ABC SCHOOOL SUPPLIES, INC. (1982–present)

Dept. Controller, Furniture Division
Reported to Chief Financial Officer. Coordinated four other department controllers in cost accounting and tax returns. Prepared monthly sales analysis and department comparison reports. Developed new cost accounting system *which resulted in $500,000 tax saving.* Supervised staff of four who *handled 30 percent increase in volume without adding additional staff.*

WALTERS ELECTRONICS CORPORATION (1978–1982)

Assistant Dept. Controller
Co-conducted financial audits. Developed reports and recommendations for President and CEO. Implemented computerized cost accounting system *which resulted in $145,000 annual payroll savings.*

Sr. Accounts Receivable Clerk

Analyzed accounts receivable systems. Revamped system, which *increased productivity by 25 percent*. Implemented improved collections system, *resulting in collecting $50,000 in past due accounts*.

Education

B.A. Pace College

Try this with your own work experience. Start with a simple chronological listing of the jobs you've had:

1. _____

2. _____

3. _____

4. _____

5. _____

Now rewrite this list, concentrating on features and benefits. Look for the bottom-line results that will get an employer anxious to meet you:

1. _____

_____

_____

2. _____

_____

_____

3. _____

_____

_____

4. _____

_____

_____

5. _____

_____

_____

The Functional Résumé

A functional résumé highlights your accomplishments and abilities and puts your strongest selling points right up front. You should use a functional résumé when you're just entering the job market, when you're reentering the job market after a gap of any length, when you're changing careers, when you've had many different and possibly unrelated jobs, or if most of your work has been temporary or free-lance and consulting.

My daughter Laura put together this functional résumé when she heard of a job opening as a counselor in a crisis center. When she spoke to her potential employer on the phone, she found out that the job also entailed some research and translating skills. Just out of college, Laura's experience was mostly volunteer work and college research. She decided that the best way to let the employer know that she had all the required skills was to emphasize them in a functional format. Here is Laura's résumé:

Laura Weinstock
PO Box 456
Seattle, WA 98145
(206) 522-5485

Counseling:

- Counseled sexual assault victims and their friends and family. Established better understanding for victims of their legal rights and what to expect in court.
- Coordinated work with attorneys representing battered women and children, decreasing duplicate paperwork, lost records, etc., by 25%.
- Conducted Volunteer Recruitment and Training programs. Increased volunteer staff by 40%.

Translating and Interpreting

- Translated materials on domestic violence and parenting for Spanish-speaking shelter residents, making information accessible to 50% more residents.
- Translated technical manuals for prestigious Colombian health organization. Completed two weeks ahead of deadline.
- Interpreted for French- and Spanish-speaking clients of Bed 'n' Breakfast establishment, resulting in 35% increase in clientele.

Research

- Researched and co-wrote report on U.S.-sponsored Costa Rican Nutrition Project. Report was sent to Costa Rican government.

- Researched and wrote article on the increase of malaria among NYC immigrants. Paper published in prominent medical journal.

Work Experience

1984–6 YWCA—Inner City Recreation Counselor
1986–8 NEIGHBORHOOD LEGAL RIGHTS CENTER—Volunteer

Education

B.A. Cornell University

Laura wanted to emphasize her abilities in three different areas. The functional résumé can also be used to highlight major accomplishments in a single field.

Try redoing your chronological résumé as a functional résumé:

Major Accomplishments:

1. _____

_____

2. _____

_____

3. _____

_____

4. _____

_____

5. _____

_____

Work Experience:

1. _____

_____

2. _____

_____

3. _____

_____

Last But Not Least: The Customized Résumé

This is the most job-specific résumé and the one I recommend as the most effective sales tool. During your telephone interview with your prospective employer (which we'll discuss in Chapter 26), you find out as much as possible about the job—at least the job title and some of the major responsibilities. Then you customize your résumé so that your accomplishments and what's required match up as closely as possible.

Yes, this does take time. But it makes it very easy for an employer to "put you in his picture"—to see how you would fit into this job. The more specific and clearly focused you are concerning the job objective, the fewer extraneous, and possibly negative, impressions you will make.

This is also the best résumé to use if you don't have much work experience or if you've changed careers several times. You may want to leave out your work history altogether, or at least deemphasize it by using this style résumé.

The general format to follow for this type of résumé is:

1. Job objective, written specifically to suit this job.
2. Major areas of expertise, *emphasizing transferable, marketable skills*
3. Examples of specific accomplishments
4. Work history (if it is decent)
5. Education (if it is relevant or outstanding)

Here is an example of a customized résumé. Shirley McDonald is applying for a job as a senior sales account executive for a cable television company. Through her research, she discovered that the firm is a young, progressive organization looking for "real go-getters" who can expand their markets. Shirley included only those achievements and abilities that directly relate to this job opening. Her customized résumé looks like this:

Shirley McDonald
2100 Cedar Lane
Richmond, VA 23375
(314) 336-2256

Objective: Senior Sales Account Executive

Abilities:
Dynamic, results-oriented account executive specializing in selling intangibles. Exceptional negotiating, problem-solving, and closing skills. Proven ability to develop new markets and maintain profitable relationships with established clients.

Major Accomplishments:

■ Initiated new marketing concept which resulted in $1 million in new business over a two-year period

- Developed ongoing relationship with long-time competitor's client, bringing in $100,000 business to firm
- Ranked number one in sales in fiscal 1988
- As manager, doubled sales productivity in six-month period through revised hiring and training systems

Work History:

1986–present	U.S.Broadcast Media, Inc.—Media Sales
1983–1986	Investments—Investment Sales
1982–1983	Midland Capital—Investment Sales

Imagine you're sending your résumé to your ideal prospect for your dream job. How would you customize your résumé in that situation?

Objective: _____

_____

Abilities:

_____

_____

_____

_____

Major Accomplishments:

1. _____

_____

2. _____

_____

3. _____

_____

4. _____

_____

5. _____

_____

Work Experience:

1. _____

2. _____

3._____

You should choose the résumé style that shows you in your best light and the one you are most comfortable with. Whichever format you go with, remember to be result-oriented. You aren't writing a résumé to show off what you've done; you're trying to show employers how what you've done will benefit them.

RÉSUMÉ DOS AND DON'TS

There are no hard and fast rules in résumé preparation. Many people combine formats to come up with a résumé that suits their needs and personal style. However, there are some basic recommendations about what to do and what not to do.

1. *Your résumé is the packaging that attracts the buyer.* Make sure it says good things about you. Sloppy reproduction, typographical errors, and/or dirty, wrinkled paper will most likely result in immediate action— right into the "circular file." *Have your résumé professionally typed and reproduced on good quality paper.*

2. *One page is the best length.* Two is acceptable if necessary. If you go to three, it means you're not being selective enough.

3. *Just as in the direct mail letter, use dollar figures and percentages whenever possible.* Include result-oriented information, not every single function you performed in each job.

4. *Don't list personal activities.* Do include such items as business-related activities, associations, awards, and abilities.

5. *Don't list personal information,* such as height, weight, age, or whether you're married, single, or divorced.

6. *Don't list references on your résumé.* You don't want anyone who isn't strongly considering you to call your references. Give out references only after the employer shows real interest.

7. *Don't include salary history or the salary range you're looking for.*

8. *Do have someone else check over your résumé before you send it out.* Ask this person to proofread it carefully and make sure there are no errors.

A RÉSUMÉ ALONE IS NOT AN EFFECTIVE SALES TOOL

No matter which style of résumé you choose, it's still not the most effective selling tool. A busy boss may quickly skim over your résumé looking for what he thinks are his exact requirements. Never send a résumé alone. Always include your direct mail piece as a cover letter to convince the employer to read the résumé more carefully and see how your experience and abilities can benefit him and his company.

Some people send résumés with cover letters that read,"As per your request, here is my résumé." This is nothing but a waste of paper. You want to use every selling tool you can, so send your direct mail letter along with your résumé. That way, no matter which résumé you send, the potential employer will still receive a personalized, benefit-oriented, targeted letter.

The résumé has been a standard part of the job search for many years and will probably remain so for a while to come. But résumés aren't necessarily going to keep their traditional format. How will they change? You may have to plug in your VCR to find out. . . .

25

2,001, the Video

The Visual Résumé

Sales and Marketing Principle #25

Packaging has a major impact on why a customer purchases a product or service.

SEEING IS BELIEVING

Samantha McIntyre walks into her office in the Slumberland, Inc., headquarters. She's anticipating a busy day ahead. The company had advertised for a new production manager last week. Since Samantha was going to be out of town all week, she'd instructed Todd, her assistant, to tell anyone who phoned to send in his or her résumé.

Todd greets her at the door with, "Wait till you see the response we got!" Samantha smiles, shrugs her shoulders, and says, "Okay, Todd. I'm ready. Set up the VCR."

What has the VCR got to do with checking out résumés? Well, there is a new development that takes the résumé into the age of instant communications, the age that has produced the car phone, the fax machine, the CD player, and, of course, the VCR. The video résumé is emerging as an effective way to stand out from the competition and let prospective employers know exactly who you are.

At this moment, when video résumés are not yet the norm, they can be effective attention getters. Simple curiosity will get many employers to look at them. "If I received a video résumé from someone, I would stop what I was doing and put it in the VCR immediately," says Judd Saviskas, vice president and director of human resources at Doyle Dane Bernbach in New York. "Of course, this wouldn't take the place of a final interview—there's nothing like sitting eyeball to eyeball—but I'd definitely take a look at the video."

The video résumé isn't meant to take the place of a final interview—or even the first interview. Its function is the same as the written résumé's: to get the employer's attention so that he or she will feel compelled to find out more about you. Video résumés are gaining in popularity now and may well be standard in the twenty-first century.

People today are accustomed to receiving information through electronic media. John Kelman, President of RES-A-VUE, a video résumé company in Milford, Connecticut, feels that video résumés are a successful sales tool because we live in an electronic society. We are conditioned to watching commercials and news programs where we get what we need to know in fifteen- and thirty-second chunks of information.

A video résumé usually lasts three to seven minutes. "A successful video résumé," says Kelman, "is a combination of *Nightline* and *Entertainment Tonight*." It contains preliminary information about the job candidate which appears on the screen, followed by the job seeker describing his or her abilities and accomplishments.

Your video résumé would be an extension of your direct mail letter. You would send the letter with the video. In this case, the letter would contain only one AAA, and the video would reveal two or three others.

Like a written résumé, a video résumé can be tailored to fit your job target. Electronic editing processes can change and replace small sections of the video to make it specific to the type of job you're seeking. But this process is costly. Video résumés can run anywhere from $300 to $17,000 to produce. "The way to look at the cost," says Kelman, "is that it is an investment in your future."

Video résumés can be especially effective in fields with more open, less conservative traditions. For example, advertising, public relations, marketing, and other firms used to visual representations of their work would probably appreciate the effort and innovative spirit of a video résumé.

Video résumés may not be for everyone. If you're not photogenic, have a weak, breathy voice, or are incorrigibly stiff and uncomfortable on tape, this isn't for you.

MOVE OVER, HOFFMAN AND STREEP

"One minor detail," you say. "I'm no actor. How can I go in front of a camera and not make a fool of myself?"

If you're really camera shy, you may be only asking for trouble. But a video résumé doesn't demand acting ability. It should simply be a natural, relaxed presentation of who you are, a vehicle for many of the same selling skills described earlier in this book.

In my presentation and interviewing seminars, I often have participants role-play, and I videotape them. In almost every case, people felt they were much better than they thought they would be. You will probably find the same is true for you.

AN ACTOR PREPARES

No actor or actress would dream of doing a film without rehearsing. You shouldn't either. You're going to be on camera talking anywhere from three to seven minutes, so you'd better practice, practice, practice. You may not have to do all seven minutes in one continuous shot, but you do want to appear as natural and as professional as possible.

Since you have your AAAs, you know what you want to talk about. Just talk into a tape recorder without having anything memorized, so that you sound natural. Then write down what you've said and memorize it. You don't have to be word perfect. You're not reciting a speech.

If you own a video camera or know someone who does, make practice tapes. Note your appearance, your clothing, your mannerisms, your speech habits. Then when you're ready for the real thing, you'll be calm and natural.

If you own good equipment, you may want to make your own video résumé. Be objective about it. If the end result looks amateurish and unprofessional, you'll do more harm than good. This is not the impression you want to give a potential employer. If the video doesn't show you in your best light, don't use it.

Although home video technology is advancing rapidly, it's still not up to professional standards. Steve Stein, executive producer at ARC Audio/Video in New York City, suggests that you shop around and get quotes from several video producers before you do any taping. Local cable studios can often refer you to video producers. You can also rent cable studio facilities and camera operators. (A two-camera shoot is better than one. If you can afford it, it's worth it.) If you choose to use studio facilities, you should hire a director and makeup artist as well.

There are seven ingredients necessary for a topnotch video:

1. A strong attention getter
2. Benefit-oriented presentation
3. Lively vocal presentation
4. Positive body language
5. Appropriate attire
6. A simple setting
7. Proper lighting

1. *A strong attention getter.* You've piqued their curiosity by sending the video. Now you've got to start off strong so they know this isn't just a gimmick. You should begin with a statement such as, "Hello. I'm Elaine Canfield, and last year I had the honor to be included in the national top twenty insurance brokers for a Fortune 500 company." This will keep the employer tuned in and his finger off of the rewind button.

2. *Benefit-oriented presentation.* You should include two or three benefit-oriented AAAs. Because it's not as easy to customize a video as it is a written résumé, use your strongest and most generic benefits: Choose a situation where you saved your company time or money, increased production, or discovered a unique solution to a long-standing problem. It is possible, but it can be costly and time-consuming, to shoot additional footage after the original has been completed. However, video résumés will be easier and less expensive to produce as technology advances.

3. *Lively vocal presentation.* Your voice can convey confidence or give away your real nervousness. Be aware of the volume of your voice. Speaking too loudly or too softly will distract the viewer from what you're saying. Focus your nervous energy so that it gives your voice color and animation. Be aware of your diction and pronunciation. Practice speaking into a tape recorder; play it back and listen for vocal variety, clear articulation, and energy and enthusiasm.

4. *Positive body language.* We are a visual society; people make judgments based on your appearance and body language the moment they see you. Most negative body language is the result of nervousness. You can eliminate a lot of that fear if you remember that the employer *wants* to like you. He wants to sit back and enjoy your video.

Your gestures and mannerisms are important in a video. Since you probably won't be moving around much, even small gestures become noticeable. Use strong, deliberate gestures; don't fidget in your chair or play with your tie clip or earrings. Don't twist your fingers together or clench your clothes in your hands. Once again, allow your nervous energy to animate you.

Do whatever is most comfortable for you. If you want to stand up, do so. If you stand, don't stay completely still—it will look unnatural. Move around just a little. Or if you start by standing, move toward your desk or chair and then sit down. Don't make any movement that will distract from what you're saying.

5. *Appropriate attire.* Since this is going to be more of an all-purpose résumé than the written version, your attire should be appropriate for a variety of potential employers. In this case, it's better to be on the conservative side. Wear clothes that are comfortable for you. You don't want to be fidgeting with a too-tight shirt collar or a blouse that needs to be adjusted every time you move your arm. Stick with colors that come across well on TV: blue, gray, pale yellow, and beige. Avoid bold patterns. If you wear jewelry, keep it simple and clank-free. Big bracelets or dangling earrings are taboo—on video, jewelry can be enormously distracting.

6. *A simple setting.* No elaborate backdrops or special effects are necessary. Just a simple, comfortable chair in front of an uncluttered wall will do. Or you might prefer an office setting. Whatever you choose, it should not distract from the most important element in this video—you.

7. *Proper Lighting.* Lighting is the key to flattering the subject. You should always be lit from above. If at all possible, do a one-minute sample take, then see how you look. You should be pleased with your appearance; if you think you look terrible, it's probably poor lighting. If everything checks out, go on and make the full-length version.

SOME ON-CAMERA ADVICE

▪ Talk to the camera as if you were talking to a friend.

▪ Make eye contact with the camera, but don't just stare straight ahead into the lens. Look away occasionally, just as you would in any conversation.

▪ Don't wait until the camera is ready and then "turn on." Your energy level should be high, but not exaggerated.

▪ Nervous energy and extra adrenaline make us unconsciously increase our rate of speech. We start talking faster than usual. If you deliberately slow down your speech a little, it will come out at a normal rate.

▪ Check sound levels before you begin so that you'll know if your volume is right.

▪ Practice voice and speech exercises beforehand so that your diction is clear and understandable.

▪ Focus on your selling points. Be brief and talk about benefits.

▪ Smile as naturally as possible. A smile at the opening of your video is warm, attractive, and invites the audience to relax and enjoy.

SOME WORDS OF CAUTION

Video résumés aren't for everyone. Since they're a fairly new concept at this time, an employer may think it's too "gimmicky." Or he or she may not have ready access to a VCR in the office and may not want to view the tape during personal time at home.

If you want to send a video résumé, I suggest you call first. You can use this call to establish and build rapport with the employer. Or speak to the secretary and find out if there is a VCR in the office before you send the tape.

Never send the video by itself—be sure to include your direct mail piece as your cover letter. It's a good idea to restate some of the information that's contained in the video so the employer has written reinforcement of who you are and what you can do for him.

AND NOW FOR THE AUDIOTAPE

Be prepared for unusual situations as you continue your job search. A colleague of mine, looking for a telemarketer for his office, actually designed a system for candidates to record an audio résumé.

He set up his answering machine so that it instructed the caller as to what information to leave. This allowed him to "audition" candidates and choose people who sounded professional, confident, and qualified over the phone.

A smart caller would have listened to the instructions, then hung up and created a script for himself to read into the tape. That's what I suggest you do if you ever run into this situation. Then you can call back and be sure you've included all the pertinent information without that spur-of-the-moment nervous tension.

You can also produce your own audio résumé. The same problems and considerations that pertain to the video résumé apply to an audiotape one as well. Make it short and to the point—five to seven minutes should do it. It has to be just as carefully rehearsed and prepared as the video and it isn't as easy to customize as the written résumé. You may also run into the same kind of resistance that applies to the video résumé. And once again, never send a tape without a cover letter to serve as your introduction.

FAX TO THE FUTURE

Another technological advance changing traditional avenues of finding a job is the fax machine.

A fax can be very useful when an employer is in a hurry to see your materials. A fax (facsimile copy, sent over telephone wires) can be sent across town or across the country in a matter of minutes. If it's important that your direct mail letter or résumé be received in that short a time, by all means fax it. Many neighborhood copy shops or stationery stores now have fax service available. Prices vary, but it's usually less than using one of the express mail services.

The one drawback of faxing letters or résumés is their appearance when they're received. Fax copies simply don't look as good as the original. The quality of the copy often depends on the quality of the fax machines involved. Fax paper is usually specially coated and not as sturdy as most computer or typing paper. Unless the employer tells you otherwise, I think it's worth the extra time to send a neat, professional-looking letter and résumé. You can always send it by overnight courier if time is an important factor.

Choose the type of résumé that best expresses who you are and what you can do for the company. Remember, the point of the résumé—on paper or on tape—is to get someone interested in learning more about you.

The next chapter will show you how to take advantage of that interest, how to build on it, and how to use the concepts of telemarketing to set up an interview.

26

Telemarketing

Tapping into Your Telephone Connection

Sales and Marketing Principle #26

The only way to close a sale is to get to the real decision maker.

PHONE PHOBIA: ITS CAUSES AND CURES

I'll never forget my first job-hunting experience. I was ambitious. I was enthusiastic. I was ready to go get 'em. I went over my CCI, reviewed my accomplishments, researched my sources with great gusto, and sent out targeted, well-written, benefit-laden direct mail letters. I kept an appointment calendar next to my phone. If I wrote in a letter to Mr. Joseph Adams that I would call on the thirteenth, I would write Joseph Adams' name in a bold, strong hand on the thirteenth. Soon I had many such names penciled in, and the day I sent my letters out I flipped through the calendar with great anticipation. Everything was going fine.

Then it began to hit me. On the ninth I felt a slight twinge. On the tenth I noticed I was getting a little jumpy, and by the eleventh I was really starting to sweat. As the time for making the calls got closer, my anxiety level increased. I was afraid to pick up the phone.

What is it about the telephone that terrifies us so? I would think to myself, "What's the worst that can happen? Can the person on the other end jump through the phone and harm me physically? Of course not. The worst that can happen is that he'll say no." But that "no" loomed large in front of me. One no would send me scurrying back to do some more research, write another letter, or any other task that would keep me from making the next call. I went through this with every call—until I realized that my anxiety and imagination were getting the better of me, and my fear of rejection was coming across on the phone.

Phone phobia is a common phenomenon. The fear of rejection is very strong; we take it all very personally. Not everyone you contact is going to buy. But all marketing campaigns are based on the law of averages: The more calls you make, the higher your average return. Your job search is a marketing campaign; you have to expect that you will get a certain percentage of rejections. You may get five appointments for every fifty calls you make—but those five appointments will be with people who are truly interested in what you have to offer.

Phone phobia takes other forms as well. You may be embarrassed to call. You may assume that you're interrupting someone's busy schedule, using up their valuable time. The truth is that your time is valuable as well, and if you didn't have a good reason to call you wouldn't be doing it. You are calling with something of real value—an offer that can help solve the other person's problems, free up his time, and benefit his organization. If *you* don't believe in your value and the value of your offer, neither will he.

Keep making those calls. Don't let all your hopes ride on one phone call. It's like planning a party and inviting only one guest. If that guest doesn't show up, there is no party. But if you invite fifty people and one guest doesn't show up, you can still have a very successful evening. And remember that practice makes perfect. Your first follow-up phone call may be agonizing, but the second call will be a little easier, and the third easier still, until one call will get you a yes. As you keep on going, your technique will improve and the number of yes's will increase.

THE PHONE IS NOT YOUR ENEMY

"Personality plus" is how most people described Diana when they met her. In social situations she was witty and confident, and in business meetings she handled herself in a calm, professional manner. Ask her to make a phone call, however, and Diana fell apart.

Reluctance to use the phone was holding Diana back. She was being considered for a promotion at the pharmaceuticals company where she worked, but her supervisor had doubts about making her a manager. Most of Diana's work was outstanding. But when asked to make a phone call, or to follow up on important projects via the telephone, Diana stalled and stalled. Sometimes her supervisor ended up making the call herself rather than wait for Diana to do it. Sometimes it took Diana days to work up the courage to make a call. She always felt as though she were intruding or would sound foolish or incompetent.

One day Diana saw her daughter playing with a toy telephone, pretending to talk to her friend across the street. It gave Diana the idea to make her own pretend calls. The next time her supervisor asked her to make a call, she wrote down what she wanted to say and pretended before she dialed. When she did make the call, she referred to her notes so she wouldn't be nervous and forget what she wanted to say. After only a few weeks, Diana was able to make phone calls with the ease and confidence she displayed in other areas of her life. Her supervisor recommended her for the promotion.

The phone is not your enemy; it's a natural extension of you. Before you begin your telemarketing campaign, practice making calls until you feel really comfortable "reaching out to touch someone." Call people not for business but for pleasure. Make more calls than you normally do. Now is the time to catch up on those calls you've been meaning to make for months. Call friends and relatives. Call stores for information, call the library for research information, call anyone you can think of so that using the phone becomes an easy, pleasurable experience.

Make sure you're physically comfortable as well. If you're calling from home, try to set a separate work area for yourself so you'll feel more professional. If you're calling from your present job, remove your phone from the clutter on your desk so that it has a "home of its own." George Walther, one of the country's foremost experts on telephone communications, says in his book *Phone Power: How to Make the Telephone Your Most Profitable Business Tool,* "The physical space works as a 'mental anchor.' When you turn to that place in your [home or] office, you shift into your 'professional communicator' mode."

THE ETHICAL ISSUE OF JOB HUNTING ON THE JOB

If you're presently working and are job hunting, you shouldn't be making calls from office during work time. It's okay to use coffee or lunch breaks to make calls, but be sure you use your phone credit card number; don't charge the calls to your office.

A young man I'll call Martin was in a great hurry to improve his position in life. He was dissatisfied in his job as an assistant food service manager in a large corporate cafeteria. In order to speed up his job search (and save himself some money), Martin used the office phone to make his phone calls. Unfortunately for Martin, his manager received the phone bill before Martin found another job. "I would have given you a very good reference if I'd known you were leaving, Martin. Now I see you're not as honest as I thought you were," the manager said. "I'm afraid I won't be able to give you a recommendation after all." As the saying goes, crime doesn't pay. Don't close doors just to save a little time or a few cents.

There are cases, if you've been laid off or let go, when the company will allow you to make such calls while you're still on the job. Just be sure that you behave ethically in all your dealings.

TAKE ADVANTAGE OF YOUR ADVANTAGES

You'll all set up. You've got your phone areas designated, you have paper and pencil nearby, an appointment calendar, and copies of the letters you sent out. You're ready to make your phone calls. If your confidence is still a little shaky, remember that when you're making a call, you have several advantages over the person on the other end:

1. You know more about the person you're speaking to than she knows about you. You know there's a strong possibility she'll be interested in speaking to you. You may know some of her problems and are prepared to offer your assistance. She'll be impressed with your knowledge and preparation for the call.

2. The person on the other end is not prepared for you, while you have spent a long time preparing for this call. Since you are prepared, you'll be ready to handle any objections or answer any questions she might have.

3. You have a strong objective firmly in mind, which gives you the edge in the situation.

4. The person on the other end is being asked to make a quick and unexpected decision. The only decision you have to make is what to say next.

BREAKING THE PROTECTIVE SECRETARY BARRIER

One common problem you may face is that the person you wish to speak to is probably not the person who answers the phone. You want to speak directly to the decision maker; you want to speak to the person to whom your letter is directed. More than likely, you will first have to get past the protective secretary, who is answering the phone because the decision maker is in a meeting or is preoccupied and unavailable to speak with you now.

■ *Technique #1: Be polite but firm.* When you call and the secretary answers, immediately state who you wish to speak to. "Ellen Peterson, please." Don't ask a question or even have a question in your voice. Make a statement as if you expect to be put through immediately. Many times you will be. But you should be prepared for a good secretary to do his or her job—and part of that job is to screen the boss's calls. However, secretaries are also used to fulfilling requests. Make yours one the secretary can't resist. Repeat frequently that you want to be put through.

If he or she says "Please tell me what this is about" or "What is this in reference to?" you can say "She's expecting my call," because she is. You wrote in your letter that you would call on this date. Or you can simply reply, "It's personal; please put me through." This usually works right away.

The secretary's job is to screen out bothersome, unimportant calls. You shouldn't be calling if that's how you feel about the call you're making. You want to convey strength and conviction and the feeling that yours is a call worth putting through.

▪ *Technique #2: The direct approach.* You can try the direct approach by saying, "I recognize that you are protecting your boss's time. This will only take a minute or two. Please put me through." You should try to build a relationship with the secretary, so that he or she will know who you are the next time you call. If you've built a good rapport the secretary might put you right through the next time. Always remember that the secretary is doing a job. Don't argue or be offensive.

Remember also that the secretary can be a great source of information, starting with the boss's title and the correct pronunciation of the boss's name. This is an important point; people are very sensitive about their names. My son's name is Ian—pronounced Eye-an. All through school, he took an immediate dislike to any teacher who couldn't get his name straight. If you're calling someone with a difficult name, be sure to find out how to say it, then write it down phonetically on your copy of the letter.

And don't forget the secretary's name. Write that down also. If you call back again, be sure to use his or her name. If you do get through by being rude or devious, the secretary will certainly remember this and could very well keep you from being hired. Remember the saying: "What goes around, comes around."

Since many secretaries have a good deal of influence with their bosses, you want them on your side. Many bosses won't even set up an appointment if the secretary says, "That person was rude when she called."

If the secretary has been helpful, don't forget to thank him or her when you call or send a note later. The secretary will remember that too.

▪ *Technique #3: Get the message.* If the boss isn't available, ask the secretary when would be the best time to call back. Find out if the boss usually comes in early or stays late. Ask for a specific time to call back. However, try not to make it sound as if you're free to call anytime at his or her convenience. You can say, "I'll be available at two o'clock. Would that be a good time to reach her?'' Let the secretary know that your time is valuable as well.

Don't be tempted to divulge your exact purpose to the secretary. There is an old sales slogan that goes "The more you tell, the less you sell" and that applies here as well. You don't want to give anyone the opportunity to rule you out or turn you away prematurely.

As Jeff and Marc Slutsky so aptly put it in their book *Streetsmart Teleselling: The 33 Secrets,* "Never try to sell your product or service to buffers or filters. Only sell them on putting you through to the decision maker."

What if the boss is out when you call? Should you leave a message? Robert Shook, co-author of *Successful Telephone Selling in the 80s,* says, "You don't want to tell the secretary any more than is necessary, but if you keep calling back and don't leave a message, he or she will probably recognize your voice and become annoyed. You can leave a message saying 'It's personal,' or 'It's confidential.' "

■ *Technique #4: Wait for the beep . . .* Here's the scene: You're going along making your calls, doing just fine. You've gotten through a few times, spoken to a few secretaries, and you decide to make one last call. You dial. It rings. You hear a click, and then a strange, metallic monotone voice comes on and says:

"Hello. This is the XYZ Company voice mailbox. Ms. Peterson is not in her office right now. If you wish to leave a message, please wait for the beep. . . .''

As we move into the twenty-first century, more and more organizations are installing "automated voice mailbox" devices, or corporate answering machines. If the person isn't in, you may leave your message just as you would on a home answering machine. I would not recommend this, however. You can develop a relationship, and possibly an ally, with a secretary, but it's hard to make friends with a machine.

If you call at several different times of the day and always reach a machine, try circumventing the system. There's usually a message to callers that says, "If you have a rotary dial, or need further assistance, please stay on the line." In that case an actual human will answer and you may be able to ask the operator for information about your prospective employer's schedule.

If you still can't get through to the boss, rehearse a message to leave the next time you call. Make it an attention getter—use your direct mail letter as the basis for your script.

■ *Technique #5: Make the telephone operator your personal secretary.* Another excellent way to get through to the decision maker is to use a person-to-person call. Though this can be time consuming and expensive, it does work. You may not know it, but you can make local person-to-person calls. What you are actually doing is hiring the operator to serve as your secretary and make the call for you. You'll need a cooperative operator. If you don't get one, keep trying until you do.

After you dial Operator, ask him or her to hold the call because you have some instructions to give. Then say you want to speak to Ellen Peterson—and only Ellen Peterson—and if she is not there to please leave a message that you called. That's all. When Ms. Peterson returns she will have a message that you called person-to-person. After two or three of these messages her curiosity will be whetted and she'll probably pick up the phone next time you call. One of the advantages to this is that people still have a certain respect for long distance (and especially person-to-person because so few people use it), and if the operator says person-to-person they will assume it's long distance even if it isn't.

After three calls and three telephone messages from you (which haven't cost you anything), you can instruct the operator to inquire when would be the best time to call. You can then call back directly when you know the decision maker will be in.

THE BEST TIME TO CALL

From my own experience, I've always reached the people I've wanted to contact by using a combination of these phoning techniques. No person is unreachable if you really want to get through. The best times to connect with busy people are before work, during lunch, and after work. If you have asked the secretary, you know which of these times would be the best to try. You might even try on Saturday mornings, when many executives come in to catch up on extra work without a protective secretary to take their calls.

I gave this advice to Glenn, one of my seminar participants who was having a difficult time reaching someone he really wanted to work for. The secretary was pleasant, but not exactly cooperative. I told Glenn to call between eight-thirty and nine in the morning, and again between noon and one. After three days, Glenn got through to the employer at twelve-thirty in the afternoon. "Oh," said the boss, "You just caught me. My secretary's out to lunch and I came back to the office earlier than I expected. What can I do for you?"

WHAT TO DO WHEN YOU DO GET THROUGH

Finally, the secretary does put you through. Or isn't there. Or is out sick. You've made it past the "bodyguard" and now you're speaking to the decision maker. You must go directly after your objective. This is not the time to try to make small talk; you must grab attention immediately. One major disadvantage of the phone is that the other party can simply hang up on you if you haven't given sufficient reason for her to stay on the line.

You should always start off by calling her by name right away. Say, "Is this Ellen Peterson?" (use her full name if you know it—and you should). If you feel more comfortable saying Ms. Peterson, that's okay. Then follow immediately with your name and the fact that you're following up on the letter you sent. This is important because she can't see you; you don't want her to spend your phone time thinking, "Who is this person? Am I supposed to know him? What does he want?"

Once you've introduced yourself and reminded her of the letter, take a deep breath and go for it. Start right in with a powerful benefit, and then request an appointment.

> Ellen Peterson? This is David Clark. I'm the sales executive who wrote you a letter last week saying that I added eighteen new accounts last year in a territory that was supposedly saturated with our product. I know I could do the same and more for your company. I can come in and see you on Wednesday the tenth at quarter to four, or Thursday the eleventh at quarter to ten. Which would be best for you?

The reason for the quarter hour is a subtle one. If you say you can come in at two or three or nine, the assumption is that the interview will take an hour, and she may not have an hour to spare. If you use the quarter hour, the assumption is that the interview will be only fifteen minutes long.

PERSISTENCE PAYS OFF

Remember that your goal is to get an appointment. You must be persistent, because it's not very likely that the prospective employer will say yes right away. You will need to keep coming back to your objective. Be prepared for all kinds of responses.

You may hear, "I'm sorry, I haven't seen your letter."

Your reply could be, "I'm sorry you haven't seen it. But I would be very happy to tell you more about myself on Wednesday at quarter to four or Thursday at quarter to ten. Which would be better for you?"

Or she might say, "I've seen the letter. That's all I need."

Then your reply would be, "There is really much more that I could tell you in person. Would Wednesday or Thursday be better for you?"

If she says "Tell me more about what you've done," give her one accomplishment that was not in your letter. Persist, adding, "I can tell you more on Wednesday at quarter to four or Thursday at quarter to ten. Which is better for you?''

Keep coming back to your objective. If you reveal too much over the phone, the boss may think she has enough information to make a decision right then. This is not what you want.

If she says ''I really don't have time to see you,'' say, ''I know your time is very valuable, but also I know I have something valuable to offer. I will only take up fifteen minutes of your time, and I'll be in your neighborhood next week. Would Wednesday or Thursday be better for you?''

If she says she'll be out of town for three weeks, try to set up the appointment for when she returns. Offer to drive her to the airport, bring in her favorite breakfast—whatever it takes (within reason) to get that appointment.

You are using a technique called ''the broken record,'' calmly and persistently repeating your point. By remaining calm and pleasant throughout, you avoid being annoying, but you do get your point across. Be assertive, not aggressive. Be charmingly persistent. If the employer gets annoyed, say, ''This same persistence, Ms. Peterson, is an example of how I will apply myself to all my work.'' Make it flattering to her that you care so much. Your objective will be reached when you get a definite response for an appointment.

DON'T FORGET TO NETWORK

Never hang up empty-handed. If the answer is no, go for some leads. Ask if there is anyone else in the company (if it is large enough) or if anyone she knows elsewhere who might benefit from your services.

Be specific when asking for referrals. This is a technique that I teach in my sales seminars. If you are selling coffee makers and you run into a no-sale situation, you might just say, ''Do you know anyone else who would like to buy a coffee maker?'' Chances are the prospect will say no. But if you're more specific and say ''Do you know anyone who's been complaining about the quality of their coffee lately?'' you get the prospect thinking along a specific track. ''Oh yes,'' he might say. ''My neighbor down the street was talking about that just the other day. She may be in the market for a good coffee maker. Let me give you her name.'' The prospect is then doing someone else a good turn by helping to solve their problem.

So instead of asking ''Do you know anyone else who might be interested in speaking with me?'' ask, ''Do you know anyone who's been complaining that they can't find new markets in their territory? Perhaps they would be interested in seeing me." You might get referred to a colleague in a related field who is a likely prospect. You can respond by saying, "I appreciate that information, Ms. Peterson. May I say that you gave me his name?" Then you can call and say, "Ms. Peterson of XYZ Company suggested I call you. . . ."

YOUR ATTITUDE COMES THROUGH

As any successful telemarketer can tell you, your attitude comes across strongly and makes an immediate impression. If you're uncertain and apologetic over the phone, your prospective employer can only assume you'll be that way on the job also. He or she is much more likely to respond to someone who sounds confident and enthusiastic.

Think about people you enjoy listening to, people you like. What are some of their attractive qualities? Are they optimistic or pessimistic? Do they express interest in you and the world around them or do they seem self-centered and preoccupied? Attractive qualities (qualities that are not only pleasant, but that actually *attract* other people) are not hard to acquire. Everyone has positive and negative qualities. But the more you focus on the positive qualities, the more dominant they become.

Natalie Tremain was out of work and depressed. Natalie (and many others at the plant) was laid off when the textile company she worked for was acquired by a large conglomerate. An excellent manager, Natalie knew many people in the textile industry, but she was losing momentum in her job search. She tried making calls, but after two or three unsuccessful attempts, she was reluctant to go on. She would stop, watch TV, do some errands. She would make another call or two, then stop again. Finally, Natalie called her friend Joanne, another job seeker, to see how she was managing.

"Oh, I'm doing fine," Joanne told her cheerfully. "I've already got three interviews set up for next week, and I've got lots more calls to make."

"Didn't you get a lot of rejections?" Natalie asked. "How do you keep going?"

"Yes, I got some rejections," Joanne replied, "but I figured those people were losing out on a good thing and I went on to the next call. I schedule a time for making phone calls and then pretend that I'm at work and this is the job I have to do. I've spoken to some very nice people who seem really interested. I'm going to make some more calls right now as a matter of fact."

Natalie thought about Joanne and her attitude toward rejection. She tried it out herself and found she was able to make several more calls that day. She even set up an interview with someone she'd been particularly nervous about calling. When Natalie changed her attitude and her "work" habits, the responses she got changed too.

If you admire what someone else is doing, imitate his attitude. Try it on for size. Associate with positive people. Natalie listened to Joanne and imitated her attitude. If someone you admire has a lot of enthusiasm for his work, follow his example and see what happens. Act as if enthusiasm is a part of you and soon enough it will be. Act as if you're interested in helping others meet their needs and soon enough you will be. You'll find that these truly are attractive qualities and people will respond positively to them.

TRICKS OF THE TELEPHONE TRADE

Grab a person's interest through positive and negative motivation. Positive motivation persuades your possible boss it is well worth his time to see you because of your specific offer:

> I added eighteen new accounts to a saturated territory. I know I could do the same or more for your company.

Negative motivation lets the boss know that there is something missing in his present way of working, and that you have the answer to this problem:

> I know that the tri-state area seems to be saturated with electrical suppliers. What you need is someone who knows how to find untapped buyers in this area—and having done just that for my last employer, I know I can do the same for you.

■ *Visualize.* Try to imagine what the person on the other end looks like, so that you are speaking to a real person. Know what you expect from him. If you don't expect a positive response, why bother to call?

■ *Be prepared before you begin.* Have copies of your letters handy, and any phone numbers you will need. Have blank paper and pens or pencils ready. Keep your calendar open next to the phone and make sure you have all appointments, personal and business, written down. You don't want to forget an important appointment because you didn't write it down or make two appointments for the same time because you didn't have your calendar handy.

■ *See yourself on an equal footing with the person you're calling.* You are just as intelligent, competent, and deserving of success as the people you are speaking with. You have information and ideas that they need, and you are convinced that what you have to offer will benefit the prospective employer and his or her company.

Rehearse, relax, and breathe deeply before you begin.

▪ *Use a technique called bunching.* Prepare all your calls and know how many you will do at one sitting. Group them in geographical areas. If you're calling long distance, be sure you're aware of time zones.

USE YOUR VOICE TO HELP GET YOUR FOOT IN THE DOOR

Your voice is your calling card. Since he can't see you, the person on the other end is going to judge you by how you sound. Your voice can be a great help to you, but it can also be a serious liability. It can give you away as being nervous or unsteady—or it can convey the impression of courage and self-confidence.

Pay attention to your voice if you want others to pay attention to you. Listen to yourself. Practice by reading aloud, reciting in the shower, reciting poetry in the car. Listen to how classically trained actors such as Peter O'Toole or Meryl Streep use their voices as instruments of feeling.

The voice, as we hear it over the phone line, is made up of several different components: speed or pace, volume, tone, and diction. Each of these can be worked on separately and then together.

Pace

Listen to how the other person speaks, and match your rate of speaking to his:

▪ A fast talker will have no patience with you if you are too slow.

▪ If the person on the other end speaks slowly, match it. People who speak slowly are usually suspicious of fast talkers.

If your speed is much different than his, he'll feel uncomfortable without knowing exactly why.

The average rate of speech is about 150 words per minute. People think at a rate of four times faster than they speak, however. So if you are going too slowly, you'll lose the attention of your listener. Speak too quickly, and people won't be able to follow what you're saying. Pace yourself. Study public speaking techniques. Remember to breathe and take natural pauses.

You can practice pacing your speech with the following rhyme. Say the first line very slowly, the second line quickly, the third slowly, and so on. Then repeat the rhyme, saying the first line quickly, the second line slowly, etc.

> Hey diddle diddle
> The cat and the fiddle
> The cow jumped over the moon.
> The little dog laughed
> To see such a sport
> And the dish ran away with the spoon.

Not So Loud

Many of us tend to speak too loudly on the phone. Speak in a normal tone, as if the other person were sitting right next to you. If he can't hear you, he'll let you know. Keep the mouthpiece about half an inch from your mouth and speak in a calm, low pitch. Tape record your voice during a normal phone conversation and listen to make sure you speak at a moderate volume.

Practice controlling the volume of your voice by saying the word *no* over and over again, starting very softly (almost whispering) and working your way to very loud (almost shouting). You'll gradually learn to recognize when you're speaking too softly or too loudly.

Variety Is the Spice of Life

The telephone is not an accurate reproduction of your voice quality. People's voices sound higher over the phone than they do in person. Vary your pitch and rhythm so that you are not speaking in a monotone. Using a tape recorder helps because you need to make adjustments based on how the other person hears you, not based on how you think you sound.

To practice pitch and inflection, say the following, letting your voice follow the words:

> Let your voice come down evenly, smoothly as a sigh.
> Then evenly up and ever so high.
> Hold your tones level and high today;
> then level and low tomorrow, I say.
> Let tone glide high,
> then slide down low.
> Learn to say no, no, NO.

Or recite the "do, re, mi" scale, going from a high tone to a low one. Or try the numbers one through eight, going up the scale and coming down again.

Your tone of voice reflects your attitude. Nervousness, resentment,

27

Face-to-Face

A Guide to the Ultimate Sale—
The Job Interview

Sales and Marketing Principle #27

A sale is a series of planned questions to uncover needs, build trust, answer objections, and gain commitment.

EXPLOIT YOUR NERVOUS ENERGY

You are a thoroughly prepared salesperson. You've studied your product inside and out, you have a full slate of AAAs, you've done your homework on the company and the person interviewing you, you've practiced and perfected your marketing skills. Now you're about to put it all together face-to-face. A thousand questions must be going through your mind. "What do I do?" "What do I say?" "What should I wear?" "What will he expect?" "What do I do if she asks me about salary?" "What should I say about the fact that I never finished college?" "What if he thinks I'm too old?" "What should I say about the time I got fired?" "Suppose he says no?" "Suppose he says yes?"

Your heart starts beating rapidly; your "fight or flight" response is telling you to turn around and run; you're sure you've got the wrong day, the wrong address, the wrong . . . everything.

Everyone is nervous before a sales call. It's all right to feel this way; it's a natural human reaction. Interviewing is not something that comes naturally. You learn how. Don't let your nervousness scare you away— use it to your advantage. Turn that surge of adrenaline into positive energy; it will keep you alert and on your toes. Nervousness becomes a problem when you aren't prepared for what you have to do—if you don't feel you have enough information or you haven't practiced enough.

THE BOY SCOUTS WERE RIGHT

You will find that your nervousness decreases in direct proportion to the amount of preparation and practice you devote to interviewing skills. There's only one way to keep nervous energy from turning into debilitating fear—and that is, *Be Prepared.*

You're already better prepared for this interview than you think. You have a career inventory of at least ten and probably more AAAs. You've spent sufficient time assessing yourself and recognizing your value, you've done your homework, and you have been steadily improving your ability to sell yourself. It's taken research, organization, networking, initiative, confidence, marketing and selling skills, and perseverance to get you this far—*and these are all skills any employer will value.* You're well ahead of the game before you even step through the door.

Don't let your nervousness get the best of you. Don't fall into the trap of thinking that everything rides on this one interview. If you don't get this job, you will leave no worse than when you came in. And you will have gained valuable practice in interviewing.

HOW DO YOU GET TO CARNEGIE HALL?

I'm sure you've all heard the famous New York story: An old man is walking on the street in Manhattan one day when a young man with a violin case comes up to him and says, "Excuse me, sir. Can you tell me how to get to Carnegie Hall?" And the old man answers, "Practice, my boy, practice!"

In any skill-building process there is no substitute for practice. Remember the first time you rode a bike, or played baseball, or sang in front of an audience? I'm sure you were nervous, and probably not very good. But the more you practiced and repeated the experience, the easier it got and the better you got. The first time a pilot takes off in a 747 must be a nerve-racking experience. But after twenty or thirty flights it becomes second nature to the pilot. So it is with interviewing skills. That's why you work to get as many interviews set up as possible. You may not want every job you go after, but you do want to practice interviewing.

Even before you go out on your first interview you can practice the interview situation. Have a friend or family member role-play with you. Use your research and background information to prepare a list of questions you think you might be asked. Have your partner play several different potential employers. Ask your partner for feedback on how well you listened, how well you responded, and how you presented yourself in general.

During my job search, I went on over sixty interviews. I got so I couldn't wait to be interviewed. And I received several job offers—not because I was perfect for each job—but because I had honed my interviewing skills so sharply.

THE TWO-OBJECTIVE INTERVIEW

You have two objectives when you go in for a job interview.

1. To get a job offer
2. To get information about the job and the company

You always want to get a job offer. Even if you aren't sure if you want the job, you want to secure a job offer. You can always turn it down. Not only is it good practice for you to go after the job offer, it's a confidence booster. Just remember not to lead people on and allow them to think you're going to accept a job if you have no intention of doing so. If you're called back for a second or third interview, and you've definitely decided this job is not for you, there's no point in wasting everyone's time.

The second objective is to find out as much information as you possibly can about the job, about the company, and about your potential boss. Without a lot of information from your prospective employer you'll never be able to make a sound decision as to whether or not you want the job —and whether to accept the job or not should always be *your* decision. Keep this in mind: You're not just going to be interviewed, you're also going to interview your prospective boss.

Every interview is a question-and-answer session, with both sides trying to get the information they need within a limited time frame. An ideal interview situation should be give and take, with each person asking and answering the questions.

HOW TO READ THE PROSPECTIVE EMPLOYER'S MIND

Through the entire interview, the employer is really only asking you three things:

1. *Do you have the ability to do the job?* And can you do it better than the other people I've seen?

2. *Do you really want to do this job?* Are you excited and motivated by it?
3. *Will you "fit in" and be part of the team—and make me look good?*

Therefore, each of your answers should be another way of saying, "I do have the ability to do this job well, I very much want to do this job, and/or I will have no problem fitting in with your team." Listen carefully to the question being asked. Which of these three categories does it fall under? A simple question like "When can you start work?" may be asked (1) to get a factual answer, and (2) to find out how excited or motivated you are to begin your new position.

Listen carefully to all questions you're asked. The less you're thinking about yourself and what you're going to say next, the better the interview will go. If you're busy thinking instead of listening, you will lose your concentration. Suppose an employer is asking you a question about why you left your last job and you're busy wondering how much money he's willing to pay you. How will you be able to answer the question? It will probably take you by surprise and you won't be able to answer in a calm, intelligent manner.

Be responsive to the employer and he will be responsive to you. Be an active listener. Nod your head. Let him know you agree with what he's saying. Not only will you give better answers by paying close attention, but you will lose your self-consciousness and anxiety as you concentrate on asking and answering questions.

THE MORE YOU TELL...

Karen was being interviewed for a position as assistant convention services manager at a large Atlanta hotel. The job required dealing with staff, suppliers, and hotel guests. During the interview, the manager said, "This job entails a great deal of problem solving. Can you give me an example of your problem-solving abilities?"

Not having written out her AAAs beforehand, and not quite sure what the employer wanted to hear, Karen stumbled through a story of an argument she had with one of the suppliers at her previous job. Then, thinking perhaps this wasn't a good enough answer, she continued on and told two more stories of disagreements she'd had with her supervisor. Karen was a good worker and, told correctly, any one of these stories would have shown her to be a creative problem solver. But because she wasn't prepared and hadn't asked the manager exactly what he wanted to know, she came across as someone who couldn't get along with others.

Once again, the old sales proverb holds true: "The more you tell, the less you sell."

Answer *only* the question that's being asked. Answer truthfully, simply, and directly. If you're not 100 percent sure of what the interviewer means, ask a clarifying question. Interviewers are notorious for asking questions that you should not or cannot answer properly without more information. Don't hesitate to ask for it. A favorite opening gambit by interviewers is, "Tell me about yourself." Interviewers will often ask this at the very beginning of the interview, before you've been able to get much information. You should always counter by saying, "There's so much I can tell you, but I want to focus on what's important to you. What specifically do you want to know?"

The more general the question, the more important it is that you ask a clarifying question. If the interviewer says, "What accomplishments have made you most proud?" You might say, "I've done many things that have pleased me. What areas are you interested in?" Don't answer until you know what he or she values most. You can dig yourself into a hole if you're not careful. For example, the interviewer may be looking for someone who is highly detailed and quality control–oriented, and detail work may not be your strong point. A general rule of thumb is: *Never answer any question unless you fully understand the reason behind it.*

SELLING YOUR BENEFITS

Don't forget the sales techniques you've been studying all along. You used the concept of benefit selling in your direct mail letter, in writing or taping your résumé, and in securing an interview appointment. By now you have a good handle on this technique. Remember your AAAs when you're answering the employer's questions. If an employer says, "This is a very busy office. I need someone who can keep track of many activities at once. Can you do that?" your answer might be, "I'm very organized." (That's a feature.) You could continue with, "In my last job I created a wall chart that let everyone see at a glance the projects that were under way, who was working on each project, and when the due dates were. That way we were able to shift staff when necessary to meet a deadline. My department never missed a deadline in two years." (That's a benefit.)

Never mention a feature without going on to mention a benefit. Study your AAAs so you can pull one out at any time and use it to sell yourself into the job.

TOUGH QUESTIONS, SELLING ANSWERS

No matter how well prepared you are, tough questions will come up—questions that may make you feel uncomfortable or are difficult to answer. I've listed several standard tough questions, which I will discuss in a moment. You should anticipate these kinds of questions and be especially well prepared for them. The trick to handling tough questions is to answer in such a way that any possible negative is immediately replaced by a positive picture of yourself and your abilities.

For example, if you're applying for a job in a field in which you have no direct previous experience, the interviewer might ask, "Have you ever worked in the garment industry before?" You might say, "I've worked in interior design and I know a lot about fabrication and fabric designers." Or you might say, "In my last job I was transferred into a new division of the company and my supervisors were very pleased with how quickly I learned and adapted my skills."

Here are some other tough questions you may be asked:

▪ *"What are your major strengths and weaknesses?"* Always clarify this question by saying, "What do you feel are the strengths necessary to excel in this job?" This is a great clarifying question because it shows the employer you are someone who wants to excel.

You know what your strengths are from your CCI. Sell the success factors that relate specifically to this job and give examples of how you have applied those qualities. Reveal only your strengths, even if you disguise them as weaknesses. Everyone has weaknesses, but some are "safer" than others. You might say that you tend to be a bulldog—you never let go of a problem until it's solved. Or you get impatient with people who don't work as hard as you do. Or you're too much of a perfectionist, but you're working on it. Occasionally, it's all right to admit to a minor weakness; that is, if you're a super salesperson, you might say, "I closed three times as many sales as anyone else on our sales force. My boss would get after me, though, because I didn't always do such a great job with the paperwork. But I have improved, and I'll continue to work on that problem."

▪ *"I'm not sure that you have the experience (or training) to handle this job. Do you?"* This is a question you should be prepared for. You know from your research what this company is looking for. But the employer obviously sees something about you he likes, otherwise you wouldn't even be in this interview. He's looking to you to help him find a way to get around this problem so that he can hire you.

If you were selling vacuum cleaners, you'd know that your model is smaller than some others and doesn't have as much suction power. But yours can get into small nooks and crannies, places other vacuums can't reach. That's the benefit you'd sell. When you're selling yourself, look for the benefits you have that others (even those with more experience) may not possess. Be confident. Let the employer know how your other strengths and skills can more than make up for your seeming lack of experience.

Say you're in an interview for a position as executive assistant to the head of the fund-raising department for a large medical center. You haven't worked in fund-raising before. You might say, "It's true I haven't worked in a fund-raising office before. But in college I was very active in the Office of Special Events. Even as far back as high school, I was involved in fund-raising—I raised 75 percent of the money my choir needed for a trip to Washington, DC. I know your department puts on dinners and charity auctions, and I feel my background in college, plus my other organizational abilities, will be very helpful to this department. I'm ready to give 110 percent in order to make up for any lack of experience I may have."

■ *"Where do you see yourself five years from now?"* What this question really means is, "Are you going to be around for the long haul? Or do you just see this job as a stepping stone to your next career move?" Reassure the employer that you anticipate being very happy in the prospective job and that you'll be looking for ways to continually improve and grow. Sell your sense of commitment and give examples of your record of loyalty and reliability.

■ *"Why did you leave your last job?"* You must never lie or put your old job down. Another old sales proverb says, "Never put down the competition. It just makes you look cheap." Don't make excuses for yourself. If you were fired, say so. (The interviewer will inevitably find out if you don't.) You needn't go into detail, but give him a general reason why things didn't work out. "My supervisor and I had very different ways of working and things just didn't work out. But I gave it a good try and learned a lot on the job while I was there."

■ *"What makes you think you're qualified to work for this company?"* A defensive answer would be to say "I've done . . ." and rattle off a list of reasons why you're qualified. A nondefensive answer would be to say, "That's an interesting question. Actually, you're in a better position to answer that than I am. What do you feel is the one thing that would make me qualified?"

■ *"Can you work under pressure?"* This is a definite candidate for a clarifying question. Ask the interviewer to explain what he or she means by pressure. You might find out this is an extremely high pressure position and not one you want to take. Or you may find out that you've worked under similar conditions before and would have no problem dealing with them on this job.

■ *"Do you like working with people or things?"* This is a loaded question unless you know what the job is. As Dustin Hoffman said to the director in *Tootsie*, "Which answer will get me the job?" You have to have more information before you answer this one.

■ *"What sort of money are you looking for?"* Never talk money until you know there's a job offer. No matter what, wait until the interviewer is sold on you. That might mean waiting until the second or third interview. *A good salesperson always establishes value before talking price.* First, you show the prospective buyer all the wonderful features and benefits of the product he's considering. Then, when he's convinced this is the one he must have—that's when you discuss price.

The more time the employer invests in you, the more he or she has at stake. If the employer asks you this question early in the interview, you can counter with, "Is this a job offer?" If that seems too direct, say, "I think it's more important that we talk about your needs first, and if I'm the right person for the job we can talk about salary later on." Then ask another question: "What would you say is the primary skill needed to succeed at this job?" Negotiating for money will be covered in Chapter 29.

YOU HAVE THE RIGHT TO REMAIN SILENT

One of the great formulas of success came from Albert Einstein. He said, "If A equals success, the formula is $A = X + Y + Z$. X is work. Y is play. Z is keeping your mouth shut."

Remember that no law says you have to answer every question when it's asked. If a question makes you very uncomfortable, you can always try a diversionary tactic. You could say, "Mr. Smith, would you mind if I asked you a question that just came to mind?" And there are some questions that federal law mandates you do not have to answer at all. The Equal Opportunity Commission has strict laws about questions relating to age, criminal record, financial affairs, handicaps, national origin, marital or family status, race or color, religion, or sex. If you feel that questions being asked in any one of these areas are not directly related to job requirements, you can legitimately refuse to answer (pleasantly, of course). For example, if working on Saturdays is a legitimate job requirement, a question such as "Will you be able to work on Saturdays?" is allowed. But it can't be used as a subtle (or not so subtle) way to find out your religious beliefs. If you have doubts, you may want to reconsider working for the person who asked the question.

WHAT, ME ASK QUESTIONS?

"Hold on just a minute here!" you say. "If the boss is the one asking all the questions, how am I supposed to get the information I need?"

Now, that's a smart question. And the answer is, in order to achieve your second objective—which is to get enough information for you to decide whether or not you want this job—you're going to have *ask questions*.

You are following two tracks during your interview. The first and most obvious is, "What is your problem? What can I do to help?" Your secret agenda is, "Is this the right job for me?" Every question you ask should come from one of those two contexts.

TAKE CONTROL: DON'T BE AN INTERVIEW COUCH POTATO

Dennis came to me because he had been looking for a job for almost a year and hadn't had any luck. During my first meeting with him, I understood why. Dennis was a very passive personality (at least in an interview situation), and he seemed so laid back and unaggressive that it was difficult to see how he'd ever be successful.

We went over the "rules" of interviewing until Dennis became comfortable with taking a more active role in the process, answering questions with energy and enthusiasm and asking questions of his own. Within three weeks, Dennis had two appealing job offers.

Employers are looking for energetic people. They don't want you to sit through an interview like a bump on a log, letting the interview go by without having any input. Remember, you're the salesperson here. You have to make the sale—it won't make itself. In order to do that, you have to take control.

You take control in an interview by asking questions.

What would you do with the rest of your life if you won the million-dollar lottery? I got you thinking about it, didn't I? Just by asking one question, I changed the direction of your thoughts. My book *Smart Questions* is based on the fact that a question is one of the simplest, yet most effective ways of taking and remaining in control of any conversation.

By asking the right questions in an interview situation, you can steer the conversation in the direction you want it to go. The impulse to answer a question—any question—is automatic. A question is like an electric shock to the brain; we feel compelled to answer. This is true for you—and for the employer as well.

The more questions you ask, the more control you have. Each time you answer an employer's questions, regain control of the situation by asking another question. For instance, if an employer asks you to describe your greatest strengths, follow your answer with, "What would you most like for a new employee to bring to this job?"

If you sit back passively and let the interviewer pick you over to see if you have the goods, you will learn little about the job. Before the interview, make a list of questions you would like to have answered. Carry the list in your purse, your briefcase, or your pocket and don't be shy about pulling it out. Smart interviewers appreciate a flair for asking good questions—and the thoughtfulness and professionalism it takes to prepare them ahead of time.

Choose your questions carefully. Always use open-ended questions that require more than a yes or no answer. For instance, don't ask, "Is this the kind of job where I would have authority to make decisions concerning budget?" Instead say, "What kinds of decision-making authority would I have regarding budgets?" Use some questions to get facts about the job itself. Use others to find out the employer's needs so that you can let him know how hiring you would fill those needs.

THE RULES OF THE GAME

The interviewer usually sets the style and tone of the interview. If the interviewer is very good (and you can't count on this), he may suggest that you feel free to ask questions throughout the interview. A less secure interviewer may say, "I'm going to tell you a few things about the job and then ask you a series of questions. You may ask any questions you have when I'm through." Usually he talks so much there is no time left to ask your questions. Or he may not set up any game plan, leaving you wondering how he's going to proceed.

You have no way of knowing how the interview is going to be conducted until you get there. All the more reason for you to be thoroughly prepared. Do your research and you will already know enough about the company to be able to ask smart questions. So you are armed and ready.

When the potential employer sets up the rules, the next step is up to you. You may choose to go along with his game plan, or you may politely object. For instance, if he or she has stated that you should save all your questions for the end, you might interrupt at a point near the beginning and say, "Excuse me, would you mind if I asked a question here? I need to clarify something you just said." The interviewer probably won't realize that you are changing the plan and will more than likely be glad to explain what he or she meant.

When you go in for your interview, assume it's going to be a normal situation with an even exchange of questions and answers. You want to get control immediately. Remember, the person who asks the questions gains control. Try to ask the first question—pleasantly and politely. You can begin by expressing interest in your interviewer or by making an observation about the office or view. If you can find out something about the person ahead of time, it gives you a distinct advantage: "I saw in *Business Today* that you just got promoted. What are the things you feel have contributed to your success here?" Or, if you've come through a recommendation, you might casually ask, "How do you and Jaimie Gerard know each other?"

It's always to your advantage to know the inside "lingo." Martin Shafiroff, a managing director at Shearson Lehman Hutton, advises job seekers to "read up on the business before you go in for an interview. Talk the language they talk. Bring up what you know in conversation, ask questions about what you've read. You'll stand out from the competition."

Whether you ask your questions as the subject comes up (and you may have to bring it up) or read from your list at the end of the session, there are always questions you can ask to keep you in control and give you the information you need. A list of the kinds of questions you'll need to ask is included in the next chapter.

Most of your time should be spent asking questions and listening carefully to the answers, not talking endlessly about yourself without a sense of what the other person wants to hear. Your questions also give the employer clues about your interest level and how well you prepared for the interview. You will be judged not only by the answers you give to the interviewer's questions, but also by the quality of the questions you ask.

One of the best interviews I ever had was with a very sharp and smart sales manager. Knowing I had had two previous careers, he asked what made me think I would be satisfied in this job, since I had so many interests. I took my time and thought about it. Then I asked him, "Does your job satisfy all your interests?" I was eventually offered the job, and I'm sure it was because of that one question.

REMEMBER YOUR SELLING ABCs

When the interview is coming to an end, remember your ABCs: Always Be Closing. Don't be afraid to ask for the job. Say, "I would like very much to work for your company. What can I do or say to help you make a favorable decision on my behalf?" The interviewer might just tell you what else is on her mind. You'll know what her objections are and how to deal with them.

If the interviewer says "I'll call you and let you know about the job," don't be passive. Set a specific time for you to call her back. If you are refused and you really want the job, press for a second interview: "Ms. Employer, have you ever wished for a second chance to make a better impression? I'd like that chance, since I really want to work for you. Can we meet again next week?" This has worked magic for me in many cases.

GETTING IT ALL TOGETHER

Everything about the interview counts—from the minute you arrive to the minute you leave. Get there early if possible and be polite and friendly to everyone you meet. Don't smoke or drink, even if offered. Coffee or tea is acceptable, as long as you make sure there is somewhere to put the cup down when you're through with it. You don't want to be left holding it awkwardly throughout the interview.

Find out about the office environment before you visit. Is it formal or casual? Does everyone dress alike or do they prefer a creative flair? If you're not sure, conservative is always best. You can always wear something different to the second interview. I once went on a job interview looking too chic, wearing an avant-garde coat, too much makeup (at least for this particular company), and a severe haircut. They were interested enough to ask me back and I had another chance. For my second interview I came back in a camel's hair coat, just a drop of makeup, and a different hairstyle. The boss said, "You seem different." Eventually I was offered the job (although I didn't take it), and I'm sure I wouldn't have received the offer if I hadn't changed my appearance.

The impression you make on the interviewer carries over into the job itself. If you position yourself as strong, capable, and ambitious in your interview, you begin to establish your reputation and power base for after you're hired.

FOLLOW-UP: THE SECRET OF SALES SUCCESS

"I attribute a lot of my success in this business today to follow-up procedures I established at the beginning of my career," Jackie Burton, president of Burton-Luch Public Relations, told me recently.

"When I first started out, I had to work very hard to 'sell' my clients to newspaper and magazine editors and TV producers. I made it a habit to follow up my initial sales call with a personal note, along with any requested materials. I'd call again to make sure they received the package and perhaps give them another idea of how they could showcase my client. Every time I booked a client, my first order of business was to send a thank-you note or card. I sent notes no matter how it turned out, because I knew the editor or producer spent time trying to make it work.

"These people remembered me, and later on, when I had other clients to promote, they were happy to hear from me again. Selling is a complex process, but for me it's the follow-up that makes it work."

Many top sales professionals feel the same way, and follow-up should be an important part of your sales effort. The day after each interview you go on, the follow-up process begins.

Keep a record of how the interview went. You can make a form for yourself to keep on file. Here is a sample for you to copy or adapt:

Date of interview: _____

Name of company: _____

   Address: _____

Name of interviewer: _____

   Title: _____

   Phone number: _____

Job position/title: _____

   Main responsibilities: _____

_____

_____

   AAAs discussed: _____

_____

_____

_____

_____

Salary or range mentioned: _____

Follow-up:

   Thank-you letter sent: _____(attach copy)

   To call back on: _____Call made: _____

   Next step: _____

Positive/negative impressions: _____

_____

Summary of performance (What did I do well? What can use improvement? Was I well prepared? Did I ask enough questions? etc.):

_____

_____

_____

_____

_____

No matter how you feel your interview went, follow up with a letter thanking the interviewer for the meeting. Include a brief reference to your most relevant AAA and remind him that you'll be calling at the time you discussed (and be sure you do).

One manager told me, "I often judge job applicants by their follow-up actions. If a candidate is really interested in the job and is as conscientious as she says she is, she'll call me back. Then I know I can trust her word."

EIGHT KEYS TO GETTING A YES

Here are eight secrets to getting an offer at the job interview:

- Be prepared.
- Be ready to turn negatives to positives.
- Ask questions to keep control.
- Listen actively to content and intent of questions you're asked.
- Don't answer any question you don't fully understand.
- Ask for the job.
- Follow up.
- Practice so much that you will be relaxed and comfortable enough to let your best self shine through.

A good way to be prepared is to know the kinds of questions you'll probably be asked and the kinds of questions you should be asking. Study the next chapter, practice with the questions provided, add some more of your own, and role-play until you're ready to face any interview situation. You're on your way!

28

How to Handle Objections
Like a Pro

Answering Tough Questions

Sales and Marketing Principle #28

The person who asks the questions controls the sale.

EMPLOYER #1: "It doesn't look like you have much experience in this field. What makes you think you can handle the job?"

EMPLOYER #2: "So you've been a volunteer for five years. Do you have any real work experience?"

EMPLOYER #3: "You were terminated from your last job. Why?"

EMPLOYER #4: "You don't seem to stay at any job for very long. Why have you moved around so much?"

These are all tough questions. But if you read them over, you'll find that not one of these employers said, "I don't want to hire you." What they did was ask a question or, in sales terms, raise an objection.

One of the hardest lessons salespeople must learn is that an objection is not equal to a rejection. As we discussed in Chapter 22 on becoming a salesperson, an objection is what you hear when a buyer hasn't yet made a positive decision.

When employers ask you tough questions, they're really hoping you'll show them the reasons they should hire you for the job. If a prospective boss asks "Why were you fired from your last job?" and you answer "Personality conflict—my boss was uncommunicative," what impression will you make? Perhaps your last boss couldn't communicate well, but that doesn't tell this employer why he should take a risk and hire you.

We often accept objections at their surface value because it's easy and comfortable. If an interviewer says "I can't afford to hire you," we can comfortably accept that and tell ourselves, "I didn't get this job because he doesn't have the money. It wasn't *my* fault."

Sometimes we take objections personally and feel hurt and disappointed. How do you overcome this fear of rejection and failure and go for the close? Remember my motto, "Success is turning knowledge into positive action"? Well, this is the perfect place to make that motto work for you by using the knowledge you already have and by being open to learn more. If you're reading this book, it means you're willing to learn more about the process of becoming a successful salesperson.

SIX SUREFIRE STEPS TO HANDLING OBJECTIONS

When objections come up, you have the chance to answer the question, to offer more evidence, to restate your case, to show the prospect the real value she is getting for her money.

Here are six steps to follow to be sure each objection is handled to your—and your prospective employer's—satisfaction:

1. *Be an active listener.* Let the prospect know you hear and understand her concerns. Ask yourself, "If I were in her place, wouldn't I have the same concerns?" Never argue or put the interviewer on the defensive. A simple statement such as "That's a good point; I'm glad you brought it up" or "I understand how you feel" can let the prospect know you and she are on the same side. Don't interrupt or assume you know what the interviewer is going to say, even if you've been asked this question many times before.

2. *Ask the prospect to explain the objection to you.* Ask yourself, "Do I fully understand the problem here?" If a prospect says "I think you may be overqualified for this job," ask "Why do you think so?" or "What do you mean by that?" She might say, "Well, I'm not sure we can afford to pay what you'll probably be asking." Then you know she really is concerned with money, and not with your qualifications.

If you hadn't asked her to clarify her objection, you'd have wasted a lot of time trying to convince her you're right for the job. Once you know she's really objecting to the "price," you can continue to establish value for her.

3. *Translate every objection into a question in your mind.* Treat each tough question as a challenge, not an obstacle. Ask yourself, "What's the missing information that's keeping this prospect from going ahead with the sale?" When a prospect says "I don't think you have enough background in this field," respond as if she had said, "Can you tell me

what other qualifications you have to make up for your lack of experience?"

4. *Answer the objection.* Ask yourself, "How can I help this prospect solve his problem?" Everyone has the right to a question or an opinion, even if it's wrong. Answer the objection by emphasizing benefits. If a prospect objects to a flaw or weakness, don't try to ignore or gloss over it. Say something like, "That's a very good point. It is true that I don't have a lot of experience in this field, but my background in social work is perfect for the kind of interpersonal skills and understanding you need for a job in human resources. And I'm very eager to learn."

5. *Sell the benefits.* Ask yourself, "Do I know which benefits are most important to this person?" The stronger the connection between your abilities and the prospect's needs, the fewer objections you'll hear. For example, you're interviewing for a position as bank customer service representative. You assume the boss is looking for an outgoing "people person." That's true, but she's also looking for someone who can work on his own, because she travels a lot. So you would do best in the interview by selling your independent nature.

6. *Confirm the answer.* Make sure that you've answered the objection with no misunderstandings. Ask yourself, "Are we both satisfied that the issue is resolved?" Ask the prospect, "Does that answer your question?" or "How do you feel about that?" or "Does that take care of your concern?"

Practice these six steps before you go into a real interview situation. Ask your favorite role-playing partners to come up with as many objections as they can think of. Ask them to go from the sublime to the ridiculous, from "You don't have the right qualifications for this job" to "My astrologer says the stars are not in the proper alignment." Then the next time an interviewer starts talking astrology, you'll have your answer at hand and your technique well established.

THE PERFECT SALES OPPORTUNITY

Interviews make us nervous because we don't know exactly what we'll be asked. It's that old classroom syndrome: You know you know the material, you're pretty sure you'll pass the test, but you're afraid there'll be one question you just won't know how to answer. You break out in hives just thinking about it.

An interview is not a test. There are no right or wrong answers. As a matter of fact, the more questions you're asked in an interview situation, the better off you are. Why? *Because each question you're asked is another opportunity to sell yourself.* Every time a potential employer asks you a question, he or she is really saying, "Tell me why I should hire you."

Improving your interviewing skills requires preparation and practice. Your hard work will pay off, however. In a recent survey I took, all of the employers I spoke to said they used interviews as their primary means of selecting future employees. That means no matter what type of job you're seeking, no matter what your experience or qualifications, you can't get a job without being interviewed first. Obviously, the better you are at being interviewed, the better your chances of getting the job.

In a moment I'll present a list of commonly asked interview questions. They are also excellent selling opportunities. Study the questions and think about how you would give a positive, benefit-oriented answer.

For instance, suppose an employer were to say, "I see you only stayed on your last job for four months. Why didn't you stay longer?" How would you answer? If you weren't prepared, you might get defensive and say, "It wasn't my fault. I had family problems and I had to go home and stay with my mother."

A better answer would be, "I was doing well on the job, but then my father had a stroke and I left to help my mother at home. I learned a lot during that time at home, and it helped me make a decision to go into this field. . . ."

Use these questions for practice and role-playing. Ask a friend to study the list of questions and then set up a mock interview situation. This is an excellent way to practice your selling skills, build your confidence, and get out from under the shadow of the giant question mark.

Here are the sample questions:

Why are you looking for work at this time? _____

_____

_____

Why do you think you're qualified to work for this company? _____

_____

_____

Why did you leave your last job? _____

_____

_____

What are the things you want most from a job: money, power, satisfaction, etc.? _____

_____

_____

Name three people in your life who've influenced you most. _____

_____

_____

Can you tell me about a problem you had on your last job and how you solved it? _____

_____

_____

What do you do in your leisure time? _____

_____

_____

What are the main responsibilities of your current job? _____

_____

_____

What were your major accomplishments in your last job? _____

_____

_____

What impact did these accomplishments have on your organization? __

_____

_____

What did you like most about your last job? _____

_____

_____

What did you like least about your last job? _____

_____

_____

What do you think are your greatest strengths? _____

_____

What do you think are your greatest weaknesses? _____

What are your long-term career objectives? _____

Why should we hire you? _____

Why do you want to work for our company? _____

Why do you want to change jobs (or careers)? _____

Your work experience seems to be all volunteer. Have you ever had a "real" job? _____

How competitive are you? _____

Are you willing to work overtime? _____

SELLING SPECIFICS: QUESTIONS FOR SELECTED JOB CATEGORIES

The questions I've just listed are asked in all kinds of interviews. You may also be asked questions that apply to the specific industry or position for which you're applying. Accountants, for example, may be asked questions that apply strictly to that field. You should develop several AAAs that pay particular attention to your technical and specialized skills. If you don't have direct experience in the field, develop AAAs that show how your own background and experience relate to those that are called for in this job.

Information interviews are good sources for finding out what questions might be asked of you. Tell your information source that you're planning to look for work in her field and ask her to give you an idea of the questions she might ask of a potential employee.

Take careful note of these questions; then you'll be prepared when they come up in real interview situations. Here is a sampling of questions that might be asked in five of today's hot job markets:

Accountant

What different accounting activities were you responsible for? _____

_____

_____

Did you develop systems and controls on your last job? Can you describe them? _____

_____

_____

What computer systems do you know? _____

_____

_____

What types of budgets have you worked on? _____

_____

_____

What types of financial analysis have you done? _____

_____

_____

Computer Operator

Tell me about the equipment with which you've had hands-on experience: _____

_____

_____

Where did you get your training? _____

_____

_____

What was the nature of the work you did? _____

_____

_____

With what software are you familiar? _____

_____

_____

Can you learn other systems easily? _____

_____

_____

Electronics Engineer

What are some unusual technical problems, and how did you solve them? _____

_____

_____

What different types of circuits have you worked with? _____

_____

_____

Can you describe a project you worked on from conception to finished product? _____

_____

_____

What management responsibilities have you had? _____

_____

_____

Nurse

What were your duties on your previous job? _____

_____

_____

What supervisory experience do you have? _____

_____

_____

What made you go into nursing? _____

_____

_____

What is your nursing specialty? _____

_____

_____

What is your experience with Medicare and insurance claims and forms?

_____

_____

_____

Employment Personnel Officer

What kinds of jobs were you asked to fill? _____

_____

_____

What were your sources for finding new employees? _____

_____

_____

Have you ever written job descriptions? _____

_____

_____

What job evaluation systems have you used? _____

_____

_____

Were you responsible for any orientation or training programs for new employees? _____

_____

_____

Using the examples I've just listed, develop a list of at least five to ten questions that relate specifically to your field of interest. Use your research, your own experience, and your information interviews to help you out.

1. _____?

_____

_____

_____

2. _____?

_____

_____

_____

3. _____?

_____

_____

_____

4. _____?

_____

5. _____?

BRING YOUR OWN LIST OF QUESTIONS

As you've learned, your second objective at an interview is to get as much information as you can about the job and the organization. That means you should be prepared with a list of questions to ask the employer. You should bring your list of questions with you.

The questions you ask the employer are also selling tools. You can't make a sale without asking questions. You want to ask questions to uncover the employer's wants or needs; you want ask questions to find the emotional reasons the prospective boss would have for hiring you.

Some questions you might want to ask are:

- "What are the key responsibilities of this job?"
- "What do you foresee as possible obstacles or problems I might have?"
- "In terms of my major responsibilities, how much actual authority do I have?"
- "What changes or improvements would you like to see in these responsibilities?"
- "Of the people who have had this job before, what were the characteristics of those who performed well? Of those who didn't?"
- "If you hire me, what would your specific expectations be?"
- "Why is the position open?"
- "What would you most like for a new employee to bring to this job?"
- "How many people have held this job in the last five years?"
- "Who would I be working with on this job? Is it possible for me to meet them?"

- "How is job performance evaluated here?"
- "How is it rewarded?"
- "Does the company promote from within? How and how often?"
- "How many women and minorities are in middle to upper management?"
- "How are decisions made here?"
- "What is a typical day on the job like?"
- "What is your overall philosophy about training?"

QUESTIONS FOR YOUR FUTURE

Everyone wants a job with a future, and in these times of mergers and hostile takeovers, it's vital that you get information on where the organization is headed. You don't want to give the impression that you are simply applying for this job as a stepping-stone in your career. However, you do need to consider the future. The best time to ask questions regarding the company and its future plans is toward the end of the interview. You might ask:

- "What are the usual career paths like for new employees?"
- "I see that the company is expanding its markets into the Northeast. Where do you see the company moving?"
- "What are you doing in terms of human resource planning to make that happen?"
- "Have you had any major layoffs or cutbacks in the past few years? Do you anticipate any in the near future?"
- "If so, how would my job and/or department be affected?"

One of the most important questions you can ask is: "What can someone coming in at this level and performing in an outstanding way hope to achieve?"

Make a list of at least ten questions you would want to ask at your next job interview:

1. _____

_____

_____

2. _____

_____

_____

3. _____

_____

_____

4. _____

_____

_____

5. _____

_____

_____

6. _____

_____

_____

7. _____

_____

_____

8. _____

_____

_____

9. _____

_____

_____

10. _____

_____

_____

Asking the right questions can be a major factor in getting a job. But getting a job, just any job, is not your ultimate goal. There are certain benefits you need to ensure a fulfilling, financially rewarding future. The next chapter will show you how to go after what you need and get it.

29

Negotiating for Your Future

How to Ask for More and Get It

Sales and Marketing Principle #29

A successful negotiation is a win–win situation—but the person who asks for more usually gets it.

I don't know about you, but I'm a die-hard movie fan and I love to watch the Academy Awards. A few years ago, Sally Field performed in a wonderful picture called *Places in the Heart* for which she won Best Actress honors. She was being recognized by her peers for an outstanding performance in her chosen career. She stepped up to the microphone and millions of TV viewers waited to hear her thank her mother, her father, her high school drama coach, and her beautiful family for all their love and support.

Instead, she walked up to the mike, tears in her eyes, and said, "You like me! You really like me!" It was a touchingly human moment—a reminder that no matter how rich or famous we may get, the ultimate achievement often appears to be having people *like* us.

Why do I bring this up in relation to negotiations? Because our ability to negotiate is heavily tied up with our self-image and self-confidence. Sometimes we are so thrilled just to be recognized that we are willing to accept less than we deserve. If you have been searching for a job for a while and one is finally offered to you—especially one that you are very excited about—your first reaction may be to shout "They like me!" and feel lucky to accept what is initially offered.

The fact is that when you are offered a job, your bargaining power is greater than it will ever be. If you're saying "I'd better not ask for too much or they'll just go hire someone else," you'd better think again. You have just successfully convinced this interviewer of the valuable contribution you can make to his organization. Don't undermine that effort by selling yourself short. The interviewer wants you for the job—and he doesn't want to begin the costly, time-consuming search process all over again. So you are actually in a very good bargaining position.

CHECK YOUR EGO AT THE DOOR

Negotiation is above all an exercise in logic and clear thinking. Whenever emotion supersedes your reasoning power, you have lost. If you let your ego get in the way and respond to an offer with "Who do you think you're talking to? *I* can't accept an offer like that!" you're not going to get much farther in the bargaining process. Getting angry or frustrated if things don't go your way doesn't help at all; it only gives the other person an advantage. Since negotiation is a form of problem solving, if you fail to communicate your specific problems, needs, and bottom-line positions, you will probably not get what you want.

Negotiation requires objectivity. You may be tempted to take a job (1) simply because you like the person who is to be your boss, or (2) because you think that he is such a nice guy he'll give you other concessions later. Liking your prospective employer is a consideration; however, that person may be fired tomorrow, or be transferred or promoted, or go to another company. Don't make negotiating decisions for emotional reasons.

Communication is the key to negotiation. The better you communicate what you want and why you want it, the better your chances of getting it. We're back to the principles of good salesmanship again: If you can demonstrate the benefits of your suggestions to the other person, he's likely to agree with you.

POWER, POWER—WHO'S GOT THE POWER?

As Herb Cohen, negotiating expert and author of *You Can Negotiate Anything* points out, "Power is based upon perception—if you think you've got it then you've got it. If you think you don't have it, even if you've got it, then you don't have it."

Anyone can be a good negotiator. Many of us are afraid to ask for what we want because we don't feel we deserve it. When you are negotiating, it doesn't matter how you feel. It's how you *act* that counts. Think of what is more important to you: living through a feeling of uncertainty and discomfort for a short while, or living for a long time with the consequences of being unable to stand up for yourself. Feelings pass quickly. You may never get another chance at this negotiation again.

Ted and Frank were both job hunting at the same time. Each was offered a job as a purchasing agent at a large manufacturing firm. Ted was offered a starting salary of $24,000. He had hoped for at least $26,000 but was afraid he would blow the deal if he asked for anything more. He accepted the offer.

Frank was also offered $24,000 to start. He too was willing to accept the money—providing he was assured a place in the company's training program and tuition reimbursement toward his M.B.A. The employer agreed.

Five years later, Ted was struggling to pay for night school in order to earn his degree. Though he had moved up to a supervisory position, without further training he had very little opportunity to move up farther. Frank, on the other hand, completed his M.B.A. and did so well in the company training program that he was promoted to a management position after only three years. There was very little difference between Ted and Frank in terms of ambition or ability. The major difference was in their attitude toward negotiation at the time they were hired.

THE ULTIMATE SALES GOAL: MUTUAL SATISFACTION

When I was a kid, a favorite uncle of mine used to love to play tricks and practical jokes. One of his favorites was to make some outlandish remark, such as, "Wanna make a hundred bucks? I've got it right here in my pocket. Let's flip a coin and see who gets it. Okay? Heads I win, tails you lose." This classic no-win situation taught me the value of learning to negotiate.

Kids are naturally great negotiators. They'll trade peanut butter for American cheese or a toy truck for a frog, and everyone comes out a winner. They know what they want and they go after it.

I once watched a small boy in the park struggling to slide down a snow-covered hill on a big, brand-new sled with fancy painting and steering mechanisms. The problem was, it was just too big for this little boy. Sliding next to him on the hill was an older boy using one of those round plastic sleds with a rope across the middle. Instead of going over and grabbing the sled he wanted (which is a popular negotiating style, not only among children), the little boy sized up the situation, went over to the older kid, and started a conversation. "You look like you're all scrunched up on that round sled," he said to the older boy. "Your feet are hanging over the edge. I bet you could slide down really fast on this big one. And you could steer it better too!" The older boy was thrilled to ride on a new, classy, steerable sled, and the young kid had a lot more fun on the simple plastic one. That's a win–win negotiation.

Negotiating is something we all do frequently in our daily lives without even being aware of it. We negotiate for who will take out the garbage or who will drive the kids to school. We negotiate about which movie to see or whether to have Chinese food delivered or go out to Burger King. We give a little, we get a little.

Negotiating is a specialized form of problem solving. There are some problems that you can solve yourself. Problem solving becomes negotiation when two people or groups start from opposing positions and attempt to find a compromise, each side hoping to give up as little as possible and to gain without the other side losing.

Every business owner knows a deal isn't clinched until all the details are ironed out, the price settled, and the goods delivered—or, as Yogi Berra put it, "It ain't over till it's over." All the selling skills you've been learning and practicing throughout the job search culminate in negotiating the price of your product. If you seem convinced that what you're asking for is fair and proper, then others will be convinced too.

Negotiating is not about winning. It's not about making unreasonable demands and expecting others to "take it or leave it." Negotiating is about options. It's about asking yourself and your opponent one important question: "How can we come to a mutually satisfying agreement?"

You do this by posing "What if . . . ?" situations. "What if I give you this and you give me that? Would that satisfy both our needs? What if I take less of this and more of that? Would that be agreeable?" The more options you come up with, the more room you have to compromise.

IF YOU DON'T KNOW WHAT YOU WANT, WHAT CAN YOU HOPE TO GET?

If you don't know what you want out of a job, you'll be tempted to take anything that's offered without examining the consequences. There are many other factors to consider besides money. You must clearly decide what is most important to you.

A young friend of my daughter's came to me for advice about a job she'd been offered as an editorial assistant on a small magazine. It was a publication Linda admired and respected, and she was thrilled to be offered a position there. But they couldn't afford to pay as much as Linda would have liked. She was prepared to go into negotiations and fight for a much higher salary.

We sat down and went over her goals. Making a lot of money was not as important to Linda as having a career in journalism. This magazine would be fertile ground for a young journalist's on-the-job training. When she thought about it, Linda realized she was willing to accept less money if they were willing to give her a chance to write.

In negotiations, it came out that the magazine was agreeable to giving her occasional short assignments with the possibility of full-length articles later on. She took the job. Linda later told me that even if she had been able to get that higher salary, she wouldn't have been happy there without the writing opportunities.

Before our discussion Linda was prepared to go in and battle for more money. But that wasn't what she needed to make her happy. *Had she not clarified her goals, she might have blown the whole deal for something that was not her highest priority.*

KNOW YOUR LIMITS

The next step after clarifying your goals is to set your limits. Start with what is least acceptable. Linda was able to accept a lower salary than she had hoped for, but she wouldn't have been able to work for no money at all. She had her rent to pay. Before she went into negotiation, she had to determine what was the lowest figure she could realistically accept. You have to know your cutoff point and resolve that you can't accept anything below it.

Next, determine the maximum you can ask for within reason. If you're negotiating for a company car, you can't reasonably insist that it be a Rolls Royce. Start with the maximum reasonable request and hope that you'll get it. If you don't, you negotiate down from that point. You never want to let your opponent know what your least acceptable level is or he'll go right for that. If you ask for too much you can always settle for less. But if you ask for too little, it's almost impossible to bargain upward.

Ask the following questions of yourself:

- What do I want to get out of this job?
- What are my real needs (other than money)?
- What is the most I could get?
- What is my bottom line?
- Where specifically can I compromise?
- What concessions could I make that would hurt, but that are still possible?
- Do I have a clear understanding of what's at stake, what issues are involved?

ADAPTING THE PERFECT PLAN

Don't be upset if things don't go exactly as you planned. A good negotiator is always flexible. Patience is valuable in negotiations, but you may also need to be quick—to alter your strategy, to pick up on a new factor, or to go in a different direction altogether. Trust your instincts and allow yourself to absorb new facts as they are presented. Remember that one of the most sought after success factors is adaptability. Your demonstration of this factor can convince the employer he's made the right choice—and he may be more willing to see things your way.

As you are presented with shifting opportunities, you may decide to forgo certain prizes in order to get new ones. Stay alert to these shifts by constantly asking yourself these questions throughout the negotiations:

- Why is the employer insisting on this particular point?
- How does this affect my bottom line?
- Am I still within my range?
- If the employer makes this particular concession, how can I help him save face?

MONEY TALK

Never talk money until you know there's a job offer. By the time you're talking money, the interviewer should be really sold on you. The more time he or she has already invested in you, the more you're worth.

There is a principle of economics that is particularly applicable here: *Money follows value.* If you (or the employer) want to talk about money before you've established your value, you'll be on the short end of the stick.

In most cases, you don't want to discuss money until the second or third interview. At that point, you'll have a pretty good idea of the employer's level of interest. By then you've also gotten enough information about what the job entails to make an evaluation of how much you think you should be paid. Also, if an employer asks very early on "How much money are you looking for?" he may be trying to screen out candidates. He may really be asking, "Are you overqualified for this position? Or underqualified?"

You shouldn't answer this question early in an interview. You can easily and calmly reply, "It's too early to discuss salary at this point. I don't know enough about you or how I can help you and your company." Then you can change the subject by asking a question. (Remember, the person who asks the questions gains control of the conversation.) Should the employer then return to talking salary, go for a trial close: "Does this mean I have the job?" or "Is this an offer?" If he says no, then repeat the fact that it's too early to discuss money and ask another question.

Getting Down to Brass Tacks

What happens when you do reach the point when money talk is appropriate? Try to get the employer to mention the money figure first. If you get him to disclose his acceptable range first, you'll know whether or not it's even worth pursuing. You may find it's even better than you hoped, and if you had suggested a figure first, it would have been too low.

When the interviewer asks you how much money you're looking for, you should ask whether there's a possibility of negotiating. Some salaries are fixed—the employer doesn't have any power to negotiate. Many jobs have a salary range that can be discussed, and some jobs have an unlimited salary budget. So ask the employer directly which category this job fits into. If you're asked "What are you looking for?" say (with a sense of humor), "What I think I'm worth and what you think I'm worth may be very different. What are you offering?"

If the job has a salary range, ask what the range is. If the employer says "The range is $22,000 to $25,000," you should reply, "$25,000 sounds like an acceptable figure."

If the employer asks "What's the minimum salary you would accept?" don't answer. Tell him you're not looking for the minimum. Say, politely, that you are looking for a job that is both intellectually (or creatively, or whatever is important to you) challenging as well as financially rewarding.

One important piece of advice: Don't accept an offer immediately, even if it's a good one. Let the employer know that you're seriously interested and that you know you could make an outstanding contribution to this company. But you need to consider the offer for a few days. The employer will wonder what other offers you're considering and may even increase the offer in a few days. If not, you can always call and say you've decided to accept the offer.

Thinking it over also gives you the chance to make sure you have negotiated well and got what you needed. Once you've made an agreement, you can't very well go back and say, "By the way, I forgot to ask for . . ." If you've asked for time to consider, you can say, "I've been thinking over your offer and on the whole it seems very fair. But we haven't discussed . . ." That way, you still have the negotiations within your control.

Playing Your Cards Right

Negotiating, like poker, is not always about holding the best cards. A good poker player is always looking around, staying aware of body language and nonverbal signals—yours and the other players'. Your eyes can reveal a lot about you. When you're asking for what you want, look directly at the other person. If you're constantly shifting your gaze or looking down, the implication is that you don't believe in what you're saying. You have nothing to be embarrassed about. It's okay to ask for what you deserve.

Never treat your counterpart lightly. Listen attentively and agree as much as possible that his suggestions are good, although perhaps not what you had in mind. If you disagree, do so respectfully. The best way to turn a negotiator hostile is to make him feel his suggestions are being dismissed or ignored.

Pay attention to how the other person is acting. Ask yourself, "Is this person sending any nonverbal signals? If so, what do they mean?" Such signals can tell you when to hold the line and when to push forward. If you're in an interview and the prospective boss is giving you her full attention, then suddenly begins to fidget in her chair, perhaps you've said something to turn her off. Try and find out what it was, or ask a quick question to change the subject.

THERE'S MORE AT STAKE THAN MONEY

We negotiate in order to meet our needs. Companies, in the past, have assumed that all their workers' needs were the same and benefits were designed for the "average" worker. It wasn't practical to make a separate deal for each person—the bookkeeping and paperwork would be much too complicated.

Today much more emphasis is paid to individual needs. Computerized systems make it possible for even large organizations to devise customized benefits plans. It's up to the individual to make sure she has the ability to negotiate for those things she deems most important.

NEGOTIATING FOR THE NEW BENEFITS

When looking for a job, you should be looking for an environment that protects your employability and is responsive to your needs. The interview process is no longer based solely on what you can do for the company. Roberts T. Jones of the U.S. Department of Labor sees a need for people to take a much more active role in negotiating their own futures. "You've got to ask yourself, 'What can this company do for me?' " he says. "It's not enough to bargain for wages anymore; you've got to structure your contract at the time of your employment. That's when you should be bargaining for training, health care, child care, work schedules, even severance pay."

As work and workers have changed, the things employees consider important have also changed. An article in the August 1987 issue of *Personal Administrator* discussed the new generation of "family sup-portive companies." In exchange for tax breaks, reduced employee ab-senteeism, and increased worker morale and productivity, some companies were expanding their benefits to include the following options:

▪ *Cafeteria-style benefits.* Many progressive companies are offering "cafeteria-style benefits," a "menu" of benefit choices like health insur-ance plans, life insurance, and child care subsidies from which you select those that appeal to you most.

At St. Luke's Episcopal Hospital in Houston, Texas, employees are allotted a certain amount of money and then given a list of benefits from which to choose. If you want more benefits than the allotted dollar amount will pay for, you can make up the difference yourself. If your choices cost less, the extra money goes back into your paycheck. It's a little like *Wheel of Fortune,* where you get to go on a shopping spree with the amount of money you've earned and you get to keep the leftover money for the next go-around.

Employees at St. Luke's have been very pleased with their individual benefits packages. And the company discovered that not only was the flexible benefits program a major attraction for new workers, but present employees cited their benefits program as an incentive to stay with St. Luke's. Many other organizations around the country are experiencing similar success.

▪ *Child care.* Child care is one of our country's greatest concerns. Unlike earlier times in America, where only one parent worked and the other stayed home with the kids, it's now the norm for both husband and wife to be working.

Some companies provide on-site day-care centers; others subsidize child care costs. In 1980 there were only fifteen to twenty companies nationwide that had such programs. By 1987 at least a thousand had subsidized child care programs, and that number has grown since. The increasing number of single parents in the workforce is another reason this issue has become a strong negotiating point. Whether you have a family now or are planning to have one, you'll want to find out what kind of child care benefits are available to you and to make sure some provi-sion is made in your benefits package.

▪ *Flextime and job sharing.* One of the most significant negotiable ben-efits is flextime. This usually means that a company will keep its doors open from about six in the morning to eight at night, and workers choose an eight-hour shift within that time. Everyone is at work at some point between nine in the morning and three in the afternoon. Take, for exam-ple, a husband and wife who both work for the same company. The husband works from six to two daily. This lets his wife get the kids up and ready for school. She then goes into work at ten and works until six. In the meantime, her husband is home when the kids get out of school at three. This kind of schedule gives both parents time to be with their children and saves on day-care costs.

Another version of this is job sharing, where two employees split one shift. I have a cousin in California who was looking for part-time work. An experienced legal secretary, she also goes to school part-time. When she applied for part-time secretarial work at several large law firms, they all said no. Then she ran into another woman, a single parent, who was also looking for part-time work. They presented themselves as a team and now are sharing a legal secretary position.

My cousin works from nine in the morning to one-thirty in the afternoon. Her "partner" comes in at one and they discuss the day's projects. My cousin then goes off to school, and her counterpart takes over until five-thirty. The situation works well for both women and their employer is more than satisfied with the arrangement. Some states, including California and Arizona, now have "Shared Work Unemployment Compensation" to provide unemployment benefits for people on reduced work schedules. Flexible scheduling often gives employees a greater sense of responsibility and emphasizes the value of the work performed rather than hours spent working. As this value increases so does their productivity, which benefits both employee and employer.

Before you begin your negotiations for your new job, sit down and make a list of all the possible factors that would make this the ideal job for you. Here are some of them:

- *Monetary:* Salary, salary potential, bonuses, commissions, profit sharing, royalties or residuals.
- *Position:* Title, authority, responsibility, office, support staff, budget, career potential.
- *Benefits:* Life and health insurance, training, vacation time, flexible scheduling, child care, tuition reimbursement, company car.

SECRETS TO NEGOTIATING POWER

Getting what you want takes a winning combination: asking the right questions, mastering your selling skills, and a strong belief in your worth and value to the job. It also takes practice in skillful negotiating tactics. Here is a summary of what it takes to be an effective negotiator:

1. In order to plan your negotiations, you have to have a good idea of the potential employer's wants and needs.

2. You are in your strongest negotiating position when you are first offered the job.
3. Before you begin negotiations, you should conduct a careful economic analysis of what you would like to get from the negotiations, what you would be willing to settle for, and what is your bottom line.
4. You should show a sincere personal interest in the employer as well as interest in the company, and talk in terms of those interests.
5. Negotiating with a win–win attitude will generally result in a more equitable result than a competitive me-against-you attitude.
6. It's usually a good idea to take up less controversial issues first and always establish areas of agreement and an attitude of acceptance.
7. You must always establish value before you begin negotiations.
8. Your eyes give you away. Look directly at your negotiating partner without wavering or lowering your lids.
9. The mouth is also a giveaway. Always begin negotiations with a warm smile, even if you think you're about to disagree.
10. You come to an agreement only when a final concession is made by one person who feels that the other party will make no further concessions.
11. One of the best and most effective ways to have your negotiating partner accept your position is to have him participate in the reasoning process that leads to your point of view.
12. Always be an active, attentive listener. You may not agree with the other position, but you should never ignore it.
13. Before you leave the negotiations, always sum up the key points so you are sure that both parties have a clear understanding of the agreement.
14. Be honest and fair and expect your counterpart to be the same.
15. Studies show that a negotiator who initially asks for more and offers to give less usually winds up obtaining more and giving less.

By this point you have become a super salesperson. Don't sell yourself short. You know your value to the employer. You're not asking for anything you don't deserve. You're not trying to get something for nothing. Negotiating is a way for both of you to come out ahead. Keep this in mind, and you'll always be a winner. It's your work, it's your life. It's your choice. Don't settle for less than you want or less than you deserve.

30

A Final Look Forward

Sales and Marketing Principle #30

Marketing yourself is a lifelong process; use it well and enjoy your success.

MARKETING YOURSELF CONTINUES...

Ask a millionaire how he (or she) has done what he's done, and he'll tell you, "Blood, sweat, and tears." Ask a millionaire *why* he's done what he's done, and he'll tell you, "For the love of it."

One reason I wrote this book was to get an important message across: The real secret to success is to love the work you do. Ninety-six thousand hours of your life will be spent working. How sad to spend all that time unhappy, underpaid, and unfulfilled.

Marketing Yourself has given you the tools for success. You've learned how to be sold on yourself and how to sell yourself without selling out. You've discovered what qualities employers consider essential in the people they hire and how to improve and enhance your own success factors. You've explored your options and created a marketing plan that gives you focus and direction. I've shown you how to use professional sales techniques to get employers to buy what you're selling. The rest is up to you. *Success is turning knowledge into positive action.*

TAKE THE RISK; GET THE REWARD

The sales and marketing skills you've learned here give you choices about your work you never had before—and the ability to combine the work you love with the thousands of options that are out there now and are growing every day.

I know that it's not always easy to follow your dreams. There are bound to be problems and setbacks. But I believe in the power of setting goals and working toward them.

Who knows what the future will bring? World events are more astonishing every day. At the end of the nineteenth century, no one could have foreseen how rapidly the world would change. The twenty-first century will bring political and technological changes no one now can imagine. What I do know about the next hundred years is that we will have to make many choices in our lifetimes. It will be a century of choice and change.

The basic principles and sales techniques presented here will enable you to market your talents and abilities into the twenty-first century. The more you welcome the future's challenge and possibility, the more you'll get in return.

If you are resistant to change, you may see the future as a time of chaos that will disrupt your life. But if you embrace change, you'll do very well in the years ahead.

Perhaps we should take a hint from the Chinese language: The symbol for *crisis* in Chinese is made up of two parts—one for risk and one for opportunity. You can't have one without the other, and you don't get the reward without the risk.

YOUR MARKETING FOUNDATION: THE THIRTY BASIC PRINCIPLES

This book is dedicated to the millions of Americans whose dream is to live up to their potential, love their work, and get paid what they're worth.

The future is yours for the taking. Marketing yourself is a process fueled by your dreams and accomplished by solid sales and marketing techniques. The thirty basic principles behind this process are the foundation for your lifetime career planning success:

1. Marketing success depends on the quality of the product and the ability of the salesperson.
2. Attitude is more important than aptitude for sales and marketing success.
3. If you don't believe in the value of your product, no one else will either.
4. An effective marketer isn't resistant to change, but views it as a challenge and an opportunity.
5. With so many similar products and services today competing for the same markets, the commitment of the salesperson is often the deciding factor.
6. Increase your selling power by improving your communication:

Be sure that your message is received the way that you sent it and meant it.

7. Selling is creative problem solving: how best to get what you want while giving the customer what he or she needs.

8. Marketing often requires quick and confident decisions. That doesn't mean you have to be right all the time—we learn from all our choices.

9. The best sales question you can ask yourself is, "How can I do it better next time?"

10. Marketing must be consistently future-oriented for a product or service to survive in a rapidly changing world.

11. The more we rely on our own sales and marketing abilities, the more self-assured we become.

12. Interdependence and trust are the essential relationship builders.

13. The success of value-added marketing lies in knowing what people want and giving them more than they expect.

14. The more you know about your product, the easier it is to sell.

15. Success comes from building on your strengths, not from correcting your weaknesses.

16. People want to know the features, but they buy for the benefits.

17. You sell a product best by selectively emphasizing features and customizing benefits.

18. Effective marketing is the result of careful planning.

19. A successful marketing plan is based on an understanding of current economic trends.

20. You increase the odds of making a sale by knowing what the buying public wants and needs.

21. The odds continue to increase by knowing specifically where your buyers are located.

22. The art of closing a sale is the ability to sell to the right person in the right way at the right time.

23. The secret desire of every prospective buyer is, "Make me an offer I can't refuse!"

24. In the age of customer service, mass marketing is not as effective as an individually customized sales approach.

25. Packaging has a major impact on why a customer purchases a product or service.

26. The only way to close a sale is to get to the real decision maker.

27. A sale is a series of planned questions to uncover needs, build trust, answer objections, and gain commitment.

28. The person who asks the questions controls the sale.

29. A successful negotiation is a win–win situation—but the person who asks for more usually gets it.

30. Marketing yourself is a lifelong process; use it well and enjoy your success.

THE VALUE OF DREAMS

Never underestimate the value of dreams: Your future success is based on the dreams you have today. Ignore the scenes of the past that told you otherwise.

You're sitting in a classroom listening to an uninspiring teacher drone on about a subject in which you have no interest. Suddenly sharp tones ring through the air and you know you are being singled out: "Pay attention!" the teacher snaps, "You're daydreaming!" Perhaps you should have been listening at that particular moment; but I hope it didn't stop you from dreaming altogether.

Eleanor Roosevelt once said, "The future belongs to those who believe in the beauty of their dreams." Those who truly believe in their dreams are willing to work for them, to take the necessary steps to turn fantasy into reality and wishful thinking into positive action.

Jack Lemmon, one of my favorite actors, is an example of someone who followed his dreams. His father, a baker, envisioned the day when he would proudly bring his son into the family business. When Jack announced he was going to New York to become an actor, his father was heartbroken.

His father asked, "Is this your dream, Jack?"

Jack said yes.

"Do you love what you do, Jack?" his father asked.

Jack said yes again.

"Then go and do it," his father said. "I understand what it means to love your work. The day that I don't find romance in a loaf of bread is the day I quit."

I couldn't agree with him more.

Bibliography

Abrams, Kathleen S. *Job Prep 2000*. Wassau, WI: Entwood Publishing, 1986.
Anderson, U. S. *Success Cybernetics*. North Hollywood, CA: Wilshire Books, 1975.
Beatley, Richard H. *The Five-Minute Interview*. New York: Wiley, 1986.
Beck, Joel. *Telephone Prospecting and Marketing* (audiocassette). Phoenix, AZ: General Cassette Corp.
Bettger, Frank. *How I Raised Myself From Failure to Success in Selling*. New York: Prentice-Hall, 1949.
Bolles, Richard Nelson. *What Color Is Your Parachute?* Berkeley, CA: Ten Speed Press, 1987.
Boyan, Lee. *Successful Cold Call Selling*. New York: AMACOM, 1983.
Butler, Diane. *Futurework: Where to Find Tomorrow's High-Tech Jobs Today*. New York: Holt, Rinehart & Winston, 1984.
Cetron, Marvin, and Marcia Appel. *Jobs of the Future: The 500 Best Jobs— Where They'll Be and How to Get Them*. New York: McGraw-Hill, 1984.
Cohen, Herb. *You Can Negotiate Anything*. Secaucus, NJ: Lyle Stuart, 1980.
Cornish, Edward, ed. *Careers Tomorrow—The Outlook for Work in a Changing World*. Bethesda, MD: World Future Society, 1983.
Danna, Jo. *Winning the Job Interview Game*. Briarwood, NY: Palomino Press, 1985.
Didsbury, Howard F., ed. *The World of Work: Careers and the Future*. Bethesda, MD: World Future Society, 1983.
Elam, Houston G. *Marketing for the Non-Marketing Executive*. New York: AMACOM, 1978.
Feingold, Norman S., and Norma Reno Miller. *Emerging Careers: New Occupations for The Year 2000 and Beyond*. Garrett Park, MD: Garrett Park Press, 1983.
Feingold, Norman S., and Avis Nicholson. *Getting Ahead: A Woman's Guide to Career Success*. Washington, DC: Acropolis Books, 1983.
Fraser, Jill Andresky. *The Best U.S. Cities for Working Women*. New York: New American Library, 1986.
Garfield, Charles. *Peak Performers: The New Heroes of American Business*. New York: Avon Books, 1986.

Girard, Joe. *How to Sell Yourself.* New York: Warner Books, 1979.

Gondolfo, Joe, with Robert Shook. *How to Make Big Money Selling.* New York: Harper & Row, 1984.

Half, Robert. *The Robert Half Way To Get Hired in Today's Job Market.* New York: Bantam Books, 1981.

———. *Robert Half on Hiring.* New York: Plume Books, 1985.

Hill, Napoleon. *Think and Grow Rich.* New York: Fawcett, 1960.

Hopkins, Tom. *How to Master the Art of Selling.* New York: Warner Books, 1982.

Irish, Richard K. *Go Hire Yourself an Employer.* Garden City, NY: Anchor Books, 1973.

Johnston, William B., and Arnold H. Packer. *Workforce 2000: Work and Workers for the 21st Century.* Indianapolis, IN: Hudson Institute, 1987.

Krannick, Ronald L., Ph.D. *Re-Careering in Turbulent Times: Skills and Strategies for Success in Today's Job Market.* Manassas, VA: Impact Publications, 1983.

Lathrop, Richard. *Who's Hiring Who?* Berkeley, CA: Ten Speed Press, 1977.

LeBoeuf, Michael. *How to Win Customers and Keep Them for Life.* New York: G. P. Putnam's Sons, 1987.

Leeds, Dorothy. *PowerSpeak: The Complete Guide to Persuasive Public Speaking and Presenting.* New York: Prentice-Hall, 1988.

———. *Smart Questions: A New Strategy for Successful Managers.* New York: McGraw-Hill, 1987.

Levinson, Jay Conrad. *Guerrilla Marketing: Secrets for Making Big Profits from Your Small Business.* New York: Houghton Mifflin, 1984.

Lewis, Herschell Gordon. *Direct Mail Copy That Sells.* Englewood Cliffs, NJ: Prentice-Hall, 1984.

Ling, Mona. *How to Increase Sales and Put Yourself Across by Telephone.* Englewood Cliffs, NJ: Prentice-Hall, 1963.

Lund, Philip R. *Compelling Selling: A Framework for Persuasion.* London, England: Macmillan, 1974.

Maltz, Maxwell. *Psycho-Cybernetics.* New York: Pocket Books, 1960.

Marshall, Austin. *How to Get a Better Job.* New York: Hawthorn Books, 1964.

Naisbitt, John. *Megatrends.* New York: Warner Books, 1982.

Nash, Edward. *Direct Marketing.* New York: McGraw-Hill, 1982.

Nierenberg, Gerard I. *The Art of Negotiating.* New York: Cornerstone Library, 1968.

Occupational Outlook Handbook. U.S. Department of Labor, Bureau of Labor Statistics, Bulletin 2350.

Pascarella, Perry. *The New Achievers.* New York: The Free Press, 1984.

Payne, Richard A. *How to Get a Better Job Quicker.* New York: Signet Books, 1972.

Pell, Arthur R., Ph.D. *How to Sell Yourself on an Interview.* New York: Prentice Hall, 1982.

The Prentice-Hall Miracle Sales Guide. Englewood Cliffs, NJ: Prentice-Hall, 1974.

Robertson, James. *Future Work.* New York: Universe Books, 1985.

Sales Manpower Foundation. *How to Land the Job You Want.* New York: Sales Executive Club of New York, 1975.

Schuller, Robert H. *You Can Become the Person You Want to Be.* New York: Pillar Books, 1973.

Shafiroff, Martin D., and Robert L. Shook. *Successful Telephone Selling in the 80's.* New York: Harper & Row, 1982.

Shatzki, Michael, and Wayne R. Coffey. *Negotiating: The Art of Getting What You Want.* New York: New American Library, 1981.

Sher, Barbara and Annie Gottlieb. *Wishcraft: How to Get What You Really Want.* New York: Ballantine Books, 1979.

Slutsky, Jeff, and Marc Slutsky. *Streetsmart Teleselling: The 33 Secrets.* Englewood Cliffs, NJ: Prentice Hall, 1990.

Smith, Robert Ellis. *Workrights.* New York: Dutton, 1983.

Snelling, Robert O. *The Right Job.* New York: Penguin Books, 1987.

————, and Anne M. Snelling. *Jobs! What They Are . . . Where They Are . . . What They Pay . . .* New York: Fireside Books, 1985.

Sperber, Philip. *The Science of Business Negotiation.* New York: Pilot Industries, 1979.

Walther, George R. *Phone Power: How To Make the Telephone Your Most Profitable Business Tool.* New York: Berkley Publishing, 1986.

Weinstein, Robert V. *Jobs For The 21st Century.* New York: Macmillan, 1983.

Welch, Mary Scott. *Networking: The Great New Way for Women to Get Ahead.* New York: Harcourt Brace Jovanovich, 1980.

Willingham, Ron. *Integrity Selling.* Garden City, NY: Doubleday, 1987.

Yate, Martin John. *Knock 'em Dead with Great Answers to Tough Interview Questions.* Boston, MA: Bob Adams, 1987.

Index

POSTSCRIPT

If you want to know more about Dorothy Leeds' speeches, seminars, and audiocassette programs, please call or write to:

Dorothy Leeds, President
Organizational Technologies Inc.
800 West End Avenue   Suite 10A
New York, NY 10025
(212) 864-2424
(800) 423-1169
Fax #: (212) 932-8364

Her Positive Action Cassette Learning Programs are:

Smart Questions: The Key to Sales Success. This unique and proven program will help you improve your questions to solve the mystery of the decision-making process, uncover the right information in the right way at the right time, practice surefire ways to answer objections, and close the sale. Plus hundreds of sample questions you can use immediately in your next sales presentation. The set of six cassettes and the Comprehensive Workbook costs $95.

PowerSpeak: The Complete Guide to Persuasive Public Speaking and Presenting. You can easily become a powerful and persuasive presenter by following Dorothy Leeds' proven PowerSpeak method. Learn how to overcome the six major speaking faults. The set of six cassettes and the PowerSpeak Workbook costs $95.

The Motivational Manager: How to Get Top Performance from Your Staff. Being an excellent manager is the best way to get ahead. With this motivational program you will discover your strengths and weaknesses, how to hire, coach, train, motivate, and lots more. The set of six cassettes and the Management Performance Indicator costs $95.

People Reading: Strategies for Engineering Better Relationships in Business. Gain a huge career advantage by influencing others and achieving results through reading the unique differences in people. The set of three cassettes and the Practical People Reading Guide costs $49.95.